KEEP THIS QUIET! III
INITIATIONS

Praise for Keep This Quiet!

"Margaret Harrell's *Keep This Quiet!* offers an illuminating look at Hunter S. Thompson in full throttle trying to make it as a Top Notch prose-stylist. Harrell fills in many important biographical gaps. A welcome addition to what is becoming the HST cottage industry. Read it."
—Douglas Brinkley, editor of *The Proud Highway* and *Fear and Loathing in America*

"The reader comes to feel an affinity with the trio of writers in their attempts to achieve their iconoclastic visions of success, glimpsing them as individuals beyond their work, seeing how they think."
—Kirkus Indie Reviews

"If you want to know what the Sixties were really like, read *Keep This Quiet: A Memoir*. It's all there: the openness, the hope, the ideals, the risks, the highs and lows, the travel, the love."
—Robert Morgan, author of *Gap Creek* and *Terroir*

"Keep This Quiet? Not likely. Margaret Harrell's *Keep This Quiet!* is a feast for the Gonzo soul. It's all new and a valuable addition to my collection. . . . Highly recommended."
—Martin Flynn, www.hstbooks.org

"This book is a joy to read, particularly for anyone that has that urge to express themselves through the creative arts in all their forms. In terms of its importance to the Hunter S. Thompson world I would have to say that there are not many other books out there that have the same intimate understanding of the man behind the myth."
—Rory Feehan, www.totallygonzo.org

"Thompson loved Harrell's work as the line editor on *Hell's Angels* and she here details the nature of their relationship."
—William McKeen, *Literary Journalism Studies*

"Harrell's writing is crisp and easy to follow. I found it nearly impossible to put the book down."

—Rachel Escobar

"*Keep This Quiet!* is a moving read and much recommended to any literary studies or memoir collection."

—Midwest Book Review

"While the job at Random House did offer her the opportunity to meet a lot of writers and famous people, it is Hunter that became her secret office romance. . . . A great deal of the book is personal letters from Hunter to Margaret, with Margaret's inside emotions written in the theoretical margins. Harrell is an excellent storyteller, in a story that is never about the narrative, but about the real people. Every person in the book is bold and well defined."

—San Francisco Book Review

"*Keep this Quiet!* is a riveting, soul-baring honest look into Margaret Harrell and the inner workings of one of the world's greatest writers."

—Nick Storm, owner of Storm Generation Films

"Harrell beautifully tells the story of how her relationships with the three men, predominantly Thompson, progressed, sharing intimate moments and keeping the reader turning the page."

—Portland Book Review

"*Keep This Quiet!* is at once noisy, sensual, and word-drunk, as well as quietly intimate and full of Harrell's wonder at her luck. While most readers will come to this book for the Thompson content, in truth all the portraits here—all four of them—are compelling and often touching."

—W. C. Bamberger, *Rain Taxi Review of Books*

"*Keep This Quiet! My Relationship with Hunter S. Thompson, Milton Klonsky, and Jan Mensaert* by Margaret A. Harrell is a masterpiece! I never expected to say that about a memoir."

—Ron Whitehead, author of
The Storm Generation Manifesto and on parting, the wilderness poems

Praise for Keep *This* Quiet Too!

"It is chaotic, shambolic, impulsive, complete and utter madness at times here. . . . A passionately written memoir that doesn't sit around being fit and proper and straight laced. . . . As a key to the lives of these three writers it is idiosyncratic and in an age where blandness is the norm it is a pleasure to go on her journey and find out a little about what makes these men tick and what drove her to them."

—Eric Jacobs, *Beat Scene* (UK)

"Margaret A. Harrell has done it again. In her brutally compassionately explicitly honest second autobiography, *Keep THIS Quiet Too!* Harrell manages to repeatedly pull the rug out from underneath the reader."

—Ron Whitehead, outlaw poet author of "Never Give Up"

"At times adventurous, at times sensual, *Keep THIS Quiet Too!* hinges upon the complexities of human relationships, especially the challenges posed by the heart-wrenching feelings of love that may or may not be fully requited. Highly recommended."

—Midwest Book Review

"*Keep THIS Quiet Too!* starts off as Margaret Harrell's immersion in the art, music, and literature of Mensaert, Thompson, and Klonsky but becomes something much more."

—Alice Osborn, author of
After the Steaming Stops and *Unfinished Projects*

"As she opens the door the reader is compelled to walk on through and discover alongside her. What a ride."

—Nick Storm, political reporter cn/2 Louisville KY, owner of Storm Generation Films

"In this book Margaret goes an extra few steps to open her heart and lay bare. Having read the first volume, the line was baited. Her words were jangling on the hook. I couldn't help but bite and from the first few pages she reeled me in. . . . Imagine laying oneself prostrate before someone, not knowing how things will roll. Margaret did it then with her lovers. And she's doing it now in the sense of opening her heart to her readers. I was somewhat taken aback with her honesty."

—MARTIN FLYNN, www.hstbooks.org

"Margaret's life is, as always, more amazing than any book. If I didn't know Margaret, I wouldn't believe her incredible life story. But I know her and I can tell you: all of it is true."

—FRANK DESPRIET, author of *Van Reptiel tot Robot 2.0: Evolutie van de menselijke communicate* (*From Reptile to Robot 2.0: Evolution of Human Communication*)

"Deep and provocative . . . insightful . . . unique, for sure!"

—RUSSELL D. PARK, licensed clinical psychologist, coauthor of *The Power of Humility*

"Harrell's rapturous experiences with Thompson and her transformative journey toward wholeness intelligently propel her literary presentation through and beyond literary boundaries."

—BERNIE P. NELSON, *The Mindquest Review*

Keep This Quiet! III
Initiations

Margaret A. Harrell

Saeculum University Press
USA Romania

Copyright © 2014 by Margaret A. Harrell

All rights reserved
Printed in the United States of America

For bulk or 40% bookstore discounts or signed copies,
e-mail orders@hunterthompsonnewbook.com

Cover design by Gaelyn Larrick of http://www.wakingworld.com
Interior design by Darlene Swanson of http://www.van-garde.com/
(vol. I design by Bram Larrick)

Some poetry was reprinted from *Love in Transition* I.
The computer image was reprinted from *Toward a Philosophy of Perception*.

Publisher's Cataloging-in-Publication Data

Harrell, Margaret A. (Margaret Ann).
Keep this quiet! III initiations / Margaret A. Harrell.
p. cm.
"Volume 3"

Includes bibliographical references and index.

ISBN 978-0-9837045-6-0 (pbk.)
ISBN: 978-0-9837045-7-7 (e-book)

1. Jung C. G. (Carl Gustav), 1875-1961—Correspondence. 2. Spirituality. 3. Pauli, Wolfgang, 1900-1986—Correspondence. 4. Self-actualization (Psychology). 5. Initiation rites—Religious aspects. 6. Harrell, Margaret A.—Travel. I. Title.

E169.12.H37 2014
306/.1097309046—dc22
2011909464

Saeculum University Press
5048 Amber Clay Lane, Raleigh, NC 27612

A division of Saeculum University Press (SUP)
Didi-Ionel Cenuşer, publisher
B-dul Victoriei 5–7
550024 Sibiu, Romania

The author in 1991

Twenty years from now you will be more disappointed by the things that you didn't do than by the ones you did do. So throw off the bowlines. Sail away from the safe harbor.
—Mark Twain

A Question Enters the World

I also think of the possibility that through the achievement of an individual a question enters the world, to which he must pose some kind of answer. For example, my way of posing the question as well as my answer may be unsatisfactory. That being so, someone who has my karma—or I myself—would have to be reborn to give a more complete answer. It might happen that I would not be reborn again so long as the world needed no such answer . . .

C. G. Jung, *Memories, Dreams, Reflections*

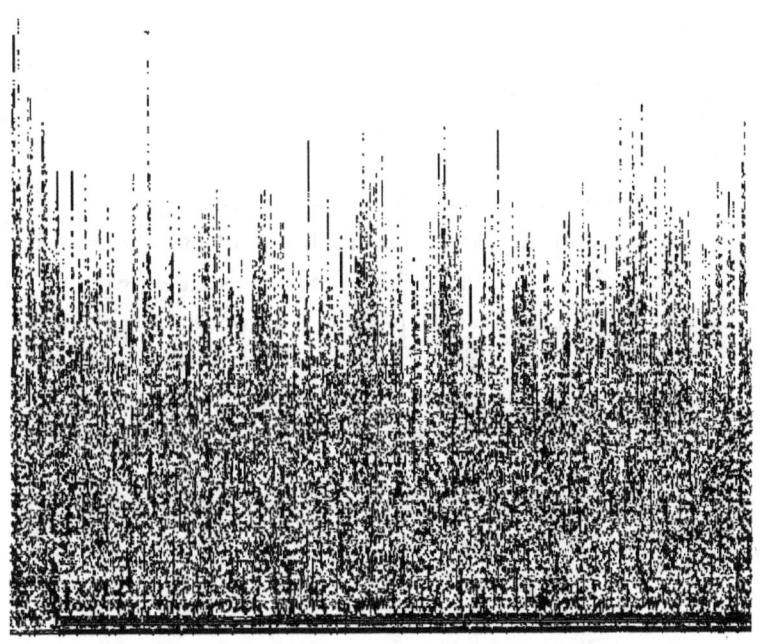
Spontaneous computer creation in the author's apartment

"It's very provoking!" [Alice] said, in reply to the Lion (she was getting quite used to being called "the Monster"). "I've cut several slices already, but they always join on again!"

"You don't know how to manage Looking-glass cakes," the Unicorn remarked. "Hand it round first, and cut it afterwards."

This sounded nonsense, but Alice very obediently got up, and carried the dish round, and the cake divided itself into three pieces as she did so. "Now cut it up," said the Lion, as she returned to her place with the empty dish.

Lewis Carroll, *Through the Looking-Glass*

Now both men [Jung and Pauli] are dead. Physics has undergone great advances with its grand unified theories and its current development of superstring theory. Yet the central question remains: What is the nature of Pauli's great dream? What is that speculum that lies between the worlds of mind and matter? Will it be possible to develop a new physics and a new psychology which are complementary to each other?

F. David Peat, "Divine Contenders"

Contents

Author's Note	xix
Prologue	3

PART ONE

Science, The Unconscious, A Constellated Archetype, Pauli and the Beggar Ulysses

On a Scientific Footing	30
Pauli and the Piano	34
Ordering Archetypes: The Brain and Consciousness—How We Make Choices	38
Procrastinating Further: Important Side Topics—Beneath the Beneath	41
A Pantomiming Archetype	47
Lines under a Window	51
Pauli: The "Missing Fourth"	60

PART TWO

Getting Back to Me: The Initiation

Threshold of the Initiation	72
Over the Threshold	87
A Master Initiation in a Personality-Level Self	92
Inside the Initiation	105
A New Christ Personality	109
To Love—*and* Remember	111
Damascus "Cook Key"	112

Watching the Hand Played—One Step Up 123
Sowed Seeds 128
Comparison—Intention to Heat 139
Newton & Alchemy 141

PART THREE

Jung, Pauli, The Meta4

In Search of a "Psychophysical Theory" 148
Gate *Eau*, Water Gate 154
More to Ponder 158
Why I thought "this" and . . . 168
Doubling Time: Greece 169
Rounding Out Zurich, 1986–87 171
Bridge: Who Am I? 178

PART FOUR

Meeting Willy and Cast, The Bell

In the Hospital 184
Jyoti's Workshops, "Willy might not survive,"
Kundalini, An Event Ball 212
Hunter Reintroduced in 1991 235
Hit Pause 238
Looking Ahead 239
Preview Volume IV: A "Naked Child" in the 1990s:
Divine Child & the "Hieros gamos" 242

Appendix I

Meditations & Exercises 245
Of Chris Van de Velde 247

Contents

Of the Author 253
Exercises Keyed to the Book 255

Appendix II
Summary of the Major Initiations 273

Notes 276
Works Cited 284
Acknowledgments 291
Artwork Credits 293
Index 294

Author's Note

The third in the series, *Keep This Quiet! Initiations* continues my memoir. As well as being a memoir, this book is indebted to Swiss psychiatrist Carl Jung (born in 1875) and Nobel Prize-winning physicist Wolfgang Pauli (born in 1900 in Vienna), who dreamed together of uniting physics with psychology. I attended the C. G. Jung Institute in Küsnacht, Switzerland, a suburb of Zurich, 1984–87.

It was in Zurich I had my first initiation. The initiation built on the sudden (to me) death of Milton Klonsky (November 29, 1981), which baffled me, made me question whether death really existed in a nonphysical sense—a question I wanted to answer for myself by experience. Did the mind that told me "Some of us have more whites around the eyeballs. I was a crazy kid. You know what I was crazed by? *Immortality*" just vanish into dust?

He went on: "*I've* died. But I've died into *me*; *he's* still around. I can talk to that kid anytime I want to."

Was his astonishing mind (that library of knowledge, beacon of sparkling insight) obliterated? Was all evidence of his lifetime decayed into soil and recycled?

I had to know. By closely following the experiences I was having after his death—in dreams and outer incidents—I hoped to find out. In that, the unconscious would help me, I believed; it had helped me as a writer since age seven.

What is the unconscious? As Jung made central to his schema, there exists in addition to an individual unconscious that contains our personal memories, a deeper, highly structured collective (or objective) unconscious that is inherited. It is, as Jung put it, "the foundation of what the ancients called the 'sympathy of all things.'"[1] The physicist F. David Peat calls it "the common ground out of which matter and mind emerge."[2] But this is only the beginning point as to what that collective-unconscious mind might be. Often I use the term "the unconscious," in cases where it is clear which is meant but also because if you are unconscious in a situation, the mind is very often drawing from both personal and objective layers.

We know that until you can imagine something, believe it's possible, you're pretty sure not to see it around you even if it is. Your eyes will skim right over it, vowing it isn't there. It seems wildly implausible, as did many experiences in this book until I had them myself. Even the eye refuses to cooperate. Peat puts it starkly: "Anthropologists have reported that aboriginal people shown snapshots of themselves usually can't see anything but a swirl of abstract colors and shapes. They don't know how to read that kind of map."[3]

Initiations break down belief systems, using powerful means to divert our neural pathways, open up our hearts; if necessary, make us take our heads out of the sand. For me, as this story unfolds, experience—often contrary to what I supposed was true—became the teacher.

These initiations, beginning in 1985 (based first on the death of Milton Klonsky in 1981, which I didn't learn about till the summer of 1982), took me to multidimensional places. Initiations are personal and transpersonal. They transform us—in this case, me. The unconscious, however, is still vital. It's just that what is unconscious is in constant flux.

Initiations individually take us across our own stopping points, our own finishing lines where ribbons are broken. We burst across, out of breath, in a turmoil, turned topsy-turvy. These things happened to me. I began to discover a consciousness level far beyond my own.

But I had to learn for myself; everyone does. And this book is the result. For a lot of people today, there are boundaries ready to be pushed aside. I learned how to say what follows over the past twenty-seven years. Now the page is turned, and I walk into the book formed of those experiences, those initiations.

In Appendix I you'll find Mind Body Spirit exercises to help you integrate and apply the ideas in the initiations into your own meditation practice.

One needs an initiation like that in Zurich only once. In my case, it shattered every assumption I took for granted. I think a lot of people can relate to the pattern of breaking through a block to the future, annihilating its obstacles. The way this comes about will create an individual story, a personal myth, or contribute to, as Jung put it, "dreaming the myth onward."

Even when we have spiritual experiences today outside established religion, we are often given Western explanations. Whereas in the East it can be more matter of fact, because of an ancient societal culture that regularly guided people in a structured way through some of these experiences.

In fact, if there was a great drought in the East, people might gather in a tent and pray and chant for rain, till the moment the guru would say "now let's all go out," and then the rain would fall. Or they might call on the rainmaker. Society expected this kind of participation—which we in the recent West don't, barring some exceptions in indigenous situations.

The following true story was told often by Jung, who got it from Richard Wilhelm, a sinologist who translated the *I Ching* and brought it to Jung's attention. Wilhelm witnessed the story below unfold:

> A rainmaker, Kiau Tschou, was summoned to a Chinese village after a long drought. The situation was dire; local rituals had been to no avail. Upon arriving from another province, the withered old man asked for a hut to be constructed and enough food and water for five days brought, then settled into solitude. There was not even a dark cloud for three days. The fourth day saw dark clouds, then rain and rain and rain. The villagers asked how he made the rain and he answered that he didn't: "When I first arrived in your village, it felt discordant, disharmonious, unbalanced, disturbed. And I felt out of sorts with myself." He had then retreated into the hut to reestablish his inner harmony. And the rain came.[4]

A Buddhist article, "Turning a Tap in Adelaide, a Downpour in London," adds:

> The rainmaker replied, "No, you don't understand. You see, where I come from everything happens as it is supposed to. It rains when it's supposed to rain and stops when it is supposed to stop. It is the same with the people too. We all do as we are supposed to as well. But when I alighted from the carriage in your province I recognised at once that you are all out of harmony and so it was no wonder that it did not rain when it is supposed to. Being here myself I became infected by your disharmony and I became out of sorts. I knew that if anything could be done then I would have to put 'my own house in order' first. And that is all I have been doing for the past three days!"[5]

I want to leave the impression that my experiences are not particularly unusual. They are, however, "irrational," counter to the left brain. But the left brain and even the ego are just a piece of us, a piece of our physical self, a piece of the "known quantity" of us, which we all know is only a glimpse, like our limited glimpse into the universe.

An underlying wish in this book is to make "becoming yourself" seem "safe," if you will, while still adventurous and *unsafe*. But the kind of unsafe that's fun. And fulfilling.

KEEP THIS QUIET! III
INITIATIONS

Prologue

As this story opens in 1984, en route to the C. G. Jung Institute in Küsnacht, Switzerland, I'd reached a watershed moment. My marriage had failed, not because of an affair but because I felt the lifeblood sucked out of me. I'd been in a deeply co-dependent relationship, jumping when my husband cracked his whip or said boo; blackmailed for thirteen years by his threats of suicide, which were not idle.

Leaving him, I lived for a year in Charlottesville, Virginia, diving into my first workshops in personal growth. At the end of a year, on a rainy Sunday, I drove a small U-Haul trailer, teetering unsteadily to the right and left in the wind for six hours, to a storage unit in North Carolina. Then flew out of Raleigh–Durham. Destination: New York–Switzerland. My mini-dachshund, Snoep, with his back legs paralyzed, perched quietly on my lap.

In my 1984 notes I asked myself an intriguing dream question, on October 5–6: I wanted to absorb the events of the fifth, "*including the phone call of HST.*" The scanty comment jogs my memory: in a New York stopover I dialed—for the first time in years—my former Yellowstone Park boyfriend, Bill Holden, and another former boyfriend, Gonzo journalist Hunter S. Thompson.

I drew a parallel: both lived in "BACKWOODS—of Alaska, of Colorado: 2 hermitlike types." I talked with Hunter "midnight–2 a.m." I found "a side of him I didn't know in his comments on women and his approaching interview with a porn queen."

(He was about to go to San Francisco for *Playboy* to research the Mitchell Brothers' famed O'Farrell strip club, a story that would balloon into a prospective book, *The Night Manager*.)

What I would give to remember more! With the notes I reconstruct how "I told Hunter I was trying out my new self in N. Y.—not drinking alcohol, etc.—and if my friends wanted the old me, I'd get new friends." HST and I had often spoken in terms of "Life Nr. 1," "Life Nr. 2"—going back fifteen years.

For instance, in August 1968, quitting my job as copy editor at Random House, I used that phrase. He had replied the next month (after covering the Democratic national convention, where riots broke out) that he was "writing bags of pages every day on Chicago"—for a book tentatively titled *Eight Years on the Road to Chicago: Notes on the Death of the American Dream—or, once again, Which Side Are You On?* He went on: "How—to change the subject—is your second life shaping up? I'm curious; the whole idea fascinates me. I'm also curious about the book you've been writing. Send word—and Happy Birthday. Love, H."

I answered, "My second life has taken a strange, unforeseen turn right off at the start. I'm using all my wits to get myself into MacDowell Colony."

When I married Jan Mensaert in 1970, Hunter said he'd lost count: "First Belgium & marriage, then the Cairo Hilton, then back to Greenville for a while. It's hard to know what's happening. I assume you're married & of course I congratulate you and Jan. Is this the third life, or the fourth? What next?"

And writing his Author's Note to *The Great Shark Hunt* in his editor's Random House office in 1977, he contemplated jumping "straight off this fucking terrace and into the [Rockefeller] fountain, 28 stories below and at least 200 yards out in the air and across Fifth Avenue." Because—reflecting on his adventures—"Nobody could follow that act. Not even me." If he survived, he predicted:

> Everything from now on will be A New Life, a different thing, a gig that ends tonight and starts tomorrow morning.
>
> So if I decide to leap for The Fountain when I finish this memo, I want to make one thing perfectly clear—I would genuinely love to make that leap, and if I don't I will always consider it a mistake and a failed opportunity, one of the very few serious mistakes of my First Life that is now ending. [Signed] HST #1.

Prologue

My nonalcohol regime I mentioned on the phone in New York was a switch from a few nightly beers. Before leaving Charlottesville, I'd been advised (by a highly reputable international psychic, Mariah Martin, a longtime educator in the fields of consciousness evolution and spirituality) to temporarily take that step; she predicted that energy in Zurich would be so high I needed to avoid overstimulating my lower chakras. With some apprehension, I told Hunter about this lifestyle change. (He may have countered with the revelation that two years before he'd checked into a rehab facility—and almost as quickly checked back out.)

When we hung up, I took out my notepad and asked my dreams to illuminate the call. The request was granted. In a dream Hunter appeared symbolically in the guise of a tap dancer while "my sister LL" (representing my alter ego) had a dance audition.

She did things not yet as well as me, such as a plié with incorrect alignment, I wrote, *but that's her inexperience, I hope.* (I associated the tryout with "testing my new image with HST.")

The dream continued, bringing in the figurative Hunter, emphasizing his smooth moves: *Another girl surprised me by being a tap dancer—really good at it. She whirls around even better than [a professional]. I watch her.*

I took it that the rhythmic heel clickings of the female tap dancer, the freedom, the flashy spins, the sense of being in sync with LL (like Eleanor Powell with Fred Astaire dancing to "Begin the Beguine"), represented HST's inner feminine, who'd responded to me tit for tat, musically in step, when I announced my "new self."

At one point, LL lets her bra slip sideways a bit, exposing a little breast flesh awkwardly. I keep my distance, while realizing this is the way you start out.

I thought that LL, in "leaning too far forward, with her breast (= emotions) showing," had illustrated my "feelings (w/ HST) I don't identify with."

On the seventh, Snoep and I flew out.

Hunter soon flew out of Stapleton International/Denver first class with "harried-looking middle-aged business men" and his girlfriend, Maria Khan, toward San Francisco airport, which was closed because of a violent thunder storm.[6] I don't think I knew about Maria. He would write of this trip in *Kingdom of Fear*: "I am in the sex racket, which is worth about $10 billion a year on anybody's computer—and I am flying to San Francisco to take on the whole city government; the mayor, the D.A., and the police chief. . . . The Mitchell Brothers—Jim and Artie—will be waiting for me at the gate . . . This is the fast lane, folks . . . and some of us like it here."[7]

I'd promised to relay my address. He'd said, "I hope to see you again someday." Two hours on the phone wasn't a lot, but it left a high. Off we went in opposite directions.

I was to start classes October 23. Arriving early in Küsnacht, I took German, yoga, ballet, and jazz and revised my secondary novel, *A Lecture upon the Shadow*. I'd written it in Morocco, about the doomed failure of my marriage with Flemish poet Jan Mensaert.

Following up on the promising contact with Hunter, I left him a machine message. Waiting for classes, I had our conversation on my mind.

October 16, I dreamed: *I'm trying to reach Hunter. I remember I spoke to him once in N.Y. & told him I was going overseas but I'm in N.Y., phoning him, & he answers. Then he's gone. I'm disappointed & disoriented. I didn't ask if he'd written as planned, either.*

Then (a few nights later in another dream): *The phone rings. The operator asks for me. I realize it's Hunter and say, "This is she," but change my mind and say, "I'll go get her." I race out of the male apartment to the female one. I see at a glance he's hung up. I say, "Damn," etc.*

In case the reader doesn't know, Hunter and I had an affair after I'd copy-edited his first book, *Hell's Angels*, at Random House. It began in long-distance calls, letters, and editing, leading up to a dramatic meeting in February 1967, when he came to New York for his book tour. And bada boom bada bing. We hit it off in person, as over the electric wires and through the words that jumped off the page.

I became convinced in Charlottesville that my life followed

nineteen-year cycles. At the start of each, I seemed to encounter a tidal wave. Something huge. Nineteen years earlier, in 1965–66, I'd met the three powerhouse males who played major roles in my life between 1965 and Zurich—Hunter, Jan, and Milton.

The meetings came tightly packed, in a fist of synchronicities, anchoring me into relationships from 1965–66 till Zurich.

I'd learned strength from these three writers. I was an aspiring novelist myself, unpublished, having begun two manuscripts. One, in Montparnasse, Paris, in 1965, on the European trip I took for that purpose—to walk in the steps of famous writers, painters, musicians in the 1920s. Sit at their café tables. Soak up the atmosphere. And begin. Which I did. Back in New York, when I met the genial Milton Klonsky, I instantly selected him as the model for my protagonist, Robert.

I had no tape recorder, but by racing to the bathroom or other maneuvers, I could scribble down and memorialize some of Milton's comments. Not only for perusal, as many were worth a fortune in my depth bank, but also to put into Robert's mouth. For instance, "This would have to be either love or despair; it's up to you to choose which."

But the "big book" wouldn't finish, and by 1980, reading Jung's *Man and His Symbols* and his autobiography, I'd detected that I'd layered his psychology of "individuation" (true identity, which requires an integration of all parts of the personality) under the story: lo and behold, hidden in the characters were my shadow; my animus, or inner-male energy—Robert/Milton being, in fact, what Jung called the "bridge to the Self." Reading Jung, I could see that as clear as day. What more did I *not* know *I knew*?

If I'd been experiencing the individuation process, outlining it correctly in my writing, wasn't it about time to explore it consciously?

I was not the first or last to whom Küsnacht/Zurich, was a magnet. Nonetheless because Küsnacht was where Carl Jung founded his original institute to promote the study of images, myths, fairy tales, archetypes, and his psychology of the unconscious, which he believed fervently was active in a major way in our lives. Dreams beckoned me to enroll.

Big Dreams shine headlights into the future. In the lead-up to Milton Klonsky's death in 1981, I'd had one. My only lucid dream ever. In it, I found myself writing in the dark—not aware it was dark (i.e., being unconscious) till reaching for a blank page, I couldn't find one.

At that instant the light came on; I saw unfamiliar masterpieces hanging as if on a wall. I was astonished. The paintings filled the remaining pages of the book I was writing, pages I'd assumed were blank. Framed, glorious, unknown portraits. I gaped. Where was this? Why had no one ever seen this illustrious art?

I watched as on an earlier half-page, then another and another, my writing vanished. Immediately, an invisible hand replaced it with scenes. Finally, I saw myself on a stage, receiving the award for my book—"number four this century because it was rare." I associated "rare" with "rara avis," which was how Jung described a patient he had at first thought beneath him, till he dreamed he had to crane his neck to look up to see her. The dream offset his waking impression. He then dismissed her as a patient, saying she didn't need his instruction.

This was a perplexing grade from the unconscious. Who inserted the pictures? Number four—what was it? For Jung, it was "an instinct of individuation." An archetype of wholeness. But I would find out that it was much much more.

In 1984, I had short, curly auburn hair, styled in Madrid. I was 5 feet 3¾ inches and weighed 120 pounds. I'd been an amateur dancer since age five, one year professional.

I did not know it yet, but the universe puts its full strength behind one thing now, and then another thing *now*. At those "tides in the affairs of men," the whole ocean is in support, even if one is the tiniest drop. Everything is *lined up*. To spring. You have only to go *with the white caps*, ride the surge.

Before tackling Zurich, I would like to set up the Charlottesville scene a little.

I moved to Charlottesville, Virginia, in September 1983, having just left my husband in March, and in October my mother died suddenly. In Charlottesville, I studied for a year at the brand-new Mind Body Spirit center called "Openway" founded by the Mexican healer-therapist Graciela Damewood—attending experiential events, including a monthly hyperventilated-breathing workshop. Graciela's philosophy was that healing involves "bring[ing] consciousness into all processes"; she focused in part on unconscious "imprints" and said, "The most essential element of healing is not a technique. It is related to the energy vibrations of love and trust." Later the Integral Healing Centre of Toronto evolved out of her work. I also had a volunteer job with psychologist Bob Van de Castle, director of the Sleep and Dream Lab at the University of Virginia Medical School. My assignment was to put Van de Castle's definitive bibliography of dreams into a computer.

I was mourning the death of my mentor, Milton Klonsky, which I learned about in July 1982, though it occurred November 29, 1981. In passing through New York City, I wheedled the unlisted phone number of his best friend, *New York Times* book reviewer Anatole Broyard, out of a sympathetic Knopf editor. But had no luck in reaching Anatole by phone.

So I wrote him in the hyperbole I felt, July 17, 1982, "Everyone else can disappear but not Milton."

I described how every year "I passed through New York, only to see Milton." Never announcing myself in advance, always finding him in his apartment. Also:

> Last September 25 in Belgium I received a strange deposit of money in my bank account, then in October learned it was for delivering medicine to a doctor in America, and that I would even get a free ticket. And I was frantic to come, because I felt—and this never happened to me before, with anyone—that Milton was very ill. I couldn't come, however, and told myself it was nonsense, but underneath I knew it wasn't (and was afraid to phone). Then Nov. 29 something quite miraculous happened.

The miraculous thing was a numinous parade in Blankenberge, Belgium (where I was temporarily living with my husband).* I saw it alone—with no other viewer—at nearly the exact time (I later learned) of Milton's death; it held me spellbound. I mentioned to Anatole I might come to New York for a day or two—"to get the fact of his death hammered into my head." I added: "I think you must be rather lost, like me . . . This time [my 1982 stopover in New York], perhaps of all times, I had so much to talk to Milton about, so much to tell him, so much to ask him. Everything had changed" (meaning I was pretty sure to leave my husband). I closed:

> How is it possible now, to pass years watching his memory grow dim? He, the "magnesium flame," as he put it. One thing there was to hold onto: whatever happened, there would be Milton, who always made the meaning of the passing years clear to me, because of whom how could I be lonely? No? How be lonely, that is, not in the way that really counts. And how not be lonely now? Except that he said when someone very close to you dies (his father, specifically), you become that person. I don't feel the tie broken, even yet. But then I don't accept the fact that he's dead. Not Milton.
>
> There's an old postcard of mine here, with just a note, in green ink, in Milton's handwriting: "Why fly? Why solitary?"

It was at Virginia Beach I learned about Al Miner.

Al is compared by many to the "sleeping prophet," Edgar Cayce. As an early computer programmer, he discovered his psychic gift quite publicly by accident in 1973, when he filled a friend's canceled hypnosis appointment. By chance, the session was with the Reverend Dr. E. Arthur (Art) Winkler, a clinical psychologist, who had also founded the Congregational Church of Practical Theology (which

---

* By numinous, I mean having a mysterious, highly charged aura around it; the word, used often by Jung, comes from "numen," meaning "a presiding divinity or spirit of a place."

Prologue

recognized all the world's greatest religions). Hypnotized, Al immediately fell into a Cayce-like trance, and a spirit group he afterwards named "Lama Sing" spoke through him. Al refused to believe his friends' account of what happened till he listened to it on tape:

> When the recording started, and Al heard the voice, he wanted to jump up and run out of the room. What he heard was obviously his voice, but not only was the accent not his, how could it be that he was speaking with them while he was having his own experience in the desert? The more upset Al got, the more everyone else laughed. Finally, Dr. Winkler brought a chair over and sat down next to Al.
>
> "It's okay," Dr. Winkler said softly. "This kind of occurrence is rare, but it does happen. You have an uncommon ability to move in the somnambulistic state of hypnosis very easily."
>
> What happened when he went back to a time several centuries in the past (while simultaneously diagnosing illnesses in the "present") became the turning point that led to his spending decades as full-time channel.

Repeatedly, in Association for Research and Enlightenment (A.R.E.) tests of psychics afterwards, Al ranked number one for accuracy.

As a writer, I hadn't wanted to learn anything through psychic readings; I wanted to find out through my intuition. However, at forty-three, when our story begins in 1983, I couldn't shake the overwhelming impression that Milton was not dead, he was guiding me. I asked around, got Al Miner's name, and sought him out. I felt it was of life-and-death importance to me to determine whether Milton was alive. I believed theoretically in an eternal soul. But that assumption had not been tested. I was severely shaken, in a quandary. This situation was way over my head.

In asking for a remote reading, I wrote, "My whole past life has been pulled out from under me like a rug."

I explained that marriage to my Belgian husband, Jan Mensaert, had "gotten me on a sandbar." In March, I'd left him definitively in our home in Larache, Morocco, despite fears he would carry out the suicide threats by cutting his wrists or doing any number of the things he'd tried unsuccessfully before. I'd stopped believing I could help him reach his potential as an artist, or that I hadn't the right to stop trying.

However, he was sure "we have a karmic relationship and should try to work things out."

Then the second very important male relationship—"with Milton Klonsky (born November 26, 1921, on Staten Island and died in New York City November 29, 1981)." I felt his passing was "the turning point of my own life, when the old collapsed and the new marched in. My trail began to appear. To me it was as if my own higher self died with him, and the highest truth. This too is probably a karmic relationship."

I was still groping to adjust, asking "whether or not I am in denial and even holding him back."

In a mismatch I had not wanted his mentoring to turn romantic (which he did, as reflected in my "big book" begun in Paris, where the semiautobiographical Paula played me).

After his death, Milton had convinced me in vivid ways that he was around. First, in dreams he told me the news was inaccurate, that he was in *re*-mission. Then there were incidents, such as when an academic parapsychology researcher stopped me to say she saw a being of white light over my head. But was I making it all up? Tremulously, I waited for Miner's response in the mail.

In confirming Milton's afterdeath presence, Lama Sing shattered the past all the more, by bringing up what (to me) were phenomenal concepts. In sum: I was on Earth "at a time when both it and [I] have embarked upon a cycle of strong spiritual development, and more than the normal sensitivity prevails."

He mentioned "a cycle beyond the Earth" whereby "major soul groupings as are involved with the Earth are also in a transitional state."

If that wasn't enough to make my jaw drop to the floor and my knees knock together, he went on: One such soul grouping had as a member Milton Klonsky, likewise myself. Milton and I had a conductor, a channel, between us, "which cannot be disrupted by the loss of a physical body," for the tie was deeper, at the emotive, physical, and spiritual levels.

Lama Sing advised that a place in me was at one with God. That Self would always "guide [me] aright."

He added that my own soul was "guiding [me] into this position," directing me to look at many things "with much more reality."

I was being asked to see if I could find "sufficient merit" in myself to accept this opportunity—not putting myself above others, rather taking everyone as equal.

He said I was being presented very beautiful opportunities, whereas to find such opportunities some were having to "depart."

Who, with matters put into such terms, would not gladly accept the steps required, with however much fear and trembling—would not feel challenged and admonished to go to the deepest point of truth within?

My main soul grouping's current project, as tersely mentioned by Lama Sing, involved assisting Earth in *its* transition (while *itself* undergoing one), with the two transitions aligning. An intriguing comment he did not expand upon. He added that "growth, when attained in the physical, which is the more limited realm of consciousness of which [my] soul is capable, creates . . . generates the soul's highest qualities."

The rest, I was left to figure out.

However, being in a particular soul grouping, he said, did not necessarily indicate level of consciousness, because—he explained—in each group there were various levels. And the least evolved were vitally important because the most evolved were only as strong as the weakest link.

Soon Miner came up to North Carolina from Florida. Driving to the western part of the state from Charlottesville to take his workshop, I continued the uprooting.

I learned what practically all the participants believed: that everyone has guides, and souls belongs to multiple spirit groups. It would take time for such a concept to sink in. Was it true?

Intense dreams continued. A sample, February 6–7: "We're trying to clean up Milton's house. He's not dead"; March 14–15: "Milton has been sent to jail for something—we don't know what—and he's let out."

Many nights, I relocated to Manhattan. June 30–31: "I'm in NY, first in an apartment where I find what Milton left me"; July 1–2: I dreamed to "lower my voice," then found myself in NY with a woman who wanted to be Milton; August 1–2: "I'm in love with Milton and go to where he is with his new girl. . . . He has no memory of how he's acted upon me while he was dead. He and the girl live together in an apartment that (relative to the distance from his old apartment) seems to be where my old NY apartment was"; August 5–6: "I'm with Milton in NY. I haven't gotten around to telling him how our relationship is changed."

August 5–6: I remember how Milton told me (in a dream) he was "coming out of Virginia"—back to life: "The returned Milton has two names. I must bring him up to date on our relationship"; August 12–13: "I'm at a place where Milton's death is being verified by an officer. For the first time ever I decide to speak, as I know this subject."

The only other channel I consulted before going to the Jung Institute was then-Hawaii-based Mariah Martin. She was recommended to me by psychologist Robert Van de Castle and Openway founder Graciela Damewood and had reassuring credentials, academic and otherwise. Mariah said she thought my soul-grouping's mission involved "mind over, no, *through*, matter." Also, "a consciousness is coming toward you."

Al Miner was so helpful that just before Zurich, I had a reading (in mid-September). I was fascinated by the concept of *soul groupings*: What were they? Where was mine?

He replied: "Quite simply your soul grouping is in a realm of consciousness, that is, existence, which is several dimensions, several spheres of consciousness, removed from Earth. Think of this then in terms of the ability to accept."

He added: "Also, or further, your soul grouping spreads itself in terms of consciousness across the spectrum of several other levels or spheres, ever striving to reach higher in that sense of that term, and ever striving to—that is, those who are beyond the least of them—striving to leave a path unto which the others might follow."

Having dreamed about a group activity, I asked if a soul-group project was under way; he said yes. Specifically, "it associates with the Christ's light," which, he added, "is simply the illumination of the universal nature of each soul by the intensification of those forces which relate to this consciousness. So it is called the pathway of return unto God, the Christ Consciousness."

The term "Christ light," or "consciousness"—as meant here—did not refer to or coincide with a religion. But was, as he put it, shedding light on "the universal nature of each soul."

He said little else—in order not, he said, to abort my life purpose. Learning certain information from such a source, he said, could do that. I had always insisted on finding out things for myself, to forge the qualities from Not Knowing. Involving sometimes nail-biting suspense.

After New York—and the phone call to Hunter—I went to Zurich in high excitement. There was so much I didn't know. For instance, the Dream of My Life about *number four*—what kind of counting was that?

Thinking numbers were numinous, Wolfgang Pauli was vitally interested in *four*. Likewise, Carl Jung. Both brought up often this *quaternio*, or four. Pauli associated *three* with reason (science) and the Trinity; *four* with the irrational, the unconscious. He thought of them as a simultaneous either/or—of equal opposites.

For Jung, four added completion: wholeness; to Pauli, it meant his discovery of a final—fourth—quantum number later determined to be "spin." Out of this grew his famous exclusion principle that resulted in his Nobel Prize.

Arthur I. Miller, in *137: Jung, Pauli, and the Pursuit of a Scientific Obsession*, notes that at a certain moment Jung told Pauli of the axiom of alchemist Maria Prophetissa ("One becomes two, two becomes three, and out of the third comes One as the fourth," i.e., the Philosopher's Stone). "Pauli's psychological journey—a story of threes and fours—[was] coming together with his scientific journey."[8] This will become important as the story proceeds.

Obviously, in view of my lucid dream, I couldn't—in writing *Keep This Quiet! Initiations*—let these clues go unnoticed. I had to chase them down. What did it mean that I was working in "number four"? To answer, I had to take a closer look at Küsnacht/Zurich.

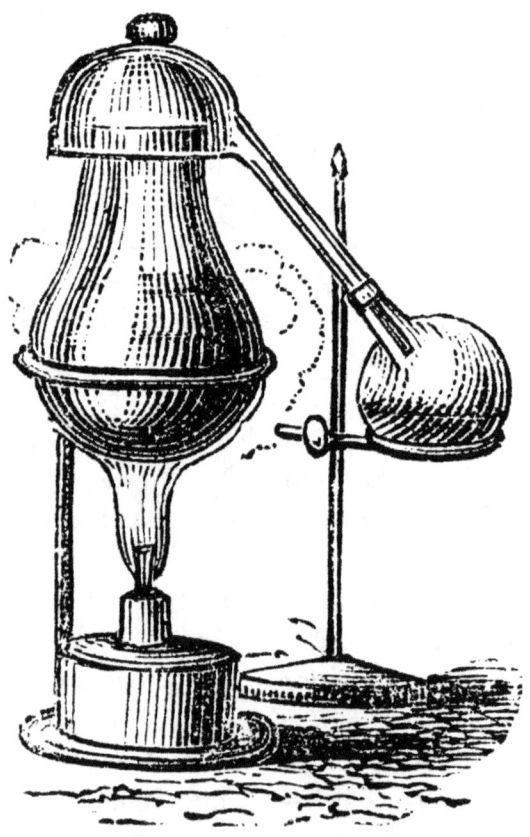

Antique illustration of Alembic distillation

Prologue

In this book I cover part of the nineteen-year block introduced to me in 1985 in Zurich.

At the C. G. Jung Institute, analysis was required to become an analyst. Though not intending that profession, I was aware of the opportunity presented; it would not come around again. So in December 1984, I began sessions with a lovely Jungian I will call Fran X. We focused immediately on my dreams.

Recounting them, I insisted she could not look into my notebook, a fancy little journal from a stationary shop. But then I left, forgetting it; I raced back to her living room; the 3x5 book had dropped between couch cushions. As we both sighed with relief, she explained that "Little Margaret" hid it. Then she held out modeling clay for my extraverted "inner child"—the opposite of the grown-up child I'd actually been (and of myself in the 1980s). She said, "You have a strong relationship with the unconscious."

What did that mean? When asked how her approach differed from the more behaviorally oriented ones, the famous analyst-author Marion Woodman answered, "Well, because I am a Jungian, I come *from* the unconscious . . . which literally *is* unconscious."[9]

Marion talks about how as a child she was two Marions and those opposites battled it out "all my life": "There was the person who lived from Monday to Saturday. She never put on shoes unless she had to. She had a corncob pipe. Hair never combed. I was *gypsy*. And when I went up to the woods, I had no fear because I had my little Joan of Arc with me and I knew she would protect me . . . On Sunday we combed my hair. Big deal. . . . I had to sit there and grit my teeth until the ringlets were in place. No pipe, nothing of that, but I did have a pretty skirt. And I loved going to the church . . . and to hear my father preach and tell a story . . . but in all the pictures on Sunday I'm clutching my skirt, like *that*. And so there was an obvious tension."

Jung had theorized that in processing information, in addition to being extraverted or introverted, everyone is dominant in one of *four* psychological types: either intuition *or* sensation and either thinking *or* feeling. I still have my Jungian Type Survey Answer Sheet. Recently, in surprise, I dug it out of a box.

A dominant *introverted intuitive* such as myself at that time (score: 25 introversion /18 intuition) would be *inferior* in sensation. I scored high in thinking as well (15). He said the inferior function—in my case, feeling (6), followed by sensation (8)—is partially unconscious.

Little Margaret personified my inferior sensation function. With extraverted sensation she (in my unconscious) would experience concrete things, like a tree or mud, for themselves (unconcerned with finding beauty or meaning in them) and be completely at ease working with her hands (or modeling clay), which I felt sure I was totally inept at.

In announcing a program at the Maine Jung Center, Portland analyst Chris Beach explains, "One of Jung's key ideas is that of staying in the tension of two opposite energies until there arises a third that transcends and resolves the opposition. . . . Within the model of psychological types, this manifests in several ways, including what happens when an individual moves from living predominantly in his/her main or heroic function (for Jung, his heroic introverted intuition came up with the big ideas) and purposely develops his/her inferior or soul/spirit function (for Jung, his inferior extraverted sensation, as he painted and carved rock [sculpting a small medieval, turreted castle at Bollingen]). Over and again, we find that when a person makes this move in a devoted and sustained way, s/he moves through initial resistance, feelings of inferiority, and wondering 'why am I doing this?' into a transcendent space where there is a sense of long time, a steady and enduring rhythm of creativity, and access to new energy within."[10]

Relevant here is a tale by the Jungian Marie-Louise von Franz that illustrates inferior sensation (with dominant intuition, like Jung)—in an extreme case.

The story: One day after von Franz lectured on early Greek philosophy, a woman in the audience who was very moved requested private lessons on pre-Socratic philosophy. Invited to tea, von Franz later said the first hour was "wasted," in her view, as the woman heaped praises on the speech, speculating on what the two might accomplish. The same thing happened in the second hour. To move

Prologue

along, von Franz brought out a book, insisting they look at it systematically. The woman "agreed," said von Franz, "but added that I must leave her alone: she had to do it quite her own way. I noticed that she was getting nervous."

When von Franz returned the next hour, the woman told her:

> she could naturally not study Greek philosophy without knowing about the Greeks, and she could not know about the Greeks before knowing quite concretely about their country. So she had started to draw a map of Greece, and she showed me the map. It had taken a lot of time. With her inferior sensation she had first had to buy paper and pencils and ink. That excited her enormously; she was absolutely in heaven about her achievement! She said that she could not yet go on with philosophy; she had first to finish the map. So by the next time she had colored it! That went on for a few months, and then her intuition picked another theme, and we never got down to Greek philosophy.

However, later this woman recalled how much it had meant to her to have Greek philosophy lessons!

Von Franz noted: "She had just drawn a map. She was a very extreme case of introverted intuition. But I must admit, in looking back, that I see what a really numinous thing it was for that woman to draw this map of Greece; for the first time she had got in touch with her inferior sensation."

That mysterious undeveloped function has access to the unconscious—standing in for it, offering Freudian slips or, as here, a hidden lost dream book. Jung explains it as a puzzle: "The least differentiated or 'inferior' function is so much contaminated with the collective unconscious that, on becoming conscious, it brings up among others the archetype of the self as well—[*out of the Third comes the One as the Fourth*], as Maria Prophetissa says. Four signifies the feminine, motherly, physical; three the masculine, fatherly, spiritual."[11]

The analysis was not to last. A few months in, I dreamed of a plane flying quickly from point A to point B, in contrast to a ground vehicle.

I realized that my intuition thought it could reach the goal fast. Knowing it to be the final session, I asked the expert analyst what to take away. She said presciently, "Remember the part of you who has secrets *and the part who likes to expose them.*"

Her words—about the two me's—were the nearest I ever come to deciphering an earlier dream: November 21–22, 1981, *one week before the death of Milton.* I was briefly subletting an apartment on the North Sea in Blankenberge, Belgium, with my husband, though most of the marriage we roughed it bohemian-style in Moroccan villages.

The year before that, in 1980, I'd bought Jung's *Man and His Symbols* in the United States and taken it back to Larache, Morocco. Curled up in the refrigerator-less apartment, where we cooked on charcoal, I read it and then at night put a pen and paper beside my bed, and an abundance of dreams gushed out.

As Milton's death (November 1981) approached, I was unaware in Blankenberge that in New York City he was rapidly nearing the end. Yet my dreams hinted at his plight. In fact, I killed off my fictitious character Robert modeled on him. But I didn't suspect that demise drew from reality. However, in whatever crisscrossing of our two fates, in the very last week of Milton's life the Big Dream below came in. I had not the remotest thought of studying at the Jung Institute Zurich (or anywhere), had not even thought studying in English in Zurich possible. Yet the message below points to it like a signpost:

> *I enter a museum dedicated to Jung and see on the wall a lifelike picture of him—almost real-looking, with bold, flowing lines as in a cartoon or charcoal drawing. I think it's a self-portrait he left on his study wall. The person with me had been an assistant of Jung's and knew the portrait at a glance. Taking it down, I hand it to him or her and ask what the most interesting area is upstairs.*
>
> *"Bipod metallic," she answers: bipod or biped. She leaves. Intrigued, I think of things with two legs, modern sculpture made of metal, with a rough shape . . . ironwork.*
>
> *Then I tell someone I want to ask a—I pause and don't say "stu-*

Prologue

pid"—question, what is bipod (or -petal) metallics?

Upstairs, I race past pottery—to the entrance of a series of rooms (3?) that I look into as down a hall, the doors open between the rooms. The nearby people give only a cursory glance in that direction. I think: so this could be a shortcut I was given in Jung's study, if that was the room—bi-something (-pod or -petal or -pedal) metallics (or mechanics?).

I felt an enigmatic topic had been assigned me, but what?

Racing past pottery—I later related this part of the dream to the lowest level of a seminal dream Jung had while traveling with Freud in 1909. Finding himself in an unfamiliar house that was "his," he investigated. Upstairs on a Rococo level were valuable old paintings on the wall; he then went down the steps to a darker fifteenth-/sixteenth-century level. Proceeding down further by way of a stone stairway into a cellar, he then descended again into a room with Roman walls, where—intensely excited—he pulled a ring in a square stone slab in the floor. It lifted.

He wrote: "And again I saw a stairway of narrow stone steps leading down to the depths. These, too, I descended and entered a low cave cut into rock. Thick dust lay on the floor and in the dust were scattered bones and broken pottery, like remains of a primitive culture." He interpreted the house to be his psyche.

With this hint nestled among others, he was able later to theorize the existence of the "collective unconscious,"* that is, in its depths the unconscious was universal, common to all people, an *a priori* substratum attempting to communicate with us, not deceive us. This collective unconscious—layering the levels of our development through history—gave us a common humanity. It was "identical with Nature to the extent that Nature herself, including matter, is unknown to us."[12] This would differ from Freud, who formulated his theories based on the personal unconscious only, which we each fill with repressed and instinctual material.

---

* This dream was variously narrated by Jung, 1925–1961, but the gist is above.

Jung did not find humans, just because of our ability to reason, necessarily superior. He appreciated the African zoological classification that put the elephant at the top, then the lion, then the python or crocodile, then humans and so on. He said, "The idea that man alone possesses the primacy of reason is antiquated twaddle. I have even found that men [male and female] are far more irrational than animals."[13]

In 1981 my dream's directive, toward Jung's "study," was primarily horizontal—befitting an *extension* of the by now richly researched symbol-driven collective depths of psyche he unearthed. It had been seventy-two years since his multistoried-house dream. On the bulletin board in the Küsnacht Institute office I afterwards saw a gray glossy snapshot of Jung so lifelike it was almost animate. He had a pipe and a long neck. It reminded me of the portrait. His journey went down and down—through levels of the past enfolded in our collective psyche. *Was the assistant in the "bipod metallic" museum personified by the therapist's parting words?*

"Bipod metallics"—did this phrase connect these two me's?

Jung went further in calling for a realliance with nature, a reconnection with the unconscious. Not knowing who we are, he wrote, "Man . . . is a top animal exiled on a tiny speck of a planet in the Milky Way . . . cosmically isolated. He can only state with certainty that he is no monkey, no bird, no fish, and no tree. But what he positively is, remains obscure."[14]

Jung predicted: "Discovery of the unconscious means an enormous spiritual task, which must be accomplished if we wish to preserve our civilization."[15] Technological invention, he pointed out, was pursued at the loss of our instincts and primeval, archaic (meaning original) self. He was encouraging not a return to a primitive state, but a valuing of qualities we'd put at risk.

The Jungian analyst Marie-Louise von Franz illustrated with the Naskapi hunter of Labrador, who lived in solitude and had no religious leader, no rituals for guidance, but instead listened to an inner voice. Von Franz said, "In [the Naskapi hunter's] view of life, the soul

Prologue

C. G. Jung Institute Library, Küsnacht

of man is simply an 'inner companion,' whom he calls 'my friend,' or *Mista'peo*, meaning 'Great Man,'" who lives in his heart.[16]

But despite Jung's insight into the need for its exploration, the unconscious is still a mighty terrain of the unknown, with consciousness a tiny tip on the submerged continent.

And so we begin where we ended the last book—in Zurich—in this dilemma that possibly held the key to my life purpose. I was divided, partly unconscious. So is everyone. But the dream said—if the assistant was the analyst—"bipod metallics" was the place for me to start.

This book took the shape it did in part because I had a hunch there was such a thing as a continuing synchronicity—as if a packed wave splattered on contact, hitting now this person, now another. Trying to say what? Further what? Out of what depths? How might I link in? In what particular intent inside that deep structure?

I thought I might be in the position, unexpected by me, to piece together part of the answer—in this glimpse behind a curtain where matter met consciousness and synchronicities spewed up encrypted bytes of data. I was hooked. While writing the book I realized: but of course, this is a constellated archetype sitting right at the bursting point.

Pauli had noticed that synchronicities, like radioactivity, *spread*.

In *Pauli and Jung: The Meeting of Two Great Minds*, David Lindorff points out that Pauli saw "matter—through his *physical* dreams—as having a meaning unrelated to the psyche of the perceiving observer, a symbolic reality in its own right."[17]

November 9, 1953, Markus Fierz, professor of theoretical physics in Basel, sent Pauli one of the seventeenth-century Cambridge Platonist Henry More's dreams. More was a significant theologian and philosopher. Shedding light on operations of the collective unconscious over time, his dream—*from three centuries earlier*—seemed to relate to a problem presented by Pauli's *twentieth-century* unconscious.

Probing the relationship of psyche and matter, Pauli had searched for how to combine irrationality (represented by the number 4) and reason (3). At the particular time Fierz sent him the dream, Pauli was looking at his own life in two phases; in this regard, he had arrived—for reasons we won't go into here—at his preference for the ancient zodiac format, 4x3=12, over 6x2. More's dream landed at Pauli's doorstep just as he mulled this over.

It ended with twelve sentences in golden letters—six he remembered, six he didn't—after which he was woken by a "trumpet call" of two donkeys (6x2=12).

Pauli believed that the six forgotten sentences symbolized the dark side of God and the desire of seventeenth-century Christianity to *separate* evil from good, repressing the dark. He thought it was time to incorporate the dark into a wholeness of the Self.

Regarding waking to *two* bellowing donkeys, Pauli thought that in building the bomb, "science had known sin." The donkey duality, he said, might reflect the fact that "God speaks to us *always* in paradoxes," which are understood over time.[18]

Years after I left Zurich, I read psychologist Arnold Mindell's revelation that his own life and work with thousands of people had convinced him of "a sort of informational wave pattern—a personal myth, relationship myth, or group vision—which moves and guides us through life." He said Jung, if alive, "would say, 'Of course, the pilot wave is what I called the individual's personal myth!'"

Mindell explains: "I need only think of my early interest in physics, the apparently improbable accidents that landed me in the applied physics area of M.I.T., how my fascination with Einstein drew me to study in Zurich where I landed one week after Jung died in 1961. My first dream of analysis was about Jung telling me to pull together psychology and physics."

Hold on. Is this the same dream, of bipod metallics? Mindell went on, "I married Amy, born on the day Jung's main collaborator in physics, the Nobel Prize winner Wolfgang Pauli, had died. Are all these things accidents? I arrived the week Jung died, and Amy 'arrived' the day Pauli died."[19]

From here—Einstein in Zurich working out his theory of special relativity, Pauli and Jung devising synchronicity there, Arnold Mindell getting an assignment from Jung in a dream—might be hypothesized a consciousness nugget, or node, if you will. Shining bright like the light on an island in darkness in Jung's so-called Liverpool dream. Let's look into it.

PART ONE

Science, The Unconscious, A Constellated Archetype, Pauli and the Beggar Ulysses

What is that speculum that lies between the worlds of mind and matter?
—F. David Peat

Each new direction of Jung was inaugurated by a dream.
—Jung Institute lecture

— 1 —

On a Scientific Footing

Now for science. I first became interested in quantum mechanics in Zurich. In fact, just before my initiation there, I was reading *The Holographic Paradigm and Other Paradoxes*. Although it was published in 1982, we are still absorbing today some of the leading-edge ideas in it, including ideas about deeper unities and laws of an underlying wholeness or inseparableness beneath matter and meaning.

I took many notes from philosophers and physicists. For instance, Rutgers philosophy professor Renée Weber (interviewing Birkbeck College theoretical physicist David Bohm): "But then you're saying that just as physics—the new physics has revolutionized the way we look at what we think of as the world out there, so you're saying the new consciousness revolutionizes the way we look at what before we thought of as the observer."[20]

And theoretical physicist Fritjof Capra. According to legend, Newton observed an apple fall, and the resulting "flash of intuition" led to his discovery of the law of universal gravitation. Capra writes, "The force that pulls the apple from the tree is the same force that pulls the planets toward the sun . . . The insight that there is uniform order in the universe is implicit in Newtonian physics."[21]

Also, Ken Wilber (later formulator of Integral Theory)—on the measurement problem:

> The mathematics of QM [quantum mechanics] can determine, with great precision, the *probability* that a certain quantum event will occur in a certain environment (at a certain place or a certain time), but it can never predict *the* precise environment itself. . . .

Thus, the particular event is not looked upon as a single entity or occurrence, but rather as a "tendency to exist," which, in this example, would be *defined* by an equation (or probability amplitude) that says, in effect: 50% A/ 30% B/ 20% C.

Now the odd thing is that the event, when it occurs, *does* occur in just *one* area. . . . When you finally walk through the door, you go through only *one*—50% of you doesn't go through door A, 30% through B and 20% through C.[22]

Then, fabulously interesting: "The event itself, if left alone (not measured), will 'propagate through space-time' according to the Schroedinger wave function, which, if squared, gives the probability of finding the event in a certain environment (50/30/20)."

Wilber continues: "When it is finally detected, it does occur in *one* region only . . . This is called the collapse of the state vector or wavepacket, because when measurement determines that the particle is in B, the probability of it being in A or C collapses to zero. The collapse of the state vector means that the event *jumped* from being a 'tendency to exist' (50A/30B/20C) to a 'real occurrence' (B)."

Therefore, the conundrum: "Does measurement itself 'cause' the collapse of the wavepacket? Does the actual particle even exist at all prior to measurement?"[23]

Well, that was then. Some of the questions have been answered. Wilber set the stage for his school of thought.

We know that everything is made of energy. But inside energy is an organizing structure. According to the Standard Model, there are fundamental, indivisible particles: fermions (quarks, leptons, and their antiparticles) and bosons. Fermions make up matter. Bosons mediate interactions, or forces. Much about bosons is still unknown, such as whether gravitons, carrying gravity, exist.

The question is, if everything else is mediated—such as electromagnetism by the photon, the quantum of light—what mediates gravity? The as-yet-undiscovered graviton? And what about the Higgs boson—it has long been surmised to exist as the missing ingredient in the Standard Model of particle physics. The Higgs particle was experimentally detected in 2012 (implying the existence of a Higgs field). When the Higgs field comes in contact with most of the known elementary particles, it gives them mass (and for their independent 1964 theory of the origin of mass in subatomic particles the 2013 Nobel Prize in Physics went to Peter Higgs and François Englert). However, mass (inertia) would not necessarily create a gravitational force in all universes. If gravitons exist, they would be the quanta of the gravitational field.

In the Copenhagen interpretation of quantum mechanics (led by Niels Bohr), when a physicist takes laboratory measurements of energy quanta, the act of measurement influences the result, causing the "collapse" of the wave of unlimited possibilities into a single form. Banishing all else, one result—in what was a field—emerges as a *fait accompli*.

F. David Peat describes how science changed with quantum mechanics: because measurements—experiments—at the quantum level require the exchange of at least a quantum of energy and a quantum cannot be divided, "the essence of quantum theory at the moment of observation is that of 'undivided wholeness.'"

He calls that "radically new in science."[24]

The Observer Theory, which many consciousness theorists, subscribe to as I do, carries the effect further. It says that when the wave function collapses—and the field of possibilities is stripped to one result—it's precipitated by consciousness.

In fact, some proponents of consciousness research turn everything upside down; they give consciousness the huge role of preceding matter entirely. Ascribing great weight to intent, many place the effects of this theory right in our homes, our thoughts.

By that token, we will find—going further—that by placing our awareness on something, we help organize it into patterns: a miracle in itself when we think about it, that by being aware, we have that much power to influence the world around us; to affect, at minimum, our perception of it. As if we could command the particles or hypnotize them to fall into line. Where do the patterns come from? How does this work? How do they keep us healthy or make us sick? Are they contagious? What don't we know?

I first became interested in this topic in Morocco, when I read about a well-known French psychologist (or philosopher; the details are vague) in *Le Monde*. This famous man believed that as he looked to each side of himself he could see the surrounding energy field (the "probable future," as it were), just by how the objects in his proximity were clustered, organized. Well, I began to try it a bit. But what I didn't know was that the idea had taken hold. It was growing. Fertilizing itself, organizing itself—becoming a pattern inside me, a pattern of attraction, of my future interest.

We're always stepping through patterns, prearranged decisions. Choices. Chain-linked probabilities of what we will do today. It's not that we don't have free will. It's that these things have been invisible to us. It's a secret of the East. Of the Great Masters. How to say it, though, is a question.

— 2 —

Pauli and the Piano

I well recall my first memory, an instant in which I became aware I existed. I was a thirty-pound, red-haired ball at the top of the stairs, listening to the voices below. Enveloped in a desperate desire, I wanted to go down. From upstairs, I only recall clearly the frozen portrait—the "tableau"—the Prufrockian dare: *will I do it?* I was two years old (or thereabouts) and walked/crawled/bumped to our living room.

I found my father in a poker game—rare for him—and I sat in one of the men's laps. He suddenly spread his fingers wide to show me his cards, carefully concealed from the others. Practically just born, I was into bets and secrets. With these clues, Jung would deduce a prototype of my personal myth.

Five years later, in great concentration I sat on a piano stool, playing J. S. Bach. It was my first recital, and partway through I forgot the end. As if glued to the stool, I stayed on it, my face scrunched up, playing; forgetting at a different chord, I started over. I repeated this process till my hands played the whole barcarolle. The tale might seem ephemeral. But was it another indicator of my personal myth? Was "remembering the end" part of it?

Jungian psychologist James Hillman, in his excellent book *The Soul's Code*, argues that *calling* ("the acorn theory") is predominant in our lives as children; he piles on examples. For instance, in the case of the future-world-renowned Spanish bull fighter Manolete, he was sickly, withdrawn, and clung to his mother's apron strings till he was gored by a bull at his first corrida at eleven, but stood his ground and dismissed the goring.

Hillman remarks: "Clearly heroism is constellated. A myth of the hero calls from within his acorn." Hillman asks if the apron strings were metaphorical, "or was he already using her apron, her skirt, as a cape?" He answers, "Of course he kept away from torero games in the street, taking shelter in the kitchen. How could this nine-year-old boy stand up to his destiny? In his acorn were thousand-pound black bulls with razor-sharpened horns thundering toward him, among them Islero, the one that gored him through groin and belly and gave him death at age thirty and the largest funeral ever witnessed in Spain."

He adds, "The entire image of a destiny is packed into a tiny acorn, the seed of a huge oak on small shoulders. And its call rings loud and persistent and is as demanding as any scolding voiced from the surroundings."[25]

Later, astounded, I ran across Pauli's 21-page essay "The Piano Lesson," which he highly prized. He wrote it in active imagination: a Jungian dream-interpretation technique that uses free association. It begins on a misty day. Reflecting on how he has long been troubled by an inability to bring together theoretical physics and depth psychology, he seeks help.

Then, inside a house in Küsnacht, an inner male figure, the master, tells him, "Time reversal." Now Pauli is a little boy beside a grand piano; leaning against it, a dark-haired lady—his inner feminine (his anima)*—wants to teach him a lesson. The music tones symbolize feelings, which, Pauli said elsewhere, were "the very thing that physics cannot express."[26] She can. In the Jungian *psychological types*, the feeling function is in opposition to the "thinking function," which Pauli, being a scientist, excels in. The dark-haired lady at times has "slit eyes."

In a translated article in *Harvest: International Journal for Jungian Studies*, Herbert van Erkelens writes that she "represents the *anima*

---

* For Jung, the anima represents a man's inner feminine, or soul, and is often projected onto outer females. The parallel projecting aspect in women is the animus (inner masculine). However, except when speaking specifically about Jungian psychology, I use the term "soul" in the more familiar language where it holds higher wisdom than the personality. In that sense, the direction of a journey like the one taken in this book is for "the personality" to become the soul. At least, that's the goal.

mundi, the soul of the world, whereas the master [a dream figure familiar to Pauli] personifies the spirit of matter. . . . The belief in strict causality [in deterministic classical physics] has in former days been used as a pitchfork to drive the world soul out of our view of the cosmos."[27]

When Pauli can't find a solution, the Chinese lady offers him the "ring i," with "i" representing the square root of minus 1, an imaginary number without which it's impossible to mathematically describe the complementarity of waves and particles. She says it represents the timeless "fourth."[28]

The dark-haired lady explains how one can play *all* the melodies, using the black *and* white keys—if only one knows how.

He gets a similar message just afterwards from a Chinese dream woman: "You must allow us to play chess with you in every conceivable combination."[29]

Had my intuition flown me into this collective/personal aspect of my journey as I tried *all possible note combinations*—to remember *the whole*—linearly/nonlinearly, as an entry card into the archetype? Was it, even at that instant then, popping in? Had my panicked, startled mind transported me outside the physical setting into the collective while *my hands* performed the archetypal movements: to play every possible combination, dark notes and light?

At age forty-five that myth, lived unconsciously, reached a breakthrough, which is where this book opens.

It is outside the scope of this book, but yet further ahead, in 2000, I would at last receive an experiential understanding of how this vision of Pauli's (and myself at the piano) might play out in the structure of Oneness, or Source, and even quantum mechanics. For now, I had a child's insight.

But reading Hillman's next comment brought everything into perfect perspective for me; significantly, "Even before there are life stories, lives *display themselves as images*" [my italics].[30] That is, cameo scenes revealing predispositions.

It had taken me nineteen years to absorb the fearlessness mentality exhibited by the males I'd orbited around, which the inner me needed me to have. The stage was set for the next nineteen. But at the boundary line, the critical moment, September 1985, a test occurred in Zurich. Would my "little self" pass—would this fantastic growth of the prior nineteen years stick—or would I have to go into a repeat, which in some ways would be delightful (but in others not!)? Passing the test, I believed, would leap me ahead in my purpose. I would be led, not as before by the unconscious, but by my deeper self.

— 3 —

Ordering Archetypes

The Brain and Consciousness—How We Make Choices

Your unconscious uses its own consciousness to reason. Even inside myself, I don't reinvent the wheel daily. Based in past action, it makes analogies, creates a line of momentum. The brain does not necessarily continue forward on the same track in cases where it appears to operate without consultation with you or me. Granted it is not openly asking, but it is making comparisons. This kind of activity, going on inside, we call unconscious.

We will examine this mode of thinking in this book.

My brain, when on its own—left unsupervised by the conscious thought process—uses an inbuilt frame of comparison. According to this framework, if I start the day in a shortcut, the likelihood is that I will continue with shortcuts straight ahead. Why? Because I set *a style* in motion. But not in linear straightness. It is chaotic—based on consciousness; the consciousness that the brain detected when I made a certain decision.

The brain will *apply* the consciousness, the calculations—what it deduced from my action—until a different style of decision sets in motion new analysis.

Then that decision too will set *a precedent*. That precedent will remain operative till superseded.

We know that the simplest choice eliminates other choices, even a thoughtless, "meaningless" act. The unconscious, however, might try to make sense out of it. *Predictive value.*

Though this may sound absurd, it's the first step to a very important fact.

Suppose the meaningless choice unconsciously charts A COURSE, like testing to see which way the wind is blowing. At least on some level it often sets up, most likely unknown to us, a sequence—a "valuing" framework. Like a pecking order.

Archetypes, as Wolfgang Pauli mentioned in a letter to Carl Jung, are "ordering factors."[31] The Jung/Pauli letters, published in *Atom and Archetype* (2001), are inside the speculative language of theoretical physics and psychology, with gems that have gone unnoticed by the mainstream public. As I read that phrase "ordering factor" last night, it opened up what I am writing today. As I slept, it led to this path into the material I have been ruminating on for days. Before that, years.

The reason a seemingly unconnected choice can forecast other choices—to the unconscious—has to do with a process of creating direction through analogy: the tendency to go in a direction. Our unconscious is always working. When my body moves, my intuition begins to interpret.

Even when I move an object with my hand, my intuition may unconsciously kick in. When I place a cranberry juice jar behind a tin of coffee grains in the refrigerator it is meaningless, I know. But that's not necessarily so. It holds unconscious information.

The unconscious loves to pick up on our secrets. In my *scale* of values I may have just placed coffee before cranberry juice.

Later in the day my unconscious may *translate that* into skipping the gym or other healthy choice. The thing may mushroom, as scale does on these tiny levels. It would be superstition to think that simply placing one item in front of the other *caused* a later event.

But the thing is, my unconscious is listening. It is getting to know me, predict me, jumping to conclusions. It can systematically attribute *placement values* as emotional preferences at that time, because my unconscious can read these SIGNALS and is conscious to what my actions unconsciously *mean*.

It is creating shortcuts and automation, easy future positions to slide into like a baseball player stealing a base: all the little choices seen as trends, pathways, predictively important, by the unconscious. For to it, when we collapse a tiny wave of possibilities with a (to us) single arbitrary choice, it can attribute *meaning* without *meaning to, by enlarging the scale,* collapsing *like* waves *in the future,* making it easy on us, as it were. Yet the opposite may be the effect.

Thus, I stopped myself from procrastinating longer on this book.

— 4 —

Procrastinating Further: Important Side Topics—Beneath the Beneath

Werner Heisenberg, a founder of quantum mechanics, came to believe that "what was truly fundamental in nature was not the particles themselves but the *symmetries* that lay beyond them." F. David Peat points this out in *Synchronicity: The Bridge between Mind and Matter*.

So to the eminent physicist Heisenberg (an originator of QM theory), the elementary particles pointed to something beyond even them. Peat explains, "The elementary particles themselves would be simply the *material realizations* of these underlying symmetries." Further, "These fundamental symmetries could be thought of as the archetypes of all matter and the ground of material existence."[32]

Even further, Peat cites Einstein's argument "that what is taken as the very essence of things, a stone for example, is in fact the complex focusing of geometry which provides the ground of all matter. . . . In Einstein's vision, the universe is like an organism in which each part is the manifestation of the whole."[33]

One little act carries a string of things with it. A whole set is pressed under one trigger. Why? How can one decision burgeon into multiple decisions? Set the larger stage? That is, make other acts much more likely. Because an unknown direction has been established; momentum continues. One procrastination is the procrastination of many things. What causes this multiplication?

The unconscious.

Not beginning something is not just omitting a single event, episode, and all it might open up. But in parallel, all it connects to more widely. How? On the personal level, by analogy. Even the perceptions of the past it changes. Connects to or associates with in the great web of connections.

Relativity in the Unconscious

The unconscious ignores time and lays things flat on a board, upon which it compares them. It brings up, as carrying energy, a thing that is *like* something else. Or unlike it. So the complementary part of some of Newton's breakthroughs is in the unconscious.

Not only because we are unconscious of it. But also because the unconscious proceeds not by adding up along a timeline but by summarizing in an entirely different manner. It has strings of relative and nonrelative things. Things that tell a common story and things that tell our story differently, which we shy away from. Or ignore, or don't see.

It defragments itself. And it pigeonholes. Our normal mind categorizes what we've explored or learned. If the information is partial, we fill in the blanks. We fill them in unconsciously. But we also fill in blanks in matters where, from a broader view—perhaps a predictive one—we unwittingly hold information.

I learned this reverse perspective in the Zurich Initiation. Finally, after many paths, I have found the way into telling that story. That is, what I learned back in 1985 that I could not put into words for two decades.

I will go back to my old practice of talking to the reader, so we can take this journey together. It is what our unconscious is always trying to do, set up a communication line. In a way, I will take the role of the unconscious now, trying to say some things about itself.

But first, a little more overview of what I boiled down as knowledge out of experience. I want to lay it out on the line first, let it dry out fresh from the unconscious, let the story build till what might seem a fairy tale seems perhaps entirely like fact.

Initiations were not unusual at this institute founded by Carl Jung in the small town of Küsnacht, on Lake Zurich, settled at least as early as the Stone Ages. A few miles from Zurich, Küsnacht was once inhabited by Thomas Mann, and Tina Turner is a current resident. It was Zurich that housed Einstein in 1912–13, when he worked on calculations for his general-relativity theory in *The Zurich Notebook*.[34]

I have mentioned one dream that led me there. In another, in 1983, I carried a child to its mother, who waited *expectantly* at the Institute door. In a reinvented language, I *carried* the baby, whom I'd received from a girlfriend of Milton Klonsky after he died.

I interpreted the child to symbolize what I'd learned in the three years since the death of then-sixty-year-old Klonsky of cancer in 1981, which launched me into an examination of afterlife questions. Could a mind of such complex wisdom die? I had never asked the question seriously before. After his death I asked it nonstop. But also, the child I "carried" must have something to do with the Institute, where her mother "expected" her delivery.

The child—part of my unconscious: three years' worth—lived there, fed by events, but while small lacked the importance to me it had in my unconscious, where it was being prepared to step into my future on a larger scale.

The connection between psychology and physics was a very important focus for Jung and Pauli, who together crafted the concept "synchronicity." As David Peat notes, it was in meetings with Einstein and [Swiss psychiatrist Eugen] Bleuler over dinner in Jung's home, during which the three conversed about Einstein's early efforts to formulate the special theory of relativity, "that Jung first began to think about relativity of time and its psychic connections." Peat also notes: "Synchronicity, as a firm concept, did not really occur to Jung until around 1929. It is remarkable that the development of this idea a year later coincided with the appearance of a new patient, the brilliant young physicist, Wolfgang Pauli."³⁵

Let's start here, where their discussions took place, which probed the meeting place of psyche and matter. That is, a physical event might "act out" the *meaning* of the *energy* present in that location.

In individual acts employing physical force we can predict the effect. It's reproducible. We measure it.

But what about synchronicity? It's unpredictable, unreproducible—that's the point. Take a statistically meaningless, random effect. Inside the numbers there might be overlooked synchronicities, which do not meet the bar of "statistically significant." They were averaged out. Meaningless.

This one insight is phenomenal to think about. Statistical experiments demand repetition. But the definition and requirement of synchronicity is contrary to repetition. It is organized by meaning, which is not statistical but one on one.

This tiny insight is in fact so huge it took me a long time to grasp. There is something so important here I did not think it through to the point—till in reading the Jung/Pauli letters one night recently, I stumbled on it. Pauli said, "In my last letter, I suggested that synchronicity should be defined in a narrower sense so as to comprise effects that only appear when there is a small number of individual cases but disappear when there is a larger number." *That disappear when there is a large number.*³⁶

He realized that synchronicity is hiding—it disappears inside the large numbers, so it is not officially recognized for what it is. It lacks that official seal because it is not the reproducible effect on which to build technology! *It's the irreproducible effect on which to build consciousness!*

Both the statistically significant basis of science experiments and the irreproducible location of meaning (in synchronicity) order our reality. One orders it to produce technology. The other gives us the means to understand.

We can look at all the statistical examples in the world and won't know enough. Because human consciousness is built around another system. In the first place, around the archetypal patterns that make their appearances at particular instances—not particular intervals—based on timing, on constellations, on the meaning that the location has if we were aware of it. This too is phenomenal, and I think I am much closer to deciphering bipod metalism, as a result.

Reading the Pauli statement was a synchronicity in itself, a very subtle one waiting for me in hiding, that many if not most people might have passed right over. For me it was a beacon in what was already a lit-up landscape.

"In quantum physics," Pauli went on, "there are not just [scientifically valid] effects that appear with large numbers instead of with small ones"—this is what got me. Arrested my attention and made me sit up in bed, starkly awake, my white hair turning young again, as it were. That was it. Large numbers erased some effects. Not that they weren't there. They just did not appear to be—were not apparent, were not possible even, in the structure of measuring by statistics and megastatistics.

He refined his statement: "In quantum physics, the observer makes a conscious choice (which always implies a sacrifice) between mutually exclusive experimental setups." The distinction is that "in cases of nonpsychic acausality . . . the statistical result as such is reproducible, which is why one can speak here of a 'law of probability'* instead of an 'ordering factor' (archetype)."[37]

In a less lively fashion, in *Synchronicity: An Acausal Connecting Principle* (1952), Jung wrote, "The experimental method of inquiry aims at establishing regular events which can be repeated. Consequently, unique or rare events are ruled out of account."[38]

---

* In the Copenhagen School of quantum physics, to which he subscribed, the only certainty about a subatomic event is its probability. This, to Pauli, was a "statistical causality" (Lindorff, *Two Great Minds,* 17).

He notes how "the experiment imposes limiting conditions on nature, for its aim is to force her to give answers to questions devised by man . . . which misses out on all those by no means unimportant aspects that cannot be grasped statistically."[39] Here Pauli and Jung's fascination with opposites is in play. Both statistical events based on large numbers and nonstatistical, unique, anomalous events count.

I dreamed in July 2011 that I was pregnant again though it didn't show. Maybe this is still the same baby, or finally the baby, after all these years waiting to go into the womb—or out. About to have her say. Maybe her birth, not after nine months by any stretch, is timed to the synchronicity that I will get to her meaning.

She is a child announced by dream, waiting till her location had been prepared. Hidden away in Jung's "study." And who was the mother? Was it the feminine? Because organizing by meaning in a timeless state is antithetical to organizing by statistically governed laws. And if so, this would be a case of the feminine (receiving, relating) meeting the masculine in this idea about the nature of reality, where technology meets awareness of higher consciousness, or centuries of wait meet centuries of progress that left it mostly out.

— 5 —

A Pantomiming Archetype

My master's thesis at Columbia University in 1962–63 focused on symbolic actions in William Faulkner. In the thesis, everyday movements such as spitting, washing, burning, squatting became unconsciously expressed carriers of meaning. But I did not extend the principle. Surely we were not walking through "symbolic actions" *that our unconscious understood.* I did not, for instance, apply the principle to the trigger to begin my first book.

In beginning my "big book" (eventually titled *Love in Transition*), I had no idea why as I sat at Le Dôme, a café in Montparnasse, Paris, in 1965, looking out a window, when a beggar, a tramp clown, *pantomimed a request for a cigarette*—mouthing imaginary smoke rings—an unconscious message was constellated. His head bobbed exaggeratedly along the length of the window. No one else appeared to care.

His gaze came to rest on me. He stared. I stared back.

My lineless, blank-sheet-of-paper face—his: gnarled, wrinkled like tree roots—the half-eaten baguette protruding from his knapsack; the audacity, the bobbing nailed my attention. But why?

Why did it address my unconscious? What underlying connection struck? What spur—to break out of the starting gate? I began *Love in Transition*—then. And *there*. An unknown architect commanded: Now. *With this scene*!

Did nature often pop up picturesque placards, calls to action, using nonverbal communication? Paint a picture for our unconscious, as sure as if a message were hand delivered? A kinetic meaning?

Latent energy sat still, didn't it? A thought did not jump

dimensions, act itself out physically in space-time—cloaked to our conscious mind, decloaking before our unconscious. Did it?

Was there a way that, just by looking around, we could see *energy configurations* of *situations* in our midst the way an animal might get its news through smell? Surely we did not have such an ability to "read" information? A book of nature?

I began to look into this. It was possible we were surrounded by maps of objects—energy configurations of situations, obstacles. Possible that as we expressed ourselves in body language, there was configuration language that matter carried.

As germs used to hold diseases without telling us, were there "ordering systems" of objects all around, in self-organizing units that silently acted like event maps, or predisposition indicators? Could they reveal to us what was highly energized and in what patterns?

Nothing like that existed, did it? Information in a book stayed on the pages, didn't it, even though we could extract it as thought? But maybe our unconscious could extract it in other ways. All these questions were to leap into my life in a vital manner, beginning in the Zurich Initiation.

In the opening of *Synchronicity: The Bridge between Mind and Matter*, F. David Peat offers some answers as to what drama the beggar enacted. What, to the collective unconscious, in its to-do list, might the scene have acted out? Peat quotes the physicist John Wheeler:

> We had this old idea, that there was a universe out there, and here is man, the observer, safely protected from the universe by a six-inch slab of plate glass. Now we learn from the quantum world that even to observe so miniscule an object as an electron we have to shatter that plate glass; we have to reach in there. . . . So the old word *observer* simply has to be crossed off the books, and we must put in the new word *participator*. In this way we've come to realize that the universe is a participatory universe.[40]

Peat adds the profound analysis: "The essence of a synchronicity

Pantomiming Archetype 49

is that the particular pattern has a meaning or value for the individual who experiences it. While the conventional laws of physics do not heed human desires or the need for meaning . . . synchronicities act as mirrors to the inner process of mind and take the form of outer manifestations of interior transformations."

In illustration, he cites the cracking sound in Freud's bookcase not once but twice when he was arguing with Jung about parapsychology; Jung felt his diaphragm harden into iron and grow "red-hot"; he predicted the second sharp crack would follow fast on the first.

In another example, Jung's doorbell rang franticly (no one was there, though his household could see the bell moving) just before he began writing *Seven Sermons to the Dead*. Of these events, Peat says they "both took place in conjunction with violent, internal states."[41]

The subject is, how does our unconscious express itself? How does it reveal and illustrate itself? Read and interpret things around us *all the time*? Never asleep, as it were, in its world.

No matter what we are doing, the unconscious has an opinion, information to measure it by. Not as we measure consciously. But it is always giving things weight. To know some more of its personal, intimate, private tools would be, to say the least, helpful.

It is time we rolled back this dynamic, relieved ourselves of some areas of secrecy and ignorance to give our awareness new subject areas.

To expand into those areas we now need to shepherd the planet, what about closing some doors of uncertainty—guarded by the unconscious—to reveal what's behind them?

I had suspected that sometimes a physical correspondence to an *unknown* meaning triggered a sense of its importance. But had not yet understood that this might mean kinetic energy (energy that moved *in scenes*, not latent like a still ball) might tell an unconscious story, where the meaning organized in a picture. Not a still shot but as if the unconscious had gained a voice, like an animal who could suddenly speak, albeit silent to us—participating in a "motion" picture of something that our unconscious knew was important. As if a dream came to life, but it wasn't a dream; it was the *scenes*, the *process*, seemingly at the outskirts of our life proper.

We had never been told that this unconscious process was visibly at play in our waking life. At least, that is what I am saying here. Let's test the idea further.

We knew what happened when we rolled a marble. But how come all these other things were always happening—to catch us by surprise? Far from our intent?

The picture concealed in a seemingly everyday scene might reveal a shot of the "ordering factor" *at that moment.*

It might be an archetype no one was aware of. Jung and Pauli discussed archetypes as ordering factors. But suppose, to carry the discussion further, we begin to introduce both the concept of chains of connection and that of pictures popping up from the unconscious not only to tell us how things stood but sometimes to energize us. That is, we might be conscious of being energized but not know *the cause.*

So let's allow these intrusions of side topics a little longer—as questions linked to experiences that seemed to indicate their relevance to an important underlying structure. Of course, I do not insist on any explanation I offer. But here are some of the possibilities presented in initiations. So, it is my life that I can look at through them. That is, if I go outside standard explanations and add in these perspectives and the unsuspected "ordering factors." *The unconscious motives, but of whom?*

— 6 —

Lines under a Window

January 23, 1938, Wolfgang Pauli had a dream he found extraordinarily significant.

There was a window at the top; to its right an uneven clock was divided in half on one side, with no division on the other.

Under the window he drew a curvy, bobbing line. Beneath that, a parallel one—peaking at shorter intervals.

The clock being high up, he could not read it. An unknown, weeping dark woman hoped to write a book but had no publisher. She was interested in "how a period of time is constituted when certain symbols appear in it." From one page a voice read ecstatically: "The definite hours have to be paid for with the definite life, the indefinite hours have to be paid for with the indefinite life."[42]

Later that year Pauli perused Jung's Terry Lectures in *Psychology and Religion*. Within these lectures at Yale in 1937, the psychiatrist analyzed some of Pauli's dreams and his great vision (of a World Clock). (More on the World Clock later.) The World Clock analysis recalled to Pauli's mind his January 23 dream of the window and two lines. He now revealed it to Jung for the first time, inserting a sketch.

After much thought, Pauli explained, he believed in "the existence of deeper spiritual layers that cannot be adequately defined by the conventional concept of time. The logical consequence of this is that the death of the single individual in these layers does not have its usual meaning, for they always go beyond personal life."

How did the unconscious depict the spiritual layers? Pauli wrote that for want of vocabulary, it used *symbols*; in his case, often—as here—"wave or oscillation symbols (which still remains to be explained) [parenthetical words Pauli's]."[43]

In recalling the baffling moment that triggered the start of my first book, I was flabbergasted. I remembered how a Montparnasse beggar desperately *bobbed his head all the way across the Café du Dôme window*—rising, sinking in an *up-down* regularity. As his lips were puckered—elaborately miming the blowing of smoke *rings*—his bouncing head traced an invisible curvy line, creating a distinctive wavy effect.

I'd gone to Paris for inspiration—all set to write a book—with no immediate publisher. As surely as a Native American on a hilltop might use a blanket and smoke to send a message, this unknown trigger mechanism brought me the signal: at this point, here, now, *start!*

Pauli went on: "The relationship to these [wave or oscillation] images is strongly affective and connected with a feeling that could be described as a mixture of fear and awe." He speculated that the curvy lines were perhaps an imago dei (image of God).

He thinks the dream depicts the anima's concept of time. And perhaps the ecstatic voice—who reads about paying for the definite hours/definite life with the indefinite hours/indefinite life—is explaining the "puzzling 'rhythms'" (lines) from a new angle; "they seem to be regulating that process . . . called 'paying.'"[44] Calculable clock time is contrasted with indefinite time, or synchronicity; in the latter a biographer puts it, "a moment seems to have a quality that relates meaningfully and unpredictably to the future."[45]

Of a much later Pauli dream, Jung says the anima's lack of *definite time* means "that she lives in the unconscious."[46]

This terminology used January 23, 1938, becomes so important to the two men that in 1950 (and again in 1952), Jung will diagram a *quaternio*—in which he opposes synchronicity (defining it as "inconstant connection through contingency, equivalence, or 'meaning'") to causality ("constant connection through effect").[47]

In the 1938 discussion, Pauli mentions having unsuccessfully attempted to relate two of the *three layers* in the dream to a "four-part object ([the] clock)." A clock should divide into four quadrants, as in his transformative World Clock. This one does not; the dream lacks harmony.

He adds, "I attach a great deal of importance to all these problems."[48]

Pauli acknowledged in 1934, soon after he first went to Jung, that the collective unconscious *intensified* his extreme polarities—by intent so that he would illustrate a collective issue: specifically, "the abrupt swing into the opposite." An issue that, he thought, was at a crisis point for our civilization.

A dream of three huge horses had told him that "in this moment [in the world] everything can turn into primitive barbarianism"—just as he himself sometimes had—if we did not embrace the lessons of Tao and individuation.[49] Individuation, by the way, did not equate with consciousness, which, in fact, could impede it.[50] In the West, Jung thought, consciousness had dangerously suppressed the "primitive disorderliness" of the unconscious.[51]

Though in the 1938 sketch Pauli drew *two* wavy lines, *not* three, in his letter he mentions the *other two rhythms*. This discrepancy will come back in later.

By 1939, a year later, Pauli intuitively believes the oscillation (wave) symbols relate to "the *attitude to death*."[52] To understand what he might mean, I find it enlightening to look at a minor comment to Jung in 1937 in which Pauli said that "the death of the individual is *always*, in a certain sense, a historically conditioned necessity, for this individual is also constantly subjected to such psychic influences, which in his lifetime could not be fully assimilated into consciousness. If the reverse were the case, there would be something incomplete about the individual life."[53] So the individual life is not over at its conclusion. Psychic influences weathered in it go on. Let's see if that holds true in the story being told here.

The book I was writing, *Love in Transition: Voyage of Ulysses—Letters to Penelope*, would unfold through a series of deaths of those I knew well.

Finally, in March 1996 in Sibiu, Romania, the first two volumes were launched. By chance, at the event I read aloud passages that developed the *beggar* image. In dream interpretation in the 1970s in Morocco, I'd used symbol books in French, which was the second language.

Through active imagination I'd detected, in word play, an

unconscious "cook-key" for the new century (that's ahead).

I'd translated "cake" as "gâteau" (pronounced "got tow"): "gate AU"—unaware of the prose poem "Le Gâteau" by a famous nineteenth-century poet, Baudelaire.

Seated on the panel, French professor Eugène van Itterbeek listened intently as I read some *gâteau* word play before the crowd. "Baudelaire," he interjected. "*Mais oui.*"

Buried in Montparnasse Cemetery, the complex Baudelaire often wrote at the open-air café La Closerie des Lilas on Montparnasse Boulevard; by 1898 a new restaurant/café yards away was challenging it: Le Dôme. There, emulating greats like Hemingway, is where I'd been transfixed by the beggar.

In "Le Gâteau," Baudelaire imagined being alone under a *dome*-like sky in a place of "irresistible nobility"—his soul felt immense—"at peace with [himself] and the universe." He pulled out bread and a flask, only to be joined by a wild-eyed beggar boy, who—offered a morsel—called it cake. A second beggar fought the first fratricidally, reducing the prize to crumbs.

Initially, writing up my Le Dôme scene, I hypothesized having a cigarette *in my pocket* and debated giving it to the beggar.

Later I discovered Milton Klonsky's prodigy poem "The End Pocket."

In it he envisioned time as a *pool table* (that had an end pocket). Like my pocketed cigarette, it was hypothetical (pool tables had no end pocket), as if in some secret complicity with my "begin" pocket. Some secret pattern of Alpha-Omega.

"The End Pocket" concluded with a plea, desperate like the beggar's but symbolic—not for a cigarette per se but for "the master" *to light our cigarettes with yours*.

Now inserting the Pauli information, it was as if I stepped right out of the collective unconscious as—at least momentarily—the "dark woman," the anima. And Pauli himself *drew the wavy line across my window*. He was known for the "Pauli effect."

Computers broke, experiments failed, a water jug overturned in Pauli's presence. More on that later.

He was an architect of synchronicity and believed it involved a "doubling," a "mirroring" (of psyche and matter). Here were *mirroring faces*: the beggar's lined, mine blank—in opposing tension across a window. As if right out of the unconscious.

What archetype in motion told me to *start? Right here?* What secret ordering process as with a searchlight slipped in and swept up these components to convey the instruction? How would it reveal psyche and physics, mind and matter? Art and life?

Discovering Pauli's wavy-lines dream was enough of a shock to get my teeth into. The issue Jung and Pauli tackled together was psyche's connection to matter, which led them to synchronicity. But they knew the theory was unfinished. It could open a door into revolutionary twenty-first-century ideas.

Pauli's dream depicted two forms of time. Was this a continuing investigation? If so (by whom? by the unconscious trying to become conscious? but what did that mean?), the progression was in human minds attracted to the next bit to "plug" into where the information was "oscillating"? That was *time* of a sort, intercepting our clock time from a big current (of "the whole"?)?

So I might as well imagine that puffing smoke (rings!) in a kinetic message—across the window between human- and particle-sized reality—it was Pauli there outside the Dôme café, drawing the wavy line with his head.

And at the same time, the Baudelairean beggar in the deadly fight in a lofty *dome*like setting. And at the very same *time*, Klonsky writing "The End Pocket," about time as a pool table where his "End" mirrored my "Begin" Pocket.

After all, it was Baudelaire who said in "Correspondences" in 1857 in *Les fleurs du mal (The flowers of Evil)*: "Nature is a temple where living pillars / sometimes let escape confusing speech; / there man passes thorough forests of symbols / which observe him with familiar looks."*

---

* La Nature est un temple où de vivants piliers
  Laissent parfois sortir de confuses paroles;
  L'homme y passe à travers des forêts de symboles
  Qui l'observent avec des regards familiers.

Well, whatever this means and wherever we are going with it, it is certainly constellated. More, in this "participatory universe," is it participating too in ways we might not have dreamed? Talking to us, and we often turn deaf ears simply because we have no idea someone/something is addressing us? Trying to make our heads turn, to startle us? The ancients would not have been surprised. The East as well. But in the West, this kind of discovery would be revolutionary to most, that, whether we believe in a higher power or not and however we define it, we are all together, minutely connected, unconsciously. And it's not just us; it's pieces of time, of space, of events, all comprising the puzzle we are constantly called upon to make better, more interesting, insert more of ourselves and our gifts and insights and creativity—our what if's—into.

By June 2012 the constellation unveiled further for me, when I read (Jung to Pauli, 1953): "What does it mean if Einstein establishes a world formula but does not know which reality it corresponds to?"

He explained: For some issues—a study of the myth and cult of Asclepius, for example—self-reflection was sufficient. However, in regards to others (Einstein's $E = mc^2$), the question is cosmic and *therefore challenges "the microcosm in the person answering the question, i.e., the natural wholeness of the individual"* (my italics). He puts Pauli's concern with his dark anima in the Einstein camp: Pauli must excavate his own *microcosm*, "and it is also why 'master' figures appear in your dreams."[54]

As for himself, Jung writes, his professional work is psychology. "I have impressive dreams about animals (elephants, bulls, camels, etc.) that *do not wish to be observed*, and when I intervene they lead to me having a tachycardia attack [very fast heart rate])."

He adds: "I am actually supposed to make the animals conscious and integrate them, which, of course, is impossible . . . According to my dreams, these animals seem to be building a road through the primeval forest and do not wish to be disturbed. So I have to dispense with psychology and wait to see whether the unconscious itself produces something."[55]

I practically fell out of my chair when reading that Jung dreamed of animals who did not want to be observed. And trying to observe them, he twice got severe heart problems. The first incident, in 1944, was a full-blown cardiac arrest; he almost died. The animals wanted to give him information through the unconscious. Speak from inside the unconscious. And yet—which is where I almost fell from my chair—the Montparnasse beggar *did want to be observed.* Was desperate. That was the trigger for me.

AND NO ONE ELSE LOOKED. Which might have been irrelevant except that it happened later on. The trigger to take cloud photographs (introduced to me in dreams) was that those clouds made sweeping panoramas of dynamic scenes impossible in waking life—and no one was paying attention.

In the beggar scene this unconscious was asking *anyone* to notice.

The "pilot wave," if you will, at work seems to be this call from the unconscious to make something conscious. It's time. Anyone will do. Any observer. Any "blank mind." Anyone who will open to a sense of possibility about this unconventional information.

In that same correspondence Pauli remembers a 1948 dream he calls an individuation process, comparing it to the *Timaeus* of Plato. Featured in it was the pioneering theoretical physicist Arnold Sommerfeld (= "the Self . . . in the form of the physics teacher"). Pauli uses the phrase "*incarnation* of the archetype." He notes how "in dreams, *gravity* often signifies the *energetic gradient* of the unconscious content toward consciousness." He speaks of "*the attraction or affinity between archetype and consciousness* (i.e., also to space and time)."[56]

Perhaps the beggar—my beggar—can now be seen as the Individuation process (wholeness, the Self) asking for more visibility, an occasion to light up.

Jung goes on: "We are virtually sealed off in the psyche [because of the way we frame the 'conception of the truth.'] . . . It was this thought that gave Leibniz the idea of the windowless monads. I must say that I do not agree with the idea of 'windowlessness' but believe that the psyche does have windows, and that from these windows we can perceive even broader realistic backdrops."

Citing the transcendental/psychic and spiritual/material aspects of reality in Pauli's Sommerfeld dream, he concludes, "Once again we are obviously dealing with a classical *quaternio*, i.e., 3 + 1 with the fourth one determining the unity and the whole."[57]

Need I say more? I'm on fire. Windows in the psyche. The Self a beggar asking to bring something from the unconscious. Bring it on the Self's terms, which evidently I accepted, however unwittingly but since I was a toddler. This was an archetype in itself—constellated.

With the significance of numbers that gave objectivity (in science) came the lack of significance of numbers in synchronicities, which gave wholeness (the opposite perspective, that nature wanted us to know as well).

In fact, Pauli answered Jung, "I could not deny *that what is in principle a statistical way of describing nature also requires a complementary understanding of the individual case*" (italics in original).

The unconscious perspective, Pauli thought, sacrifices objectivity but gains completeness. He drew a quaternio of Einstein/Pauli and Jung/Bohr. "It is the inevitable fate of physics, which operates with statistical laws of nature, that it has to strive for completeness. But in so doing, it will necessarily come up against the psychology of the unconscious, since precisely what it lacks is this unconscious and the psyche of the observer." He recommends a "coniunctio"—a sacred marriage—which "would be the finest fate that could happen to both physics and psychology."[58]

Jung wrote in *Memories, Dreams, Reflections*, "I regard my work on alchemy as a sign of my inner relationship to Goethe. Goethe's secret was that he was in the *grip of that process of archetypal transformation which has gone on through the centuries* [italics added]. He regarded his *Faust* as an *opus magnum* or *divinum*. He called it his 'main business,' and his whole life was enacted within the framework of this drama. Thus, what was alive and active within him was a living substance, a suprapersonal process, the great dream of the *mundus archetypus* (archetypal world)."[59]

"A suprapersonal process, the great dream of the archetypal world," indeed! A glue? That very elusive elementary particle called gluon? Or, what hasn't been proved to exist, the graviton? Or the Higgs boson, and some other bosons to boot? Or a concept beyond those?

Does the archetypal world dream? Build answers in giant structures with collective connections over time, inside us? Is it intent on finding answers? And if so, what question/answer did I pick up at that Paris café? We will see.

— 7 —

Pauli: The "Missing Fourth"

7/6 2012: The Window puzzle configures itself more. I picked up, by luck, *Pauli and Jung: The Meeting of Two Great Minds* (by David Lindorff). I had not intended to read secondary sources. Rather, I got my own ideas by reading the Pauli/Jung letters 1928–1952 in *Atom and Archetype*. Nevertheless, I ordered Lindorff's book, in case by skimming I caught something. And I did. (In fact, I did more than skim.)

There it was, a huge puzzle piece. Now it is time to return to Pauli's World Clock vision, which changed his life. In his vision, on the back of a black bird were two intersecting circles (one vertical, one horizontal)—with a common center. This World Clock had three pulses. Its horizontal disc was green, yellow, red, blue; four decorative little men with pendulums stood on it, and a golden ring surrounded it. The blue vertical disc had a white rim, and 4x8 divisions. Every 32 middle pulses was a "great pulse"—in which the ring advanced a complete rotation. The small pulse and horizontal circle moved in stages of 1/32.[60] The perfect harmony, Pauli said, resulted from the infusion of threes and fours.[61]

In first speaking of this World Clock publicly, in the Terry Lectures at Yale in 1937, Jung left Pauli nameless; he called the experience pivotal for "the patient"—a conversion; a "vision, in which all contrasts are reconciled." At bottom, it also meant, he said, "simply . . . the union of the soul with God."

Jung went on: "Our mandala is an abstract, almost mathematical representation of some of the main problems abundantly discussed in medieval Christian philosophy."[62] Pauli's vision came shortly after he dreamed of the "house of self-collection."

Pauli: The "Missing Fourth"

Elsewhere, Jung says the vision "aspires to the most complete union of opposites that is possible, including that of the masculine trinity and the feminine quaternity on the analogy of the alchemical hermaphrodite."[63]

In *The Meeting of Two Great Minds*, Lindorff adds, "Taking this vision to have collective significance, Jung observed that modern humans have the task of relating to the whole person or the *self*, rather than to a god-image that is a projection of the *self*."[64]

Still leaving Pauli unidentified, the Yale lectures were published as *Psychology and Religion*. Pauli read the book. Responding October 15, 1938—partly accepting, partly disputing Jung's analysis—he recounted for the first time his dream from January 1938 (with the wavy lines), which we examined starting on page 51. It had a clock as well. Pauli thought it tied in. He included a sketch. This much we know.

When Lindorff reproduces the sketch, he *attaches his own footnote*.[65] This was amazing to me. I had surmised there was a connection with my beggar/window incident in Paris. Here it came.

In Lindorff's footnote was the startling statement that no matter that *the sketch* showed *two* wavy lines, "from the context of [Pauli's] letter it is clear that three lines were intended." I checked back. Yes, Pauli outright (1) mentioned "3 layers" and (2) connected "the 'certain life' with the first (quickest) rhythm and the (temporally) indefinite life with the other two rhythms [lines/layers]."[66] Thus, implied *three*.

Lindorff concludes: "Three wavy lines were in [Pauli's] dream, not four; the clock's face lacked four quadrants, and the fourth quadrant in the picture was empty. Thus, although the dream was focused on the number three, it was conspicuously identified with four by the number's absence."[67]

Missing a fourth rhythm/line—in fact, missing the *symbol of four* entirely—meant for Pauli and Jung broken harmony.[68] Why? For one thing, Pauli was responsible for the discovery that every electron must have a *fourth* quantum number, which was, it turned out, spin. The earlier Bohr–Sommerfeld model had three quantum numbers. From here Pauli developed his "exclusion principle," for which he was awarded the Nobel Prize.

In fact, in Pauli's essay on Johannes Kepler, he depicted how this seventeenth-century scientist organized his thought around a Trinitarian sacred geometry (cf., "And although Centre, Surface, and Distance [of a circle] are manifestly Three, yet are they One, so that no one of them could be even imagined to be absent without destroying the whole").[69]

Pauli notes that Kepler had no symbolism for four in his psyche.[70] He speculated that Kepler's focus on correspondences with *three*, as an archetype in his psychology, pervaded Western science afterwards until the twentieth-century discovery of the fourth dimension of time (à la Einstein).

In the early seventeenth century even Kepler believed planets were living beings (Pauli writes, "for Kepler the earth is a living thing like man. As living bodies have hair, so does the earth have grass and trees, the cicadas being its dandruff.... As a living being, the earth has a soul." So did the other planets).[71] In agreement with the late-antiquity neo-Platonic and neo-Pythagorean philosophers, the individual soul was in the image of God: part point (center), part circle.[72] The soul (inside) was "rooted in its fixed point whence it goes out into the rest of the body by a semblance of things."

In this it was like a light, a flame.[73]

Science would remove the animating soul from matter, a change Kepler was partially responsible for.

Further, the shift from three to four in quantum numbers was paralleled in Jungian psychology. There, the inferior, unconscious fourth "function" was key. Pauli now knew that his one-sided rationality—he described himself as, in the first half of his life, a "cold, cynical atheist intellectual," which had motivated him to briefly become a patient of Jung's—originated in his "inferior function" (feeling, represented in dreams by his anima).

This fourth function lived in the unconscious but could become transcendent, the key to individuation, or wholeness. Pauli had the difficult task of incorporating this *fourth* function, the anima, who was talking to him about time, etc., in his dreams.

In devising the individuation process, Jung resurrected a centuries-old problem—*how* to progress from three to four—which wasn't as simple as from one to two, or two to three.[74] He drew a parallel between alchemy and individuation, which "starts with an unconscious content (*prima materia*) and ends with the realization of the *Self* symbol (*Philosopher's Stone*)."[75]

To reach the sacred marriage of alchemy required reconciling pairs. Among the statements attributed to early alchemist Maria Prophetissa is, "Join the male and the female, and you will find what is sought."[76] Also, the Axiom of Maria, which depth psychoanalyst Remo Roth cites from Jung's *Collected Works*, volume 13: "One becomes Two, Two becomes Three, and out of the Third comes the One as the Fourth"; the German edition ends: "so wird aus zweien ein einziges" ("in this way the two become one")[77] For some reason, this important last line was omitted from the English.

To Jung, numbers were qualitative. As a child, he wrote, "I felt a downright fear of the mathematics class. The teacher pretended that algebra was a perfectly natural affair, to be taken for granted, whereas I didn't even know what numbers really were. They were not flowers, not animals, not fossils; they were nothing that could be imagined, mere quantities that resulted from counting."[78] The qualitative aspect is indicated in my notes below, July 6–7, 1985, from a Jung Institute lecture that may have been given by Marie-Louise von Franz:

> *1 + 2 = 3. One is individuation, the godhead, feeling of being at 1 w/ nature. Can point to a still unconscious unity or to a unity on a high level. 2 = waking up out of the undivided state. The 2 parts have to remain apart by tension in order not to* melt *back into the one. . . . It can be schizophrenia, or it can be a situation where one feels: if I can just hold such a tension, it can lead to a new creation.*

Pauli would later tell von Franz "he believed in approaching three and four simultaneously." He thought the conundrum had "bottomless depth."[79]

Jung will trace "the missing fourth" all the way back to Plato, the *Timaeus*. About his diagram of psyche/physics, in which causality and synchronicity are equal opposites in a *quaternio*, Jung says in 1952, "Here synchronicity is to the three other principles as the one-dimensionality of time is to the three-dimensionality of space, or as the recalcitrant 'Fourth' in the *Timaeus*, which, Plato says, can only be added 'by force' to the other three":[80]

SOCRATES: One, two, three; but where, my dear Timaeus, is the fourth of those who were yesterday my guests and are to be my entertainers to-day?

TIMAEUS: He has been taken ill, Socrates; for he would not willingly have been absent from this gathering.[81]

Jung continues to explain: "This cryptic observation [of Maria Prophetissa the Jewess (or Copt)] confirms what I said above, that in principle new points of view are not as a rule discovered in territory that is already known, but in out-of-the-way places that may even be avoided because of their bad name."[82]

He mentions how Newtonian science forgot all about correspondences. "The revolution brought about [in 1896] by the discovery of radioactivity has considerably modified the classical views of physics." In radioactive decay it's impossible to detect the half life of an individual atom.[83]

The measurement is statistical because individual atoms may in fact still be undecayed billions of years later. But statistically, at the half-life mark *half* have decayed. So, what does this random quantum process do to cause–effect? It introduces a new idea, of acausality, in physics. During the process, it is impossible to know which atoms have decayed; the state of an individual atom is unknowable until the end.

Then Jung presents his psyche/physics diagram, with synchronicity at one pole, opposite causality. Indestructible energy and the space-time continuum are the other opposites.

The dark, unknown woman in Pauli's dream desperately wanted to publish—Lindorff says "make conscious"—her book.

Hold it. Where are we? In a sense, in my brush with the beggar, we could say that we've encountered "the missing fourth": the mysterious bouncing line traced by the bobbing tramp's head across the Le Dôme window. As if a synchronicity so empowered—passed down so often in many disguises—emboldened itself to seek me out kinetically. Confiscated the surface meaning of a hobo's act to entice me into my life's work, just like the apparition of the master speaker in my head at seven.*

Speaking of correspondences, returning home incognito as a beggar is deep in the DNA of our psyche. The shipwrecked Ulysses returned home—how? Disguised by Athena as a beggar.

In Belgium later I would see a sign go up over a new café: THE KLOK. In Flemish, "clock." Thinking of Milton *Klonsky*, I wrote what could be a description of "uncertain time":

A clock without hands
human destinies for hands
foresight
immediate sight

Klonsky had said to me, "Foresight isn't, by the way, foresight. It's immediate sight." I had, as usual when he rolled a nugget of wisdom into a handful of words, drunk it in.

He was contrasting foresight—dictionary examples include "had the foresight to invest his money wisely"—with immediacy: "seems to be happening now." The first kind was hit and miss. But there was an immediate sight with a much higher batting average.

Was that the missing fourth line—the missing understanding of time—that the beggar (Self) drew under my window, separate from Pauli's window and the smashed-physics window, but close together

---

* The experience at seven is described ahead (see page 76).

with them in another kind of time, maybe the "end pocket"? I wondered: at the termination of this astrological period, the entry to the Aquarian Age, was the Archetype of Completion—of Four—constellated? I thought so.

And it would be, in some cases, the attempt to "publish" ideas that for a long time had been in the unconscious.

And if so, how do all these pages I've added to what was to be a short introduction to lead into the Zurich Initiation set it up? Unless in some way the Initiator was exactly that beggar, that representative of the Self, who came this time not by way of a physical window but right into my apartment in Zurich (where else?). Asking if I wanted to be a participator. Bring the message carried by the anima to life.

As to what the message was, let's look at a description that, without saying so, brings back in the "world soul" of the seventeenth century, when to a hermetic alchemical perspective nature was alive. It comes from a modern scientist, Robert Lanza, as he peered down one night at a glowworm near a pond:

> There we were, the beetle and I, two living objects that had entered into each other's world. It ceased emitting its greenish light, and I, for my part, turned off my flashlight.
>
> I wondered if our interaction was different from that of any other two objects in the universe. Was this primitive little grub just another collection of atoms—proteins and molecules spinning away like the planets round the sun? Had science reduced life to the level of a mechanist's logic, or was this wingless beetle, by virtue of being a living creature, creating its own physical reality?
>
> The laws of physics and chemistry can explain the biology of living systems, and I can recite in detail the chemical foundations and cellular organization of animal cells: oxidation, biophysical metabolism, all the carbohydrates, and amino acid patterns. But there was more to this luminous little bug than the sum of its biochemical functions. A full understanding of life cannot be found by looking at cells and molecules through a microscope. We have

yet to learn that physical existence cannot be divorced from the animal life and structures that coordinate sense perception and experience.

Indeed, it seems likely that this creature was the center of its own sphere of reality just as I was the center of mine.[84]

PART TWO

Getting Back to Me: the Initiation

Jung was told someone's dream and saw it as the emerging New Religion; it would take, he thought, six hundred years.

The man was reaching down a building or tower and he looked around and saw others of all nationalities doing the same individually.
—From a Zurich Lecture: Murray Stein, May 3

— 8 —

Threshold of the Initiation

With Milton Klonsky—the star of my novel (retitled after his passing *Love in Transition: Voyage of Ulysses—Letters to Penelope*)—I had thrown away the romantic opportunity he wanted on the physical level. I did not want to throw away the opportunity with him on the spiritual level now that he was dead. I thought it was offered.

I was forty-five. I wouldn't have the same initiation now. An initiation is about transformation. I had to catch up—to get to where my deeper self could play a role directly in my life, not in the background. Where I could understand the consciousness I came out of. Had but didn't have. Not here, not now in a physical form.

If the initiation seems severe, I didn't ever see it that way. Thinking—knowing—someone cared for me that much. *That much?* Unbelievable. How, then, could I not be swept up in it?

In "The Crisis of Initiation," Jacquelyn Small explains that the current Shift of Ages from Pisces to Aquarius "will necessarily cause initiation processes to be of a higher order"—that in moving up the evolutionary ladder we'll all pass through a "burning ground." And that everyone, will feel the effects, consciously or unconsciously.

She adds that in the Piscean Age we've assumed that material reality caused what happened rather than being an effect of a "true Causal Reality that resides beyond and actually creates the physical plane." As a result, "The symbolic realities are crying out for us to take note of the lessons we are to learn."[85]

In the intense decision to leave my husband (fearing he would commit suicide if I did)—the wish made all the more intense by

Milton Klonsky's death coincident with my having just read Jung's *Man and His Symbols*, then starting a dream record, then reading Jung's autobiography—I had activated (out of my depths, my inner life) the Archetype of Initiation.

Psychoanalyst Murray Stein, in a lecture in Zurich I would attend in May 1984, said that if it were left to Jung, "God" would be translated as "the quaternio." He went on: "The new master symbol would be the concept of human wholeness." He called that—significantly to me—"the modern equivalent of the old picture symbolism of the *fish*, Christ, and whatever other symbols were used before this concept" (my italics). The Trinity had equated with perfection, he said; the quaternity went beyond that into "a new idea: wholeness."

A vital dream told me that in my case at forty-one, the soul could not just "march in" but had to find a ground-level stairs. It was in Barcelona, Spain, in 1982:

> *I was on a high plateau with the (alive) Klonsky (he died in 1981), whose upper torso stuck up from a Black Hole. I tried to pull him out but stumbled. Faced with the near-certainty of crashing to the pavement below if I stayed there, attempting to rescue him, I felt the danger was too great. I swept up spilt "milk," then descended.*
>
> *Next, on ground level, a magical-looking woman handed me a misshapen, neglected creature, assuring me that if I held it under a fountain, I would find out that the horrifying-looking thing was a delicacy. I did. Dark gook poured out, and the shriveled, chickenlike monster turned into a little fish.*

I knew this monster-fish promised transformation of an *aspect of me*. It sketched a blueprint for individuation. Individuation, Jung said, required balancing what was evolved (upper dream level) and unevolved ("inferior") in the personality, achieving a marriage with "the Self." The end should be neither a puffed-up ego nor a deflated Self.

In another lecture, the Tibetologist Detlef I. Lauf said, "If the ego is too weak to assimilate the eruption of unconscious contents, it will . . . fall into primal magical thinking. . . . The Revelation of the Self is the utmost. More, we cannot do."

As Violet Staub de Laszlo put it, in introducing Jung's *Basic Writings*, the Self is "the psyche in the totality of its conscious plus its unconscious components."[86]

Two years before Zurich, this dream indicated where my unconscious was leading; that this ignored aspect was the proverbial toad; if kissed, it would peel away its disguise to reveal a prince. In many cultures, "fish" stands for transformation. (Jung's wife, Emma, spent thirty years researching the Grail Legend, with the Fisher King's castle as a symbol for the unconscious.)

The message indicated that my ambivalence, my emotion, my confusion had aroused from within my depths a response: an answer it would work out through me. Which would lead me to Zurich. And not perfection, but the new, expanded ideal.

Little could I know that this dream was propelling me all the way back to a 1550 alchemical text, the *Rosarium philosophorum* (*The Rosary of the Philosophers*—"rosary" = "rose garden"). It was central to Jung's *The Psychology of the Transference*, but I had my dream in 1982, well before going to Zurich. To Jung the process illustrated in the *Rosarium* woodcuts compared to individuation, with the one who underwent it transferring the structure of his or her unconscious processes onto the attempt to turn lead into gold.

What picture opens the transformation sequence in the *Rosarium*? The woodcut of the Mercurial Fountain. It's well into writing *Keep This Quiet! Initiations*, on April 21, 2013, I learned this. In a half-trance or rather great lucidity, after some meditations, I just put my hand on it in Googling for something else. Suddenly, there it was, the picture below, telling me that—though I hadn't known it at the time—alchemy was veiled at the start of this quest in the dream instruction of a magic-seeming woman to hold myself under a fountain, which turns out to be an ancient symbol.

Threshold of the Initiation

The Mercurial Fountain (from *The Rosary of the Philosophers*)
Reprinted in *The Psychology of the Transference*

Another Personal Milestone

We all know we're surrounded by an electromagnetic spectrum, only part of which is visible to us—on that, we all agree. There is a range of light that is visible and a range that, equally real, equally there, is outside what we can see: infrared, X-rays, the ultraviolet we try to ward off with sunscreen. Our naked eye cannot see it, though some animals do. The same with acoustics.

I was about to find it out. But I didn't know it when the initiation began.

In fact, all our sense organs have extensions that tap into this bigger reality. I was going to be initiated into a larger spectrum.

That larger spectrum has been experienced for centuries. But it wasn't Western science; it was outside the known—testable—range.

It all started out with me as the baby who gave herself a dare in the crib. Wanting to discover a reality bigger than the one she knew upstairs. Downstairs, something big was going on. Then I got out of the baby crib and went to see.

At forty-four there was a lot I had not been exposed to. In Zurich that would dramatically change.

So far I have named two personal milestones: the instant of beginning my "big book" in 1965 and the Zurich Initiation (1985). There is a third. I was seven.

In an interview at eighty-four, Jung was asked when he first became conscious of his individuality. Answer: "In my eleventh year. There I suddenly—on my way to school—I stepped out of a mist. It was just as if I had been in a mist, walking in a mist, and I stepped out of it and I knew *I am, I am what I am*, and then I thought: *But what have I been before?*" [87]

I thought about myself at seven—similarly, *on my way home from school*. I must have in an instant realized my individuality! Startlingly, quite near my house, on the street, looking to my right at the woodsy lot overgrown with brambles (beech, dogwood, pine, elm trees with thin rope vines hanging from branches), I was struck by a realization that I was in a seven-year-old body—as if, rounding a corner, I suddenly came upon myself, or woke up. The mind inside me saw no time boundary. *Voilà*. The *I am* perceived himself based on experience *he*, but not I, knew.

I, or the consciousness, was totally astounded. It thought: *I am a great writer. And I've done nothing so far—at seven!* It was not possible. The mind inside me could not understand: *Mozart was four*, I/ it reminded my aghast self. I vowed to catch up.

So what warped time was that? What mist pulled back? Where did it disappear for years? And how did the collective unconscious, if that's what it was, produce such figures stepping into us? But Jung said no. His individuality emerged. It was he who stepped out of anonymous humanity to point himself out to himself.

Threshold of the Initiation

Now I would like to hunker down and get into the initiation.

Just after breaking with Sigmund Freud, in 1913, Carl Jung plunged into a "confrontation with the unconscious"—his term—that although turbulent brought him the seeds of his lifework. For almost a hundred years his account, in *Liber Novus* (*The Red Book*), remained inaccessible, locked underground in a Union Bank of Switzerland safe-deposit vault. Finally, it was published in 2009 as a handsome parchment-paged book. Sara Corbett reviewed it September 16 in the *New York Times*.

Jung compared his initiation to a mescaline experiment. He had an "incessant stream" of visions. In Corbett's words, "He likened them to rocks falling on his head, to thunderstorms, to molten lava. 'I often had to cling to the table,' Jung recalled, 'so as not to fall apart.'"

Had he been a psychiatric patient and not a maverick psychiatrist, she observed, he "might well have been told he had a nervous disorder and encouraged to ignore the circus going on in his head. But . . . he tried instead to tear down the wall between his rational self and his psyche. For about six years, Jung worked to prevent his conscious mind from blocking out what his unconscious mind wanted to show him."[88]

Not long after I arrived, in October 1984, I had a few lectures on "Confrontation with the Self." The class had been scheduled several times before—and always canceled. No professor had made it safely to the first day. The plan appeared jinxed. Finally, my professor showed up in the lecture hall, ready to teach—I was there—medicated, bandaged, on crutches.

Similarly, in undergoing her Confrontation, my mind-body teacher at the Institute went temporarily blind. Such a test was supposed to be awesome. Mine was coming in September 1985.

In the intervening eleven months at the Institute, I made four very important friends (all female) and attended fascinating classes on such extremely diverse topics as Mysticism, Psychopathology, the Animus, more Psychopathology, Shamanism, Myth and Relationship (for example, *double signals*: a woman complained her husband didn't pay enough attention to her; meanwhile, he was adjusting his glasses to see her while she was looking away from him; this means she really wanted to leave), Marion Woodman on addictions (a problem of control: attempting to turn life into a work of art; "the anorexic cutting meat into sixteen parts wants to make life into a rigid little box; imagine a little bird that's spent its life in a cage and when the time comes to get down, it gets in a limb and trembles with terror").

More lecture topics: Icons & Mrs. Jung, Music & Creativity, Repair of the Anima-Animus Bridge from the Self, The Tongue, Goddesses, Snakes, Absence of the Father, War (treated by the lecturer as the Archetype of the Enemy, or the shadow. In a larger sense, corresponding with invasion by the archetype in "numinous possession or militant enthusiasm . . . All values are reversed. . . . People who are angered by a broken window pane find it quite normal that a whole town should be destroyed"), Grief ("Jungian psychology is a psychology of transformation. The grief process changes us. Suffering—a center of Jungian psychology—shows us what we can bear. Grief—what we can *do*") . . .

I learned about how illness can reflect the emotions.

Just before New Year's Day, 1985, as I fell asleep I asked for long-range guidance and had a Big Dream:

I was alone at a restaurant table, and saw, standing in the center of the table, a list of dishes—prix fixe, not à la carte. It was titled: Christ Menu. To be served were 1) analysis, 2) higher math (which I knew related to the Jungian format by which the inferior function became the transcendent function, leading to individuation—in my case, through the sensation/feeling functions). A third, I forgot.

Visible nearby was a striking young male (my animus), who looked like "a Christlike rock star. He was planning to sweep into cities and thought that to tour under his name, just making appearances before crowds for a night, was enough. He was caught up in externalizing."

I was aware he wanted to give one-night Mick Jagger-like

Threshold of the Initiation

performances. I had the awareness; he was a showman. My—unconscious to me—extraverted animus was a sensation/feeling–function type. This dream impressed me. Looking inside, I could see that no longer was the "big sensational performer" on the outside only. Now he was stirring in me. This menu was an outline for individuation.

March 15, I moved from Küsnacht to a furnished apartment on Freudenbergstrasse in Zurich.

In June, I took a notable trip to Rome with the Texan Jeneane Prevatt (now Jyoti), a beautiful part-Cherokee Jungian-analyst trainee far ahead of me in psychic skills; she's an eminent spiritual teacher today.

At first, I tried to clarify whether to accept her impromptu invitation. Those days, I consulted my dreams about everything. No longer did I dream much about Milton. But when I asked for "the wisest answer to Jeneane," I didn't get a direct one. Instead, he came in strong.

June 7–8: *Milton is dying, I know, and yet he's walking around looking well. Before he dies, we want to do something. I have to go away somewhere and by the time I get back he'll be in bed. Anatole [Broyard] is there, all set to nurse him.* (A perennial dream issue: Is he dead or not? He's not dead but is going to be. He's dead but is returning.)

Still in bed, I focused mentally on a plant in my Zurich apartment. It was "dying for no reason (as if) the New York me." I shivered in grief, picturing my cascading "pothos plant at Random House, which climbed outside my office into other people's it was so alive. (But clinging.)"

It won't grow here," I wrote. "It has to die. The *me* he owned." (Milton had exclaimed a decade or so earlier: "Each of us has a self the other owns. I've missed that other self.")

A part of me faced just such a transformation as the inexplicable death of the healthy plant, I thought.

About *numinosity*—which we see in some of these dreams and which surrounded my experience of Milton's death—Jung stated in a letter (1945) to the founder of the International Study Center of Applied Psychology in Oxted, England, P. W. Martin: "It always seemed to me as if the real milestones were certain symbolic events characterized by a strong emotional tone. You are quite right, the main interest of my work is not concerned with the treatment of neuroses but rather with the approach to the numinous. But the fact is that the approach to the numinous is the real therapy and inasmuch as you attain to the numinous experiences you are released from the curse of pathology. Even the very disease takes on a numinous character."[89]

Following Henri Ellenberger's classic, *The Discovery of the Unconscious* (1970), Jung was associated with the so-called French school of psychology: "investigators who were fascinated by the discovery, first, that all of us have simultaneous conflicting subpersonalities; second, that each subpersonality lives in a different world, remembers a different past and strives for a different future; and third, that some of these subpersonalities seem capable of knowing things that appear to be impossible (telepathy, clairvoyance, etc.)."[90]

I pondered whether it had had a deleterious effect on Milton that he magnanimously critiqued the manuscript of my secondary novel, *A Lecture upon the Shadow*, about Jan and me—in which a character modeled on him played the platonic Wiseman. Might it have contributed to his death? When he finally consulted a doctor, the cancer in his lung had grown to "the size of an orange . . . weighing on his heart," I was told. This got into my imagination. In the Institute we'd studied how emotional issues, not dealt with, might become physical. I wondered what, symbolically speaking, was that great weight on his heart.

The two nights thereafter I asked about Rome, but my dreams again took the detour. June 8–9: *I'm with Milton and there's a new female. She's getting his attention a bit. I don't know how she'll fit in. He speaks of his wife. He doesn't say me. I kind of think I'm asleep and I want to ask as many questions as possible, not waking up. I say, "Who is your wife?" He says, "Moonglow."*

Then I wake. I think: *He shines on my mirror.* (Milton had once complained, "If I don't shine on your mirror, I don't brighten.")

I interpreted Anatole to be my animus in the first dream.

June 10–11: same question, same detour. Here I appeared to have a parallel history going back in time in great detail: *I decide to marry Milton. It finally occurs to me that if my eventual wish is to have him around all the time at a distance or to marry him, that means I want to marry him. I'm wondering is it wise to go to Zurich, as he has cancer—had it and no longer has. I remember he'd sent me a letter, asking for a commitment.*

(The letter was a dream memory only.)

In the dream I drew on a vast reservoir of memory that greatly impressed me as real, day by day, hour by hour. Then I hit a juncture where, in the past, I typically woke up. I tested it: *I tell my mother it was because of his cancer I became aware of my feelings for him. I tell her I had thought he was dead—suddenly it hits me—am I asleep? But dreams don't have so long a time sense. How could all that's in this dream—all my realizations, all my memories attached to this change of heart about what I really want in life—be a dream? I wait to see if I wake up, and I don't. Everything stays the same. It's no dream.*

Deciding I'm not in a dream, I reflect that my hesitancy about marrying him must mean that I haven't grasped the fact that I want to marry him *eventually.*

Here I wake, surprised. Let's look a relevant theory by Jung. As "Jung's Model of the Psyche" explains, Jung called the psyche "a self-regulating system" like the body, in which "every process that goes too far inevitably calls forth compensations.... One of the key questions raised when confronted by a patient's dream is: what conscious attitude does it compensate?"[91]

June 11–12: still contemplating the Rome offer, I note down how Jeneane (later renamed Jyoti) can do things I can't. Why?

I did not have a spiritual teacher or a guru; I'd met Jeneane/Jyoti on the cusp of my next nineteen-year lesson. I believed she was representing the growth *about to happen* to me.

Just before the trip—obviously, I went—Jyoti dreamed twice of Christ. Once he said, "I won't come . . . till the wind stops."

Flight day. The day before, after being told inwardly that I'd had a psychological split that was going to be healed and my garbage taken away, Jyoti was awakened by a garbage truck. She thought: *she's going to have a lot of help.*

En route and in our room together at the Homs Hotel (a name we found significant), Jyoti shared some of her out-of-body experiences (OBEs) and other facets of her dramatic journey that would be chronicled in *An Angel Called My Name*. Jyoti was in the midst of a kundalini awakening.*

Her previous stay in Rome, a year earlier, she told me, an entity tried to take over her body to make her an unconscious medium. She resisted. The story is narrated in her memoir.[92] Jyoti writes that before breakfast the second day, holding a pair of earrings, she started toward the mirror:

> Suddenly, a loud sound shrieked through the air. The next thing I knew I was in a dark passage and a man was speaking to me in a language not from this planet. I seemed to know and understand him quite well. I spoke to him in an authoritative manner demanding that he leave—get out of me. My vision returned at that moment and I realized I was standing at the mirror leaning on the sink, speaking to myself in this unusual language. Then in a loud voice, I said, "Get out! Get out now!" Just at that moment, the entity left taking me along with it. I found myself above my body, watching it begin to fall. I realized in that split second that if I didn't want to return, I didn't have to. Death was just that simple. With that realization, I popped back in, catching myself with my hands on the sink. My psychologist self came out, running around doing a mental check list to see if my thinking was intact. What had happened? Nothing like this had ever happened before and it was scary. I looked at [her husband] Richard, who sat on the end of the bed with his mouth open.

---

* For a definition of kundalini, see page 99.

Threshold of the Initiation

One of Jyoti's two Jungian analysts was eighty-four-year-old Cornelia Brunner, president of Jung's Psychological Club, an office she held for thirty-odd years, till her husband took over; Cornelia was in the original group who sat with Jung in the beginning of his work. She authored the classic *Anima as Fate* and translated parts of the work of Eckankar founder Paul Twitchell into German.

Cornelia recommended that Jyoti see a man familiar with such situations. The invading entity, he said, had been a spirit "caught in the astral plane," that is, "the emotional body of the earth," Jyoti writes.[93]

As she explained these things to me I was captivated. Jyoti, who was of Cherokee lineage, followed Spirit and the direction it gave.

In the latter light she had already had initiations with the Divine Mother, as when, after her first trip to Rome, she went to Medjugorje, Yugoslavia (now Bosnia), where the Madonna was reported to have appeared to six children. Waiting with the crowd in the chapel, Jyoti suddenly received the rare invitation to be admitted with a small group into the antechamber where the children regularly met the Virgin. Upon leaving the room after the apparition (which she perceived as "a tiny blue dot" moving near the children and stopping, in a cottony atmosphere heavy with spirits), Jyoti wrote, what she experienced was indescribable: "My body felt weak, and for a moment I thought I would pass out and go into convulsions."[94]

In January 1985 she undertook a vision-quest retreat in a blizzardy Alps cabin, drinking from a small spring, as the plumbing was frozen. The last night there as she walked she saw a radiance in her path, "a soft candlelight glow on the snow," and realized it came from her. She later learned to call the figure to whom she attributed this phenomenon, who would return, Metatron.[95]

It was five months afterwards, in June, that on impulse she invited me (we had met at a Christmas party) to Rome and told me some of these stories. I had been hoping for a person to prepare me for the Big Change I expected, which was introduced into my life every nineteen years. In Rome, I realized: *This is it! I asked and here's the assistance.*

She left me in Rome, for business meetings in Milan, but phoned that she'd postponed them after seeing a very high spirit entity sitting on her bed; he told her to stay in. So I was primed to have teachings myself in this amazing process she was in that was what Jung called Individuation.

With my extremes at play, I brought back to Zurich a huge mural of Genesis scenes depicted by Michelangelo on the Sistine Chapel's vault (47x20 inches) and a postcard of his *Last Judgment*. I had asked the saleslady for the *Last Judgment* mural—having stood a long time before the painting with an intense sense this was the man (the Resurrection Christ) working on my energy. Leaving at the last possible instant, I was given the Genesis scenes instead.

I also thought *The Last Judgment* somehow related to Milton. Remember that he was the first and only person I'd experienced in what appeared to be an afterdeath state and the one and only person I had to exemplify the higher self/higher mind except for, now, Jyoti.

Archetypically, for a woman, Marion Woodman had said, Jesus, a rebel, is a prime illustration of *the creative masculine*—corresponding to a high level of her animus. In Jung's charts this inner masculine comes out of the collective unconscious, where the highest, or fourth, level incarnates *meaning*, like Hermes, messenger of the gods. The third level is "the word," and as an animus projection, Milton had hovered between three and four for me. Every animus will be in one of four evolving stages. For instance, level two is the romantic, like Byron, or man of action like Hemingway. The fourth offers a bridge to the Self.

At my other extreme, a dashing Roman journalist, Claudio, drove me all over the sprawling city . . . to the Forum and the Mamertinum, the prison where by legend Peter and perhaps Paul were confined. In that cell Claudio told me the story of Peter making water spring out of the ground to baptize the guards and prisoners. Looking at the hole in the floor, I said, "This isn't the Bible, is it?" He said, "Maybe not."

After dinner he guided me through a floodlit Rome to Piazza del Campidoglio, designed by Michelangelo. Then—my notes say—to "a gold faucet," where if I stood ten seconds I could make a wish. He added, "Only one, not two." My wish: to "fulfill my destiny."

Threshold of the Initiation

The next day he drove me to San Pietro in Vincoli (St. Peter in Chains) to see Michelangelo's Moses, a marble statue nearly eight feet tall. I also was charmed by a Venetian, who thought I was thirty and could be a movie star. After much debate in myself, and though Claudio didn't insist, we had a brief affair.

Was Milton's energy in any way involved? I speculated. Not sure, but I was seeing it in faces, asking myself how that could be. Was I projecting it?

I afterwards thought the affair with Claudio was a temptation. My heart not really in it. Claudio wrote me at the hotel, inviting me back, saying he would have accepted me without last night—was following my lead. (I should have led.) I fell asleep feeling awful and blank, as if waking from a dream, and when I awoke remembered it was true.

I pondered whether Jyoti was the mother in my dream just prior to Zurich—the one I took the baby to, who was waiting for her.

Remember, again, that I was in totally virgin territory for me. I didn't have a map. I was walking blind, trying to figure out what would be much simpler, looking back today—and look much different. But then, I had to get from then to now.

In fact, in initiations—and expansion of consciousness—as people initially go to a different level of consciousness, mostly they access it through a famous spiritual entity who expresses it best personally for them. The initiation draws on a *level* of consciousness *occupied by many*. Jyoti once dreamed of looking through the eyes of now one master, now another—seeing into a plane of consciousness they each expressed.

To prepare me for the upheaval (that I was convinced happened every nineteen years), I had temporarily given up all caffeine, alcohol, and red meat.

In late August 1985, I took an exciting T'ai Chi workshop with Master Chou and was reading thought-provoking books. The comments I singled out are fascinating to me even now. For instance, "To approach the infinite cosmic intelligence, love, or insight . . . the knower has stepped aside altogether in favor of pure nondualistic awareness."[96] I wrote, "So this is the world BEYOND JUNG."

I took lavish notes from Renée Weber's interview of David Bohm, "The Enfolding-Unfolding Universe," in the previously mentioned *The Holographic Paradigm* (edited by Ken Wilber). Bohm, a theoretical physicist influenced by the Indian guru Krishnamurti, starts from the holographic brain ("I'm saying the hologram is an example of the enfolded or implicate order"). He cites in illustration a London experiment with two concentric glass cylinders—a viscous fluid running between them. If a drop of insoluble ink is slowly turned in the fluid, it would "be drawn out into a thread that was invisible and when you would turn it back, it would be suddenly visible again." This he compares to how events appear and disappear in ordinary reality, emerging from an implicate order. I wrote: "Co-Here. Space-Time = Co-HERE."

He explains how an enfolded drop that *unfolded* in ordinary reality remains part of the whole it came out of; therefore, it is not the same system as the mechanistic Cartesian model of disconnected points, "entirely outside of each other." The drop that unfolds emerges out of the whole, but we see a drop of it that has enough density to manifest.[97] Also, the implicate order is not related to time; instead, the drops unfold according to their relationship to each other.

I singled these thoughts out, but they were twigs, faint footprints, ideas I recognized but had no experience of my own yet to back up. That would come. In fact, everything was geared up to accelerate, as I'd expected. But I didn't expect the acceleration was just around the corner, in two short weeks.

I started reading *Other Worlds* by Paul Davies: "Surely science can have no more urgent a task than to discover whether the structure of the world about us—the arrangement of matter and energy, the laws they obey, the quantities that have been created—is just a random quirk or a deeply meaningful organization of which we form an essential part." He describes "a sort of frothy, foam-like structure, full of 'wormholes' and 'bridges.'"[98]

— 9 —

Over the Threshold

SEPTEMBER 6, 1985. D-DAY. MY APARTMENT: a large furnished foyer and living room-bedroom. Glazed ceiling-high orange bathroom tiles heated up the walls during a shower if I flicked the switch. The apartment, built for the landlord and landlady's son, had a lovely wood desk. An authentic Swiss down comforter covered me in bed. No TV and no telephone, which—with so much to do—I didn't mind.

I could afford to live in Zurich because the dollar was very high vis-à-vis the Swiss franc, making the rent convert to $600 a month. In two years this same apartment would rent for the equivalent of $900 as the dollar fell. But for the moment I could manage. Switzerland was notoriously more expensive than Germany and Germany more expensive than Belgium. I was starting at the top while possible—strictly because of the 2.65 value of the dollar. It would be 1.5 in 1987, and I'd be out of the country.

I had just stopped writing at the antique secretary-desk. In bed I was reading *Other Worlds* (by theoretical physicist/cosmologist Paul Davies). I paused over his description of what he called "Heisenberg's *loan mechanism,*" by virtue of which a particle that, as Davies put it, lacked the energy to get over a "hill" (a "field of electric force") might just "appear on the other side . . . having apparently *tunneled its way through*" on borrowed energy.

Only in the quantum world could this type of borrowing occur, he cautioned. Not in our macroworld; a tennis ball could never temporarily acquire energy to raise itself to an excited state and spontaneously tunnel through a net. Humans could not borrow energy, to dematerialize in one location and re-emerge in another.[99] Nevertheless, my unconscious took the idea up a notch—with a provocative dream about a *lending library*.

That night, September 6–7, I had a dream that led me into the initiation. I dreamed that as I entered my apartment I threw my coat onto the floor at the top of the stairs. The dream continues:

> I see my (deceased) father and my sister Norma neatly folding my freshly washed towels in a pile. Taking a stand, I say I'm a totally independent being—thinking that to receive their help reeks of dependency. On the verge of going further, I hold my arm out and see strings rising from the tips of my fingers. My father and sister stop.
>
> But as they do so, I see a slight flicker of emotion in my father's eyes, internalizing great disappointment. *That was Milton's emotion in his eyes. It reaches me, his unspoken feeling. The disappointment* as he gives up. I think: It's all right for him to go on helping under these totally different circumstances.
>
> *So it's my father in Milton, my father's higher development, and the Norma in my mother.* I really felt strings—invisible strings—from my two hands as I raised them to demonstrate. "*My fingers twitched by invisible strings*" [a line of poetry by Milton]. I was really touched by the sight. Got his cue.
>
> Thought, "High Eye cue."

Ruminating, I intuited the two strings represented opportunity/temptation (accepting the offer or turning it down): "two strings, two hands—the high cue, my higher destiny. Or the emotional line, the descent, caught in my throat. The normal line or the Transcendent line."

I continued in active imagination: "This is Dam-as" (*Damascus* in French).

I sensed it: this was not about dependency. In an epiphany I detected the energy, the vibration, the pattern. Which was a soul pattern of *unconditional love*.

I'd received—but did not know it—an energy transfer through my father's eyes. The "ability to accept" had just been tested.

In bed the next morning I followed my inner counsel to stay there and mediate and began to feel pulled upward.

Visions encouraged me to climb higher, past landmarks—toward an opening (hole, tunnel, top of a cathedral like St. Peter's). *Finally, after several hours* (in suspense, not knowing if I would get to whatever was up there at the top), the atmosphere "broke." I saw an opening, glided through, and was there—no doubt about it—*in a consciousness.*

It felt just like a scene from a film where characters burst through a time portal. Coining the term "wormhole," theoretical physicist John A. Wheeler envisaged the way a worm chews through an apple to traverse it end to end, making a short cut.

But back to Zurich. There was a break, a tear. Only not in physical space. In an inner peak above my head. I found myself breaking through to an utterly different inner landscape. In the heightened awareness—the atmospheric setting—I saw a man standing at the foot of a huge empty baseball stadium, rehearsing what he would say to the masses of the future he knew would one day fill the stands.

His certainty resonated in the silent air—awing me. His sole focus, in unspoken, determination—wordless but tangible in the air—to get his message right for the readers he *was sure* would occupy the seats.

I had a clear sense of fragrance: trees, flower blossoms. It was worth the hours meditating to find that break in space. Whoever he was, in such a high consciousness, I wanted to know more. He had said not a word. And in a few minutes I was out of his consciousness, back in my room in bed.

I tried to re-enter the consciousness the next morning. A shorter meditation led through another opening, this time into my father's consciousness, where I experienced visions of a movie that brought me the message I would be sent the very best teacher(s) love and money could buy.

That night I met my mother's spirit, but upon waking remembered no details—only a great love.

How could I tell a guide was there? This guide seemed to be a *he*—nameless. I assumed he personified that consciousness, that he was in some way Milton Klonsky but larger, as if Milton were inside him or could expand to become him. Or vice versa in the opposite direction. In fact, he was multidimensional and—what I didn't understand properly—*nonlocally located*. Milton, the person I believed in most, was vouching to me that this step was his recommendation.

As an artist, I had a powerful relationship to the unconscious. I had assumed my inspiration made things up. I lived in uncollapsed waves about many things and collapsed waves about others. Everyone does. Now the wave of *What I Believed* was collapsing. Moving quickly through chaos to a new point of view. I would emerge a changed person. I would have to work on creating a persona to speak from this new base. My personality would be smashed.

Importantly, I would follow my soul guidance and try out the idea that Milton Klonsky after death, as a spirit, was here in the room. However, it was not exactly he, in contrast to the dreams he'd appeared in recognizably.

I requested that *he* be brought in—the Milton I knew. This request was and wasn't granted. I felt, in a moment, a gust of energy that was as recognizably Milton as if he stood there physically. But most of the time, it was the Initiator. I was trying to at least break ground in understanding the new consciousness, dig into the hard soil, ready myself for what would take years and years of integration.

I dreamed of a plug in a wall. But it was connected to a converter. I was having a conversion.

Wednesday, September 10-11, I wrote what might sound inflated now, but it was my mind set at the time. I talked about each person being called "to live his/her own drama, his Passion Play, to incarnate, as the time has come, the potential unnoticed in him (or her), the undeveloped potential of man to be a Living Christ, incarnating the potential of transcendent love that is his (or hers) by right.

"*So my book will have a* PLOT CHANGE *in the middle. The man trying to get my attention is the inner Christ.*"

Over the Threshold

I mused on the hour in Delphi, Greece, when I marveled at *phosphorescent birds—in pairs*—streaking across the pitch-black Mount Parnassus night. I noted it had been a temptation to watch the scene with the man I did:

> He had nothing to do with the mountain moment. How many other appointments with myself have I missed that way, when my inner potential gave me a signal and she [the flirtatious aspect of me] took the opportunity to hook someone with it? Hook-cur. *Coeur* ["heart" in French, pronounced "cur"]. When I have potential energy, when I'm high, she takes the cue—my heart leaps up—my Coeur—and she comes out: Call Girl.
>
> I played with the idea of how I dealt with energy hooks in my past, hooks for my heart. Hook-*coeur*. A part of me was a hooker, not answering a higher calling.

— 10 —

A Master Initiation in a Personality-Level Self

I am asked: why does an initiation have to be harsh? Harsh? I did not see it that way. The idea never crossed my mind. It was exciting, an irresistible pull, a huge draw into the unknown, which my soul wanted.

Life was for discoveries: to learn, feel, be the most one could—that "quality of excelsis," as J. B. Rhine put it, saying I had it. To be cornered as in a cave and taught, with full attention given to the task of making me more aware, more on the inside about some secrets of life—I couldn't think of any greater privilege.

We were between semesters at the Jung Institute until late October. The initiation, beginning in September, came at an ideal time. For the next five weeks I would have no class—that is, outside the apartment. Bright and early each morning I was woken by a few audible chords or notes of music piercing the silence, without a physical source. I loved this.

The Initiator told me to call him "Milton Christ." I was looking for something concrete and familiar, and the name—kept for my private use—helped me find that.

As mentioned before but it bears repeating, this was in no way to indicate that any formal religion was necessary. Or better than another.

Had I gone to Indian ashrams in the 1960s, I might have been initiated in Zurich in terms of Lord Krishna, or, as later, Lord Ram, or who knew what personal or cultural history would have led to a different focus, a different entry point.

A Master Initiation in a Personality-Level Self

Later Lama Sing, through Al Miner, would point to how "many other entities . . . have also borne truth into the Earth, and done so with unquestionable oneness of spirit with God." He said, "It matters not how they are called. Shall we call him Buddha or Christ Buddha? Krishna or Christ Krishna? And on and on."

He went on: "It is the intent, like the fruits of a good tree, that will tell you what is being taught and from whence—what well, you see—the waters of truth are being drawn. There is but one. If you bring to us in future a variety of different names, we will answer the same."

Or as Edgar Cayce defined the Christ consciousness, it is "the awareness within each soul, imprinted in pattern on the mind and waiting to be awakened by the will, of the soul's oneness with God."[100]

The Initiator explained that first he wanted me to remove all crutches so I could go anywhere at the drop of a pin without *needs* interfering. In particular, I was to throw away the ear plugs and eye mask I slept with. Also, not turn over in the bed as I slept. And be able to sleep at any time. Also, go to the bathroom only twice a day. After a few struggles, I managed.

I didn't for a second doubt that I was in the upheaval forecast in my numerology as occurring every nineteen years, which set the stage for the following nineteen. I resolved to live up to the faith put in me by, as I saw it, more highly evolved spirits who must know I could do this—better than I knew myself.

In the fasting/purification stage, which lasted (total and semi-) at least twenty-one days, I became skinny as a rail. I was at times allowed only two teaspoons of honey a day and two glasses of water. One day, still September, I noted: "41 ½ kilos"—91½ pounds, down from 123. This quick plummet was in part due to another test: sleep deprivation. How long could I stay awake? Up to forty-eight hours, it turned out. (If I did the math in my notes correctly.) Meanwhile, I was keeping a Mental/Emotional Growth record.

Preparation is typically required to undergo any transformation process. For example, in awakening kundalini, this can involve purification and other techniques to break down preconceptions and strengthen the physical systems, including the nervous system. In my case, it was draconian the first few weeks, because, it seemed, I was far away from higher consciousness and this was a quick road closer.

I practiced receiving from and studying dreams with him. In dreams he *planted temptation* to lure me into wanting things while asleep I was renouncing when awake—such as food and sex.

I learned the beginning ropes of how to work in electricity.

The other reason for the extremeness was that I was *being purified cold turkey of physical attraction*—for a reason I will get to.

If I were to see this in hermetic alchemical terms, as in the *Rosarium philosophorum* (1550), spirit descends and matter ascends to join it. Eventually, in the hermetic version, psyche and matter symbolically wed in a Sacred Marriage in an intermediate realm.[101]

The great Chinese sage Lao Tzu (sixth century BC) said, "Do the difficult things while they are easy and do the great things while they are small. A journey of a thousand miles must begin with a single step."

Here are some notes I find illuminating, as I've forgotten all the details except highlights:

Initial events:

Fasting
All-night meditation to open Third Eye
More all-night tests
Sept. 10th—decision to keep a growth record
Daily meditations in bed, up to 20 hrs.
Visions with M-C
Meditations on Quiet, Christ, our marriage (to come)
Initiations: fasting, toilet, *Other Worlds*
Gateway: Death of Ego

Besides a growth record (mental/emotional), with a column for "Areas in which I need to grow" and another for "Areas in which growth was made," I find a list of things I experienced (in the initial crash program):

A Master Initiation in a Personality-Level Self

Delaying meals; toilet initiation; gateway ego-death initiation; landlord initiation 2nd time Milton-Christ left; ½ hr. exercise in pain; initiation: sleeping in daylight without ear plugs, etc.

Shaking-leg exercise; test of trip to Küsnacht; habit of looking for the spiritual opportunity in any situation; dealing with outside world (ability to preserve inner retreat). Test: picking up faraway signals from M-C. Self-rule, not focused on holding onto outcomes; new attitude toward the Self as not an outsider but myself with more consciousness. Realization of confusion of the Self with Initiator due to having met him as that. Adopting M-C's diet and suggestions for my clothes, etc. Creating a Solution Chart.

In a notebook I find this: "Oct. 16–17, I take the trip to Küsnacht in someone's energy. Probably his, in contact with him on a high level." A glance at my Emotional Growth record:

Emotional Growth: raising inferior emotion (based on inferiority complex and insecurity in relation to others). Raising sensation function out of the physical (the senses). Overcoming habit of emphasizing intensity rather than the meaning of an emotional experience. Progress made: . . . Growth occurred: certain hints with M-C, such as in Lone Ranger. Increased awareness of kinds of seduction in dreamwork (applied to life). Various seductive aspects I fall for in a relationship: "eternal boy" (*puer*) with inferior emotion or need of me. Ways in which I seduce: as a fantasy figure, in sex undertones, in flattery or real admiration, in air of mystery, in seeming undefined, in masochism (sacrifice). Growth: increased understanding of the past, esp. in conversations with M-C re the choice I made in 1965. His light bulb story. Growth: my reaction to his talk about his relationship with Mary. Wedding plans. Breakthrough. Centered reaction to his paralyzing my hand in strength of disapproval. Growth to do: Need to keep contact with M-C in his absence. Need to develop a sense of holiness of all things.

A Daily Routine list reads, in part:

Meditation, mental exercises, reading (*Other Worlds*, Krishnamurti, etc.), Jung Institute (classes only), spiritual exercises, prayer, Hatha Yoga and T'ai Chi (when time, perhaps outside apt.)

Music (listening)

Working on book (being stimulated)

Talking to M-C, getting to know M-C

Thinking

Caring for Snoep (restricted)

New: working/meeting with soul grouping/learning astral plane/dreamwork

No time for dance

No attempt to put everything back to "normal" that is no longer normal

With a small flat decorative glass object painted with a gateway, which hung in a window, I kept in mind that I was undergoing Death of Ego.

Not being told how this works in Eastern wisdom traditions, I found it odd and wrote:

Lack of existence of my former, personal self:

This is a very weird feeling, to be told you don't exist, though you have consciousness and your point of view. You have your own interpretation of things—yet somehow the position you used to take up has been voted out of existence. It's given a feeling of unreality to know you exist but be told you don't. That now when you say "I," it represents nothing, or at least not the subject. You no longer represent the subjective sense of the self.

A Master Initiation in a Personality-Level Self

A day in October:

> Meditate on gateway 15 min.
>
> Work on growth record
>
> Sit—15 min.
>
> Meditate on it—15 min. internal
>
> Again, 15, 25
>
> Return to growth record to make changes—15 min.
>
> Sit quietly with the changes—½ hr.
>
> Return to growth record to work on changes just made—15 min.
>
> Think about them—½ hr., ETC.

These records go on for pages/hours—longer.

> Oct. 13–14: End of dream accounts for that day: "M-C came back and I've now been up 29 hrs.

Then: "48 more hrs. initiation & 42½ kilos [normally 45]. Dream as I try to stay awake." I note: "High Energy: How to reach it; laws of the state."

I could fast extensively if not doing physical activity. Eventually, in the fasting period I stayed inside because of weakness.

My logic listened to my intuition, which told me that *if I had no predisposition for this sort of thing, it would have struck me as severe—which it didn't*. I would have been baffled. As a history buff, I was delighted that I might be experiencing—learning the details of—an unrecorded ancient esoteric process. This was one of many ideas that motivated me.

Still, to even begin to understand the initiation in non-Western terms would require an Eastern teacher seven years afterwards. I was on a step of a ladder between East and West.

In fact, anything else would have been too great a shortcut. I was taught in a way that let me discover for myself.

By late October, when the Institute opened, I was eating and attending classes. For instance, I have elaborate notes from November 1985, on Nietzsche and Dionysus, color and iconography, "Soham—Revelation." That last deals a lot with Kierkegaard and is synchronistic here. I wish I had recorded the lecturer's name. My best guess is Detlef Ingo Lauf, a distinguished Tibetologist and professor of comparative religion and philosophy at the Zurich Institute and at Columbia Pacific University in San Rafael, California. At home I was having the initiation and in class I noted down as closely as possible what this powerful lecturer said:

The Kabalistic god doesn't need to be told how great he is. If you ask a thing for yourself from God, it's a profanation, like a dog begging. You should always, in your prayer, in your behavior, try to mend divinity. This is totally different from institutionalized religion. Niels Bohr proved that time doesn't exist, that Kierkegaard was right. If time crumbles, space crumbles too. Synchronicity is all over the East.

The great innovation of Moses was the abstract notion of God. We drag God to concreteness.

Authenticity is truth to oneself. You pay a full price for that. The horrible agony of Kierkegaard—when you read the journals it's unimaginable. Kierkegaard said a revelation cannot be outside. Outside is not only blind, but there's nothing of importance there. If you look inside, you not only can effect Revelation, you can effect a kind of communication with the universal Tao . . .

There is no objective measurement for suffering. The only way to help a person is to go onto his own playground—go with him ultimately, no logic, no objective definition. With an objective definition of suffering you get nowhere. Kierkegaard cured someone who thought he was a turkey, by saying, "I'm a turkey too." They were turkeys together for a month. . . .

A Master Initiation in a Personality-Level Self

> The teacher is the catalyst for inner revelation in that each person is unique. One can go to the playground of the other and catalyze. This is the essence of the beginning, square one.
>
> Kierkegaard always uses the figure of Christ. Only the vicarious teacher—the teacher who tells you in a roundabout way—is the true teacher. Christ tells you in a roundabout way, so the revelation can come from within. The direct teaching is false. . . . The first line of the Tao: "The Tao that can be expressed is not the Tao." You have to work for Revelation with no recipes.

Leaving the Institute, I made my way back to the initiation, which continued but in a less drastic manner for several months. It opened me up to some hypotheses I think are significant.

Milton Christ, whoever he was—and of whatever relationship to me—showed me feats (called *siddhis* in the East)—regularly demonstrated by true, often hidden-away gurus there, but I didn't know it. For instance, he made the light in my living room brighter at will.

Later I read in *Stumbling into Infinity* Michael Fischman's description of the same thing happening with Shri Ravi Shankar. Also later I would learn from Shri Dhyanyogi-ji, who while attached to electrodes in California in monitored experiments would shoot his blood pressure up and dip it way down repeatedly, alarming the science team. I wasn't yet familiar with the fact that Eastern yogis study how to control matter, including their bodies. It's their specialty (yogic science), as ours is laboratory and technological science.

Once the Initiator cast a movie on my wall; again, briefly displayed his reincarnation dates on the bulb of my green reading lamp. I squinted. The dates were clear. He also once drew on the kundalini shakti, and as I looked a concave strip of light replaced the excess flesh between my thighs. I'd wanted to slim down there but not like that (it was temporary.) I would not have believed it possible.

In the East, kundalini has for centuries been considered a conscious intelligence. Dormant at birth in every human, it is coiled upside down at the base of the spine. When awakened, it moves upward. Unlocking blocks, activating chakras, it climbs to the head to unite with the divine masculine, or Shiva. Hindus call it serpent power, the Divine Mother, Goddess Kali, or other goddess names.

I did not know this at the time. The experience looked to me like the Bible and miracles, the only reference point I had. Such things had happened before, I thought; I found it reassuring; it quieted my alarm. But later, familiar with other traditions, I could have drawn up countless stories that describe great teachers working in energy in just these ways. *This, we will come back to.*

Moreover, he was not against science and assigned me to continue reading *Other Worlds*, the Paul Davies book on quantum mechanics, with him—and Krishnamurti.

On a larger scale, he more than once sent his light out through the town of Küsnacht, and I witnessed it land inside a Jung Institute classroom. Experiencing the high frequency, I found it impossible to determine who conducted and who reflected it. That is, who was picking up Milton Christ's energy directly, in affinity, and who was merely a carbon copy, able to mimic it.

It astounded me that I couldn't tell which was which. I would experience this technique many times in the years to come, but at this point such discoveries seemed shocking to me in their implications, if *cause* was so different from the way it appeared before our eyes.

He said that on three levels he was *like* me; in those he had an imperfect relationship to his feminine energy; he had lessons to learn. That would be, I deduced, because of lifetimes of people in our archetypes. Being multidimensional, he had not merely enlightened patterns but also—on those first three levels—a spectrum.

He wanted me to challenge him there by affirming the feminine; object if he told me, for instance, not to water the plants or take a bath.

On the *fourth* level, however, he was not to be disputed. There, he said, he was the Christ.

I had no physical impression that he was the Jesus I'd read about. Yet under the impact of demonstrations, I believed whatever he said. He did not go into an explanation of a transpersonal consciousness, *which in fact is what he was illustrating.* But I was as if entering the story *in media res*, after all the explanations.

I had thought "the Christ" meant a historical person and that we were entering into a period of the inner Christ. But to Jung it also meant symbolically "the Self," the image of God in each person—as was the Buddha, in a different way, "the reality of the self which had broken through and laid claim to a personal life."[102]

Gilles Quispel was another professor who lectured at the Institute. Decades earlier, learning that one codex from the ancient writings discovered in Nag Hammadi, Egypt, in 1945 had been smuggled into the West for sale, he notified Jung, whose Zurich Institute then helped secure it for translation ("the Jung Codex").

Quispel had been studying secondhand accounts of the great second-century Egyptian gnostic Valentinus for four and a half years during World War II; then, synchronistically, thirteen ancient codices—leather-bound papyrus books—were pulled out of the earth at Nag Hammadi, where they had lain buried in nothing but a red jar for almost two thousand years.

After the acquisition of "the Jung Codex" in 1952, Quispel mailed Jung a preliminary translation of a text by Valentinian gnostics (or possibly Valentinus himself): The Gospel of Truth.

It was part of the Jung Codex and revealed, as Quispel put it, that historically there was a third pillar to put beside faith and rationality in the West: a tradition "that saw in symbols and stressed immediate experience."[103] It most valued encounters with the inmost Self.

Also hidden at Nag Hammadi was the Thomas Gospel. Comprised of "secret sayings" of Jesus, it paints him very differently from the biblical gospels. Yet the source may be as old or older. When asked where to find him, Jesus in the Thomas Gospel said to look within (*gnosis* is self-knowledge): "Within a man of light there is light and he illuminates the whole world. When he does not shine, there is only darkness." He also said, "Raise up the stone and you will find me."

In the second century the gnostic strain was declared heresy and in the fourth century its books were burned.

The gnostic (inner) truth—the Know Thyself of Delphi—was not in line with imitating anyone, including the outer Christ. The archetypes of such underground, unconscious, heretical traditions led Jung to the collective unconscious, which he plunged into and retrieved from.

Listening to Professor Quispel at the Institute, stirring excitedly in my seat, I was particularly taken with how close he'd been to Jung and now stood yards away. He told us that unlike other gnostics, Valentinus did not recommend celibacy after attaining a certain level of consciousness. Spiritually mature people, said Valentinus, learned more quickly as a couple. Thus, he taught mysteries of the "bridal chamber."

Educated in Alexandria, Valentinus, his followers claimed, had received, through Theudas, an initiate of St. Paul, esoteric initiations that Paul received in his encounter on the Road to Damascus and taught only to an inner circle. So, today we know nothing about them.

It took me decades to pinpoint how initiation had put me squarely back in the gnostic camp insofar as valuing inner revelation and experience.

With regard to this fourth level mentioned by the Initiator, I later read a passage (by the famous yogi Bhagavan Sri Ramana Maharshi) in which he explains that he has no disciples. Why not? asked one of his many disciples.

The gist of his answer follows: "For the Jnani (Realized Soul), all are one. He sees no distinction between Guru and disciple. All are one. He knows only one Self, not a myriad selves as we do. So for him, how can there be any distinction between persons?" The narrator adds: "For us, this is almost impossible to comprehend."[104]

I would learn personally—after the initiation—that in the East the guru knowingly accepts the *projection* of the inner guru. He (or she) does this in representing for followers the *inner guru*'s state of being at one with God, a state they have in potential. In which case it's an illusion to think the guru really is the guru and the disciple *really* is ignorant, because the latter in fact has this state inside to discover, even if the disciple bows to his feet, which the guru sees, just as we do, as evidence to the contrary. But knows better.

Something of this perspective would help explain what the initiation, on the fourth level, took for granted. Perhaps, for the moment, I should leave it at that. I didn't have *nearly* this much myself to go on. And therefore had the more valuable (to me) experience of coming in from the unconscious with an empty, unfurnished mind on this topic. I knew nothing about what a jnana state might be.

Early on, we made excursions into Zurich. One way the Initiator communicated was with my father's watch, on my wrist. If he had something to say, the minute hand would spin wildly or stop.

At *Parade*platz (Parade Square), a bustling shopping center and tram hub—reached by walking down Bahnhofstrasse, as Pauli had done many times—he had me buy the annotated Thompson's Chain-Reference Bible.

When Milton died in New York City, I'd seen a numinous *parade* in Blankenberge, Belgium. The Initiator didn't say why I should buy a Bible, but I made the connection between *Parade*platz and the parade. I found out the importance of the Chain-Reference Bible six years after this purchase. For the moment, it sat unopened on my shelf.

After our outings, I'd instantly sit at the typewriter to pick up his reactions. What did he think? I addressed my insecurities as I delightedly felt answers pour into my head, my fingers.

The "big book" was retitled *Love in Transition: Voyage of Ulysses—Letters to Penelope*), in view of these messages and experiences I was receiving. Milton had once sent me a postcard addressed to Penelope, signed "Ulysses." It seemed apt now. Ulysses' return "home" took on great symbolism in terms of Earth's journey to a new consciousness.

In helping me edit *Love in Transition*, he had me listen in my head to song tunes, snatched phrases—see images—at the typewriter. To keep a text alive takes inspiration. If over the years I'd had to always work inside the text itself, the manuscript would probably not have survived the decades it took. Looked at repeatedly, words freeze into position. I wrote:

A plane flying high in the sky
For a TAKEOVER OF THIS BOOK
An IN-FLIGHT TAKEOVER

And then a consciousness reading WITH ME begins to coach me, sing songs, flash scenes before my eyes, juxtapositions. Everything sensed—without WORDS. How was it possible?

"I just called to say I love you
"I just called to say how much I care"

He wanted me, in writing for hours, to stimulate him and vice-versa—*not* just take down his words. In this, he appeared to be Milton. But he did not confine himself to a single form.

— 11 —

Inside the Initiation

From the start, the Initiator's goals included marriage. I could have been in the myth of Psyche wedded to the god Eros (Cupid), whom she was not allowed to look at. As a precondition, he wanted me to learn to jump into his consciousness. In my gold notebooks, October 25, 1985: "he took me into his consciousness multiple times." Prior to this period, I'd never experienced such an elevated state—though I'd been in altered states in Charlottesville in Grof-style hyperventilated-breathing workshops.

I couldn't just jump to this much higher state and resisted being told to. This obstinate point in my personality, which refused to do things on command, mirrored, he said, his.

I said it might be easier if the idea came from *me*. That if I felt forced, I harbored resentment. I didn't want to get back on that co-dependent roller coaster of my marriage. If ordered into his consciousness, I got peeved.

This, also, was part of working out his masculine/feminine balance, he said; on the three levels where like me (in many forms) he was in human patterns, he could be tempted. But on the higher level not.

When he tried to make me remember having known him before, I failed miserably. However, I totally trusted Milton Christ.

My friendly landlady next door—who used to bring me slices of her homemade carrot cake and wouldn't hurt a fly—became worried. In the early period, when I remained inside, unlike the Swiss I kept my curtains drawn. She tried the door. I didn't answer, at the Initiator's instigation. After a few attempts she called the police (convinced I was on drugs). They pounded the door. Urged on by the

Initiator, I stared at the shut barrier; then they peeped through a tiny open slit in the curtains. My heart thumped.

Seeing me alive, they could not legally force their way in, it turned out. I felt I'd passed a test.

I was well aware that no records of initiations and conversions involved meek, doubting, half-baked responses. My models (still from the Bible), such as Elijah being fed by ravens, or St. Paul blinded by light, indicated that anyone who passed through this type of experience—was transformed—was a rebel, totally submitted to the event.

No records of them would have survived otherwise, or been convincing. I was not thinking of this as a story that would survive, but I could draw no other comparisons. So this experience (and others) gave me a sense that my reactions were in line with history. From childhood as a writer, I'd taken my models from history. Here, I searched my memory for similar stories. Again, had I known other traditions, they could easily have come to mind. But I knew the West, not the East.

The more extreme an initiation, if you came out on top, the more credible and of lasting productivity, I felt it was—whether it was called Confronting the Unconscious in Jung's individuation process, wrestling with Jacob's Angel, plummeting into the Dark Night of the Soul, seeing an angel and receiving the command to write, or having a Divine Child. Or walking over hot coals. Or sitting in ice-cold temperatures in a loin cloth.

But, as with any daring soul who flirted on the borderline, one had to emerge sane for the experience to amount to something. It never occurred to me that this would lead to spending the rest of my life in a cave, for the Initiator was motivated by his concern for the world.

I thought of myself as having a conversion, of which there were many in history: all-dramatic, extreme. How could I not accept what Lama Sing had predicted was coming as a blessing? I knew I was not losing my grip. I wanted to go through this the way my models did. *Not that they had been my models before.* Sometimes one found oneself in a situation one had read about and never imagined as anything but a story. Then what? *Then this.*

Inside the Initiation

Yet I had such confidence in the Initiator, I never, from the first moment of being transfixed by his certainty inside the stadium, felt doubt.

As previously mentioned, the most extreme part stopped after the first six weeks; my ego had been uprooted. I began eating normally and the Institute reopened. I was back at class.

In the apartment we revised the manuscript that would become *Love in Transition: Voyage of Ulysses—Letters to Penelope*, which I'd worked on since 1965. Before starting the revision, he insisted on removing its negative energy; negative energy, he said, could be picked up right out of a book.

But at the Institute I learned that a student had become very ill and died. Milton Christ explained that if a person resonated with a pattern being discarded, that person might possibly fall sick.

This upset me. Could life be like that? Could discarded emotion flee to someone else? Germs were contagious, but what else was? Under what circumstances?

He acted from an entirely different perspective, where not only could spirit move through matter, but in certain conditions loose archetypical energies could "infect" our psyches, if organized in a way attractive to them.

This could be attributed, from an Eastern point of view, to karma. But the cause was a pattern. To overcome a pattern might be a life purpose. Mastering this concept, one could maneuver patterns. But we lived in them unconsciously.

A pattern could be hiding in a scene, dramatized in an action, he was saying. Organizations of energy (like bacteria) could affect us, *reaching us through our attractions*. Sometimes even an attraction that, to us, was inconsequential.

To the degree we were ultimately in a web of life, we were all learning lessons for each other. Whew. But I didn't digest it this much then.

At this point, I was asking myself if it was possible, as the Initiator said, that the student had picked up some discarded negative energy he took out of my manuscript—it was somehow contagious to her and she died? Was she susceptible to the pattern, having perhaps a lingering attraction to it that she thought she'd conquered?

This idea was appalling to me. But for the moment it was a half-conscious thought. I lived in the moment, trying to absorb what the day required. Later I would take these ideas further, with references that settled them down into known or unknown concepts. I lived, though, not in concepts but in new experience.

— 12 —

A New Christ Personality

According to the Initiator, *there was a new Christ personality coming into being.* Unlike with Jesus, this Christ (personality) was vulnerable—it needed nurturing on the surface. Inside, it was not vulnerable, he said; at the core was the first Christ. (Again, the initiation was focused through the tradition I knew best at the time. Also again, this was about consciousness, not the religion.)

In rehearsing for *The Marriage of Figaro*, Mozart flamboyantly waited till the evening before its performance to write the Overture; he began at midnight, his wife prodding him with stories if he threatened to fall asleep. Then he rushed to the performance, handing the orchestra the sheets just before the curtain rose—and calmly conducted from the keyboard. They played magnificently.

A close call, a cliff hanger—that was the new Christ personality-exterior; inside was Himself/Herself.

It was this new *personality* he was going to introduce me to, he said. But not yet. Up ahead.

It might explain to me why I had always had the inclination to look for the hidden "real" self.

Sometimes he said he had to go far out into the universe. The first time, not clear whether he was really gone, I nevertheless jumped at the chance to eat. I took my emaciated frame to the tram, which stopped at a restaurant glittering with feasts. Famished. I held the food down; then foolishly, ate an ice cream. The instant the cold dessert hit my shrunk stomach, I bolted to the bathroom. The splurge slid out.

However, I found that even if his attention was at the edges of the universe, as he sometimes had me believe, I wanted to be loyal to his regimen, and was. He returned and congratulated me, saying I'd tracked him faraway. Being a novice, I was still not really sure that he could travel far out into the universe—or that he had left at all. Everything was mind-bendingly new.

Finally, I'd mastered the task of leaping into his energy enough that he set the wedding date: November 29, 1985—three months into the initiation. The marriage would hold up in other dimensions as well.

I went shopping for an outfit and bought a rose wool sweater (with sewed imitation pearls) and a matching felt fitted hat with a slightly turned up brim. During what I imagined to be the off-Earth ceremony, I sat at my coffee table and—in honor of Mozart—played my three-LP recording of *The Magic Flute*.

It was the anniversary of Milton's death. The opera was two hours and a half hours long. Watching the twisting smoke of an incense stick waft overhead, I imagined he was in—or was—that trail of smoke. After the performance he revealed that his preference was Stravinsky's *Rites of Spring*.

Then it was the New Year, 1986, and I didn't flip the calendar page. I'd had the hunch he wouldn't stay over and I wanted him to. But finally I did change it to January 1986 and he still stayed. For how long?

— 13 —

To Love—*and* Remember

He next began *The Christ State* (channeled through my energy)—all poetry—about Earth but remaining personal. That last fact stumped me. I had found it easy to starve myself down to nothing and follow his dictation (which was highly energizing).

But how much harder was *digesting it in a form that could be communicated*; even, at first, understood by me. I could detect what belonged, what strayed off point. But *intellectually,* I could *not* explain. I could not contextualize. I had an emotional block, a boulder insofar as the material brought *me* in. I seemed to be something without a category, my ego 100 percent uprooted.

But by these counts, it seemed to me the whole Earth was uprooted. I did not know how to place this "map" of consciousness and reality on top of any map. This wasn't from the Earth I knew. It was from the man writing his book(s) (in the empty baseball stadium) "for the audiences of the future."

No matter that he was telling me that on the fourth level he was the Christ, I was down here on the three "lower" levels, so where did I fit? My ego was not yet able to grasp that perhaps even if "I" was brought in centrally, somehow it was "not about me."

— 14 —

Damascus "Cook Key"

I grappled with the question: How was I, beyond the covers of the book, to mention that he was, in writing *The Christ State* in a transpersonal/personal focus, speaking of a Christ who would return this time with "*tu*-lips"? *Tu* (the personal "you" in French) is the familiar form. And why then were the tu-lips coming over to me? With my limited framework, I was like a child who freezes, not daring to think a thought further, when letting it loose would bring me to the solution—something unthought of.

He would speak his message with *tu*-lips. I went into Zurich and bought a clown figurine—holding three red tulips. I bought another—a beautiful little statuette with white bow tie, white pants, large-plaid salmon jacket, and black sandals—with four juggling balls: three in one hand, one in the other. Also, a ragdoll clown. Clown was one of his personae.

His message drew on the Universal Mind. Yet it personalized! It concerned vital issues, archetypes, new world structure, "saving the planet."

I had never heard of a multidimensional Christ. But wouldn't it be so to be cosmic? And was some point in each person that point? And wasn't some point in each person in every person anyway? It was a consciousness aware of its "I" nonlocally. Why was I in the center, while he was a giant energy with giant messages?

Of course, I could say that I, like everyone, had this galactic consciousness. But I'd never experienced it. Or that he was many places at once, but no matter how you sliced it, it felt personal.

I felt that what he said was true. Yet I found myself in a dead-end street. *I had a message but would I ever get the authority to say it?*

The Initiator's second book, *To Love—AND Remember*, was again all poetry. It fascinated me in personalizing archetypes in an epic adventure partly of Christ and Mary inside the larger, current Earth issues. I did not dare use their names, because in this baffling slant back into history, he was—for whatever reason and inside whatever incalculable consciousness (more on that ahead)—calling me Mary. Talk about a conundrum and trap.

Once he said he was calling in the Mozart energy to write with me. At the typewriter, my fingers flew at a frantic pace over the keys—inspired—high in adrenalin. To my surprise, the Initiator rejected the writing, as too externally focused.

I named this aspect of the Initiator's energy, or consciousness, "Mozart Christ," and sometimes called him "Milton Christ Mozart." To signify the aspects of him I'd met that were meaningful to me.

The Initiator said he was going to materialize in the flesh and live with me, in a recognizable form—in fact, the just-mentioned outer model for his new human form: the jovial, kidding Mozart. But he wanted me *in his consciousness first*—again, a feat I could not accomplish at will, not rise to high frequencies on the mere intent.

After preparation one day he prepared to materialize. I was pretty panicked. Imagine sleeping in my twin bed with a materialized white-wigged eighteenth-century composer; it was too hysterically absurd for me to think of adapting to. Or believing it possible. I had heard of "materializing" but never thought about it. How could I imagine it without seeing it with my own eyes? He promised such a sight.

He began and I saw the telltale signs: a blurry, grainy form barely emerging. I was horrified. I didn't like the first impression, of which all I glimpsed appeared to be a crew cut. But tried to swallow my reaction. Instantly the process stopped.

The Initiator afterward said he'd never intended to materialize. It was a temptation, a wish in fact of his *anti-self*, which he'd known would want to take over. I should likewise be on the alert *for my anti-self*.

This was heady stuff. Had I an anti-self? (My ex, Jan Mensaert, had written a semi-autobiographical novel, *The Suicide Moz*art, in my presence, in which the protagonist was Mozart's anti-self.) The Initiator said he, and I as well, had an anti-self, which would want to—and be able to—interfere. It would attempt to sabotage the situation.

In the poetry excerpt below he elaborated on my dream of February 3, 1981. At the time I lived in Morocco on the Rue de Damas (Damascus Road). In the dream a master of ceremonies and "Dan" tested me, giving no indication why. (In waking, I'd had the *sensation of spinning* instantaneously back from an unidentified spot, where I'd been questioned about "Dan.") To me, the multilingual jumps, the spiraling word play, held pockets of energy—"syllable trails." As if energy containers, they seemed to indicate a deep *symbolic* structure spread, like mathematics, through matter, hinted at by poets.

> On the Road to Damascus
> the certificates of deposit
> All there within
> in the de-P.O. [pronounced *depot*] sit*
>
> A cement unknown to man
> an experiment with it
> a cement unknown to man
>
> When the word would come
> EAR AN†
> the second stanza
> when she would be TANZA‡

---

* P.O. (part of "deposit"); *peau*—skin (French), pronounced "po"
† I once dreamed, "The second Stanza begins with *and*." Ann is my middle name and as a subpersonality in dreams represented my inferior (transformative) "function" of working with the hands; "and" also brings in the Great Feminine sense of connectedness, as opposed to either/or. "Ear An"—of course Iran; the syllables had great energy.
‡ *Tanza*—dance (German); Con*stanza*: Mozart's wife

would dance with him
Là ci
DAR REM
la mano*
Do
REM†
DOUGH
REM
Carry out the dream with him
la mano

. . . .

Tall, almost emaciated
standing beside the Master of Ceremonies
a Master of Ceremonies in the shadow:
"When did you see Dan before?"

SEDAN SEDAN
When did you
SEDAN?

When did you see him
before?

I say, "In New York,"
not knowing why I say it
or what it means
"In New York."
Then I'm whirled back as through time
Spin-HACHE [ahsssh]
This must be
Spin-*hache*‡

---

* "Là ci darem la mano!" (Your hand in mine, my dearest)—from Mozart's *Don Giovanni*; *dare* (*dar*)—to give (Italian/Spanish); [io] *do*—[I] give (Italian)
† REM, the dream state
‡ *hache*—axe (French); spin-*hache* reminded me of spinach (makes Popeye strong).

Who would cross the goal line
Hoe *thé* * ["tay"]
Goe *Thé* ["go tay"]†
when the signal was given
Goe Thé

The mission of artists overhead
a flock of artists overhead
all in the energy pool overhead
when the signal for the run came
Go Thé

The next stanza brings in *gâteau*—cake—playing with the beggar/Le Dôme moment, when I stared out the Montparnasse café window, which numinous event in 1965 triggered the beginning of *Love in Transition: Voyage of Ulysses—Letters to Penelope*, which I would work on for thirty years (till publication in Romania in 1996), just as surely as if I'd fallen down a rabbit hole and didn't know it. As it happened, my Montparnasse scene occurred in the centennial year of Baudelaire's "Le Gâteau."

I began to think of the beggar as among other things my inner masculine energy—me—who had lost his voice. And had a slant on things I knew almost nothing about.

Was my typewriter in Morocco—little did I know—my alchemical furnace, burning, transmuting buried references in the text as the unconscious spoke in tongues and double speak?

The extract continues, merging the "Le Gâteau"/Montparnasse moment with the Rue de Damas dream, indicating what the importance was of my having unconsciously—I had no idea why I said yes—recognized this "stranger" in the dream:

---

* *thé*—tea (French); "hoe *thé*," as in "Don Quixote," pronounced in Spanish "key-Ho-tay."

† "Goe Thé"—Goethe. Related to a "go" signal. Rhymes with Dante or Qui-ho-te

Got toe
gâteau ["got tow"]
cake
cook-key
goe *thé* [tay]*

. . . .

Then the signal was beamed between them
that Dan—whom she didn't know—she remembered
For he was the man she connected with
New York

The other not visible
known only through a beam in his eye
communicating with the first through this beam
of light
that traveled from his eyes
a signal
that this part of the plan was successfully passed

. . . .

Then she would go on to the next stage with him
Then what was unknown in the plan could be unveiled

But this was a memory that must be carefully guarded

. . . .

And thus the *comedia* opened
with a mysterious test
a confrontation
a challenge to memory

---

* Tea and a cake (a *petite madeleine*) started Marcel Proust's great recollections, *In Remembrance of Things Past*. "Cook-key," the madeleine, tea, Goethe, a mission of artists overhead—some of that spinning around in this swirl or bouquet of energy-information-emotion.

And to use that memory
for the glory of God
For it was
God's energy

A child conceived waiting to be born
this child a newborn child
Not a human child
but a living child
a real child
A consciousness
An age that could accept it
that a child could be born not as a living baby
but truly existing, this baby
child of God
a birth of
a consciousness

Moving ahead, the Initiator thinks about Earth's trials in the years to come:

Out of sleep
dorm *ir**
AWAKE INNING

In some of his sons and daughters
a new climb mate
A WAY KIN

So to top our own freedom there was the
Om let
of God's
FREED Om

---

* *ir*—pronounced "ear"; *dormir*—to sleep (French), Dorm Ear; in French, "ir" is often the end of a verb involving "to go"—*sortir, partir*—thus, the connection (in the unconscious) between a "go signal" and "ear" ("-ir").

Look into the sky and see
FREED Dome

The missing event has to come in
through the hole in the ceiling
the unknown hole in the ceiling
The unknown thinness of the top of our Earth atmosphere
That the ceiling must come off

. . . .

Situations couldn't be escaped from without
a change in the Dome
The same problem would face Earth
till we removed the thin covering from the Dome
Saw the hole there
the tunnel of Death
That once through that hole
we would see beyond our own death
We would see new worlds to discover
See the future
of Earth

For Earth was in One Situation
that being a dimension
until it changed its situation
by changing the Dome
Removing the covering from the hole

A few years later I showed this text to my new Belgian light body teacher, Roland Verschaeve—the first by me I ever showed him. "This was channeled," he burst out.

Having just survived a plane crash, he'd escaped only when, as there seemed no hope left, a hole appeared in the roof of the burning aircraft and he and others from a light body excursion climbed out through the jet fuel and flames.

A double END code
DNA
VIENNA

Soaring high above this Earth
calling down to this Earth
Come in, Earth
DNA/Vienna
Remember the code
the code
CH-*ANGE**

DNA END CHANGE
END CODE
IN CO-DING
Calling from
VIE† in A

The dance
that had to be learned

Through the door
the M N Door‡
Viens§ [pronounced V N]
Viens
DNA‖ [here pronounced to rhyme with Vienna]

---

* "Ch" marked an address-coincidence trail: Milton's and my NYC telephone prefix ("CH-2"); the CH of my CHarlottesville, Virginia, postal address; then my ZuriCH zip "CH." *Ange*—angel (French). Anybody today can see the obvious relevance of Ch-*ange*, predicted in 1985, to the U.S. presidential elections 2008 and '12. The archetype of "change," here in the Zurich Initiation, connected to the consciousness of Home.
† *Vie*—life (French) is pronounced "V."
‡ MN, "Milton," the door he went through, death—a journey, expansion, higher consciousness
§ come—from *venir* (French); *viens* is pronounced V.N.
‖ As one reads this aloud, depending on the line, "DNA" is sometimes pronounced "dienna"—rhyming with "Vienna"—instead of the usual "D N A."

Damascus "Cook Key"

A new kind of man
M N
Viens
DNA

The colors change, Robert* said, but the Dome remains the same,
in circumstances surrounding an event
And yet this time
suppose
you've turned
INTO YOURSELF

Robert was the Milton-inspired protagonist in my *Love in Transition* series. The prescription for me was given:

Heart had to *ouvre*†
to Louvre

ouv-
REAR‡

Tem-
PÊTE§

T'AIME‖
PSST

Pan-

---

* the spiritually wise protagonist modeled on Milton in *Love in Transition*
† *ouvre*—open (French)
‡ *ouvrir*—to open (French)
§ *tempête*—tempest (French); "pête" is pronounced "pet"
‖ t'aime—love you (French)

AMA*

Rêve
N
NU†

In a dream Milton asked me to let go his physical form. He pointed to a barren outline, a mere structure, an empty trucklike frame. An archetype. I was to let go attachment to his physical form. Unwilling to do that, I buried my head in his shoulders.

Introducing earthshaking ideas, the initiation interwove personal and transpersonal in ways that gave me no legs to stand on: Applied Consciousness without the basics. I was supposed to figure them out.

I looked over at the "Death of Ego gate," the two-inch piece of glass I bought in Zurich. A tiny painted symbol: Ego Gate, Gate Eaux, Gate AU/O (gâteaux). Eau (water) is pronounced "O."

Indeed, a consciousness was coming toward me.

I could do it, hit, he said, a HOME run. Retrieve the consciousness that had perhaps updates to what we thought it was—if a principle in us all, a gate to FREEING THE MIND. Yet with a message so important he wrapped it up in sure delay by bringing me in personally, in a way inexplicable (to me).

Yogis such as Yogananda, in the Christ consciousness, had experienced a Light beyond religions. But I was being shown *that* in a multidimensional form—running through us—that was imperfect inside archetypes that I would hope to help *shift*. Shifting energy was what my creative impulse would be doing, whether or not "I," on another level, mostly unconscious, was writing books.

In his *Autobiography*, Yogananda called a great Hindu avatar, Babaji, the "Yogi-Christ." He wrote, "Babaji is ever in communion with Christ; together they send out vibrations of redemption and have planned the spiritual technique of salvation for this age."[105]

---

* *ama*—love (Latin), as in Amadeus, "love of Deus"
† rêve—dream; *nu*—new (French)

— 15 —

Watching the Hand Played—
One Step Up

As we remember, in the initial stages the Zurich Initiator convinced me to change my relationship to physical attraction. He said physical attraction was entangled with spiritual. And the physical, being obvious, had the upper hand.

Looking at a sizzling female, feeling one's heart race, one would rarely, in our culture, suspect that perhaps this was—insofar as the real reason for the racing heart and eyes that refused to focus elsewhere—not the trigger, energetically speaking. That under that façade, perhaps through a barely noticed nearby person, perhaps in another connection entirely, the real depth of attraction was percolating and radiating, in total anonymity.

Removing physical attraction in me (and sex with it) was the prelude to trying to create a pattern, a Sacred Marriage in physical terms.

After our spirit marriage he wanted to work in the archetype of the couple. Why not attempt to get it ready for the leap of consciousness ahead? Why not rewrite or tweak the "war of the sexes," as it were? Why not add this to his to-do list in this initiation?

The Sacred Marriage is the archetype greatly disturbing to Jung, about which he finally published a big tomb, *Mysterium Coniunctionis*.

So, the Initiator first said I had to be celibate. For several months, only my higher chakras were active. I fervently hoped this was temporary.

Its purpose achieved, a "law" might be tossed out and turn into its exact opposite. This one did.

Step one accomplished, the goal shifted. I was to try to be part of a couple pattern. So, he set up energy fields for me to go into—to attract a human being (a male who was already in his energy).

He set up the field by casting down into it (by intention, or transmission) a part of him: a memory of a relationship, experience, event he loved. This energized, vibrating memory would be a magnetic beacon to someone who had those subtle inclinations. In his heart of hearts. The catch was the Initiator would have only minor control over that person after the attraction "took."

From the Initiator's point of view, he was putting part of himself, in his transpersonality, or nonlocality, out there to be "picked up." That's the way I see it now. In other words, it was a dimension of the situation. As a memory, it was organized (in a pattern). Underlying that was the consciousness.

He wanted to create a pattern *based* in spiritual attraction, though physical attraction would be an important part too.

But there was a drawback: he was electrical; his human personality liked electricity, passion. Now that he had taken that out of me *in a physical sense,* how was he to attract "himself," who liked strong, emotive physical passion? The attraction would have to be created regardless of my not having the overt sex appeal I usually counted on.

Of the difficulty, he seemed unafraid. That is, to take on the task of destroying the archetype, at least in one instance. But then, any instance anywhere works like that, with whatever level of energy is involved.

It was a kind of St. George and the Dragon situation, where he would operate secretly, *in the unconscious.*

So he created a pattern where a male was walking—in a park once, downtown another time. He had me concentrate in the apartment beforehand till I could "see" the male. Then proceed by tram to a spot close to the location, hoping the pattern would attract us. Like two wandering magnets that found each other. On the down side, it might pivot the male into a *wild inexplicable physical attraction to someone* he met coincidentally near the location, at just that moment.

Because exact *location*—of the source of an attraction—is hard to detect if the deep attractor is not physical.

A spiritual attraction can *energize* physical attractions that mimic it. Or, let's say, express it at a lesser depth. The former, being subtle, might—by proximity—spin off an intense energization of a more earthly "photocopy." So he set up a likelihood. The adaptation (in an event) hung in suspense.

Initially *the pattern* (the format) dismayed me. He modeled it on a real event in *my* past. The fact that he chose this relationship was the first clue I had that it was spiritually based, as well as (obviously) physical. It made me think of it in a new light. Realizing that the first pattern he spread over the air in Zurich reproduced an actual past relationship in my life with someone very much alive but who knew nothing of this experiment, I was aghast.

I felt my personal life had been invaded but also validated. Because it was the relationship with Hunter he tried out. That meant that combination of physical-spiritual was not just personally memorable. In the spirit world or at least in my soul grouping, it was exactly a model they would like to re-create. At least with people similar to those in my soul grouping, it had legs.

So the plot thickens, because here was the wild, outrageous Hunter, and whom would this spirit group choose for the pattern of a male relationship with me? They found the spirit-physical-romantic-sexual-purposeful requirements of a Sacred Marriage had, in potential, an archetypal foundation fleshed out. As the Hunter relationship was not considered currently viable, under the circumstances, for distance and other reasons, evidently, it was being "recycled," as it were.

Taking the organized energy—of that relationship—the Initiator dropped it down like a dragnet. Being perceived by him as a pattern (of spiritual attraction, however physical), it was to hover like an energy bubble over the scene, which he further energized by his own loving memory. On some level, it was now prima facie *reusable*.

How? I asked. Novice that I was, I especially asked myself how it was moral to "give away" pieces of someone else or oneself.

How could a piece of my life be dropped over a location, above people? Wasn't it scandalous? Not to him. It was a sacred tool. Not the least because he considered the experiences to have been his as well, though *through* another physical person (whom he identified with, in the earlier situation). He considered himself on some level the other person.

Far from being random, for the recipients of this experiment he selected people who were resonant with his energy. Or whom, he said his energy was *in*, even potentially if strongly, to a degree he believed in or felt he could *activate*.

A word of caution, however. I was under the impression that there were differing opinions—favorites—in the spirit group around the Initiator, and that a *small* contingent, thought the relationship with Hunter could still be viable, despite obvious thorny challenges. However, it was not realistic to test the hypothesis.

Practically speaking, just imagine my being at Owl Farm. How would I act, with this initiation so fresh? How would I balance the "me" I was as a result of it with the "me" who got along with him, fit in? Not to mention that he was madly in love, which I could have guessed. Back to the plan.

Of course, the absurd—or mind blowing—idea of making unconscious energy fields, like cutting out sewing patterns, was an implication of Oneness.

It was an implication—removing religious terms—of why someone said to me that Jesus changed every cell on the planet by the *pattern* he lived.

But the odd thing to me here, as I say repeatedly, was that there was nothing abstract here except the fact the Initiator had no physical body.

I asked Al Miner for purposes of this book (as recently as 2013) if "Christ consciousness" could be interchanged with "unity consciousness" or "God consciousness," and he replied, using personal experience, that he and his wife were focused now on "removing separateness from God in our lives. We've made a number of spiritual retreats and now strive to live in the result of this intent. The result might be referred to as Christ Consciousness, meaning Oneness with God in all things. So my answer, and it is mine only, would be that Christ

Consciousness is Knowing (capital 'K') there is no separateness. The Christ Spirit could be thought of this way, but I see this somewhat differently. This is the Consciousness in action. Don't know if that helps, hope so."

So this is a consciousness initiation undergone by masters in every tradition. But that revelation was not forthcoming in the initiation. I had to figure things out.

He did not reveal his *personal* likes and dislikes beyond starting a list in my head: he liked jeans, cut flowers, rice— He stopped, realizing it was inappropriate, when he was, for all intents and purposes, transpersonal.

I was not an instant master of this situation, to say the least. The handful of encounters that blossomed led to strong, slow-burning friendships. No instant hot romances.

My question remained how on earth I would go out into the world after this, publish, have a sense of identity? For I, who had known since seven who I was (a writer) now didn't know at all. I was being given my work for the next nineteen years.

— 16 —

Sowed Seeds

Well, it's now over the time limit, and I am running to get in under the gun, to say what I made of this version of reality given in seed form and fast-firing neurons and downloads and chaos in 1985 and 1986. For I did not want to, as Kierkegaard dreamed repeatedly, die and remember there was something I forgot to say. *This.*

I could not sit up on my deathbed, as I ruminated, and suddenly, glassy-eyed and frantic, have the realization that I forgot this: *that this, in fact, might be why I was here. Of course, I knew that I'd had other challenges, lessons to learn. But that was for what we call the personality. Couldn't the soul—or the atman, the true self, the mind stream—speak at the end, say these are some things I know? Or think I know? From my point of view?*

What I knew (however I knew it and whoever that was, whatever the terminology)—that everything built up to—was a tricky communication of how spirit interlaced with matter, including mind through matter; so that the turning point into science at the end of the sixteenth century, when it split from faith, was unfinished. At most, three-dimensional.

If we run back to the seventeenth century to start over, what was the fourth dimension of those discoveries by Newton? Of that flea glass, or microscope, that Robert Hooke looked into—the first human to peer under it—and saw a flea? What split off then and there in that collapsed wave, when the ideas that created our scientific world came down, filtered, *reduced*—a few centuries' worth carved out of the larger complexity that we're now ready for? So we got science; we got technology.

Sowed Seeds

What was left back there, when we started down this road, from that download when Newton sat in his bed, envisioning his *Principia* (1687), and helped put us onto the path to the twenty-first century, with its planes and computers and technology? When he went into the same visionary field as da Vinci perhaps, but this time found not the inventions per se but the principles that would make the technological and space age come to be? What underpinnings of *that* beginning—what complement—did we filter out? Omit? Erase? To pick back up now?

What—under the radar—connecting, unifying *beginning point* was trying to come back in?

We know the initial conditions and the number of decimal points to which a calculation is carried—for instance, statistics about weather fed into a computer—determine what a meteorologist predicts. This discovery gave rise to the modern chaos theory. A forecaster will predict a hurricane, based on a certain-sized fraction (say, 1.55757) having been fed into the calculations. Another prediction may result if the fraction goes to 1.55757222222438. So all new ideas come to us rounded off—their *complexity capped*.

In the very dynamics of life they acquire complexity, perhaps making visible the very implications cut out at the starting point—then discovered through unfolding consequences of their being eliminated at the outset. This is not to say that contemporaries and forerunners didn't help Newton or that other fields (art, for example) didn't portray the gestalt of their periods, sometimes before science—picked it up and worked with it over the last three hundred years. On the contrary. But this still allows us to ask the question about the larger picture.

Now, returning to the seventeenth century, what more can we insert? Einstein added $E = mc^2$. That matter and energy are interchangeable: latent energy converts into kinetic matter. That mass is a measure of energy; likewise, energy of mass. The actual formula is $E = \pm mc^2$ (to take into account negative energy).

Suppose latent factors omitted in the Newton revolution are

re-emerging now *because we can handle them*. We have laid the foundation, not wanting to be given everything at once but rather to spread through time the opportunities to experience which *not knowing everything at once* creates.

What law? What connecting principle—or simply link, event—would add the fourth dimension to the sailing-forth of modern science through the flea-based plague (killing ten thousand a week at its high point) that, with Newton in the Woolsthorpe countryside, spared him?

What caused the modern scientific world to be inseminated, or begin the cogitations that led to its birth, in that time of death when he was passed over? The many dying, one it would center around spared, though many contributed. The idea, collapsed out of the whole, embarking to bring us from there to here.

The mass death in the Great Plague of London mirrored the pattern of collapse (above, in the superposition) of the many possible outcomes (now defunct), to arrive at the download that, over time, fell into Newton's lap. As he said about the period between the plague—in his anni mirabiles years, 1665–66—and his finished *Principia* twenty years later, "I keep the subject constantly before me."[106]

So here I sit, trying to wrap that nineteen-year course of mine into a ball, make it into a word. And, in a word, bring in my message.

Events, I would learn, have a shape. That is, an event could be diagrammed. The energy shape of it, I learned, can be *felt* with the hands. I learned the principle by *feeling the shapes of the energy of specific pages in my book—at a distance—while my hands moved through the air in T'ai Chi class in the early 1990s*. My unconscious translated diagrams in the air that my hands moved through. I gradually realized that my mind (without my knowledge) was taking the energy, and with the movement of the hands APPLYING that to the book pages from a different *location*, a different space-time—conscious of both.

The idea behind that began right here in Zurich; then the unfoldment took years, buried in time capsules, as it were; posited in hunch form, then leaving me a decade to get ready for each

Sowed Seeds

idea—revolutionary to me—that would one day make its assault on the bulwark of my brain or nerves, with me standing guard, working to steady myself as stealthily the new idea penetrated. Meanwhile, I comforted my nerves and brain cells, telling them they were not being annihilated, only stretched, changed, yet once again *converted*.

In this beginning point with the Initiator, he would make an energy organization of a geographical area, setting up emotional "turbulence," *synchronicity*—attraction: that old bugaboo of Newton, who wanted to know *just how* there could be action at a distance *without a medium such as ether*.

Holding the question for three hundred years, we discovered that space was warped, perhaps had curls, strings. Well, now add in qualities, structures of patterns—its content that like everything else tried to *replicate* and move through least resistance toward the greatest "hook."

Everything attracted, or repelled. Space was no different; the matter or potential in it was no different—the content, the nurturing womb of potential, of event organization prior to enactment in replica or even disguised variation. So though situations were not exactly conscious—no one said that—they replicated.

I couldn't speculate that far in 1986. It was what I had to learn—much beyond my capacity. At the same time, this project of saving (informing/repatterning) Earth in individual and group efforts was equally important to him, or part of the same thing.

As said, to use memories was scandalous to me but to him a sacred tool.

As an example of the kind of meeting the Initiator set up, at a T'ai Chi class I met two strangers. In a precognitive dream the night before, I'd been shown there was a deeper attraction that involved the nonlocal consciousness of the Initiator; in that sense, his nonlocally physical self.

In the dream the Initiator let me know there was either some history (related to *his* energy) or a *potential* affinity. In such a case—and in this instance in particular—the attraction was genuine, but I believed it started in the Initiator consciously. Had a spiritual base in play. There was no magic spell. No powder. No *Midsummer Night's Dream* or *Così fan tuti*. Just two lively, long-lasting friendships; in the one case I especially remember eating saffron rice in his home, practicing T'ai Chi.

To me, it seemed entirely unrealistic to expect this warm friendship to become anything at all other than what it was on the surface. He said look deeper. I couldn't.

Still, I struggled with the concept.

In fact, Al Miner, the channel of Lama Sing, had told me that some people had to leave Earth to learn the things I was going to be taught. I guessed this all made sense if my soul grouping, again according to one of my 1984 readings by Miner, had the project of "the illumination of the universal nature of each soul."

I was not encountered by a guide who wanted to speak *through* me. That, I probably could have mastered. But it was not like that.

I wrote with the Initiator:

An idea was trying to enter Earth
The madeleine in the air
Mary Madeleine
her spring
her aria
For this is her
Sea-
Son

Waiting all this time for it
Locked in the garret
the readiness of it
Man's reaching her state
For all of her would be released at once
She who had come in darkness all this way
following her soul mate
Not to be left behind but to change with him
make the spring with him

Sowed Seeds

her Sea-
Son*

This entry into the Initiator's consciousness was just the beginning—not a peak experience after which things subsided back to normal. He cracked the egg of my mind. I had read no mystical tracts or studied or entered those states. It's not clear, however, if any would have gone this far on some points.

I had the practice not to make conscious certain questions, to be *aware of them but not give them to my rational mind, or to my ego*—until and unless it becomes important to. Indeed, I hid some questions away, where the ego could look but not touch.

As he became more unspecific locally, he had—by passing every minute with me, commenting on everything, dropping everything, as I saw it, to teach me—become more cherished, more intricately the direction of my feelings, life, and purpose. I was amazed that a man could be so varied.

Still he dictated, merged with my energy—and I wrote. There were feelings flowing through the writing, and the impressions he taught me to receive in pictures, song tunes, runes—*reluctant as I was to put some of the thoughts, startling to me, onto paper*. But he insisted:

One point
One past
One man

He was calling her now out of different stories they had lived together
Calling from different points in the story
different points in time

. . . .

---

* The "sea son" reference is from Ariel (*The Tempest*) on the supposed death of the King of Naples: "Full fathom five thy father lies; / Of his bones are coral made; / . . . / Nothing of him that doth fade / But doth suffer a sea-change"

He was in all points of her past
calling to her from all points of her past
Till the time came when there must be a choice
One story must be chosen

Different stories. I didn't remember any.

But my fingers typed the words; the energy raced through me. Who would I like to go forward with? Pair with out of all points of my past? he asked. He insisted: choose "*him*" on *any level*—a tiny or large personality, his most multidimensional. To me, it was very real, despite the fact that uninitiated into a oneness consciousness, I found it all science fiction or biblical-miraclelike. Yet, doubt it I didn't.

Here the explanation begins to get vaguer because at this point *it begins to be seeds, seeds I needed time to grow.*

I was experiencing the personification, therefore a transpersonal entity state. Never mind that, to me, I was experiencing his individuality, which, however, was not to be found, he said, in outer form. But the whole Earth was based on outer-form recognition. Where would we be without it?

So I could not go out into situations he set up, radiating physical attraction. Physical attraction could come back in *after* being eradicated in me.

We had it backwards on Earth, he explained—which would have been quite fine, had we been able to divine where the intensity of physical attraction sometimes came from. The subtle signals.

Not to mention that electrical signals of PATTERNS reach us through any variety of electrical field, be it speaking to us from the TV set or whatever.

They took only if a person resonated with them. So, getting back to the seventeenth century, and what got "left out" when Newton lamented that he could not decipher the rules of attraction at a distance—yet (unknown to us till recently) spent long days in secret alchemy experiments—that was easy to redress now, with the discovery of electrical technology. As germs were carried by rats, electrical signals likewise reached our emotions and triggered them UNCONSCIOUSLY, *in delayed response*—in PATTERNS inside FIELDS.

In the Zurich apartment before going out to meet a "protégé," I would meditate to try to see the scene "in the future" in which "he" would be inside a stranger or an acquaintance in the field he set up, for instance, once in a park. If my hands began to vibrate, I knew (let's say interpreted) that an electrical connection had clicked *now* in the near "future." That an energy was operating—if in the right hand, conscious; in the left, not.

Though the transmission and decision happened at the instant I felt the vibrations, the related action took place later. But was now "set."

Over the next couple of decades I was often suddenly aware when my energy made electrical contact, including whether or not it was misread; if misread, I have never even once been able to stop the event after it was set up.

For instance—more recently—if someone's unconscious zeroed in on me during my downtime at the TV, it might give the scene undue importance and draw a conclusion—a false one—such as that I was lazy. The person whose unconscious had picked up this information and made this deduction would be completely unaware of it. A projection had been filed away. The person would later bring this unconscious presupposition into the present when something made his or her intuition focus on me.

It might violate the very core of my being. But in the intensity of the electricity, *drawing on my energy as well*, the person's intuition would feel sure of its conclusion. And be dead wrong.

In that way spiritual energy can work against itself, though we say microphysics has nothing to do with macrophysics—that the particle world is inactive in our laws, inactive in its relationship to us. Not so. It is hiding, because we did not seek it because our laws ruled it out. Until now.

This entanglement of spirit and matter or in this case electricity and events is *very very important to understand today*.

Imagine if the height of the plague had merely accelerated death, adding piles of corpses, rather than becoming that synchronistic background to Newton's laws of motion and universal gravitation.

As long as we saw everything through purely physical reality, we would be too unconscious for this time period. Events would. Events, basing themselves on physical attraction, would be too chaotic—too intense.

Absent physical contact, mass communication would transport these "plagues."

Through our technology all these patterns would be spread—just like germs before them—with no one the wiser about how this "plague" operated.

It was not air. It was not ether. Oh no? It was air WAVES. So waves did it. That was it. Not a single "cause" but waves, waves of AIR. That was it, because the air waves contained all that INFORMATION WE PUT INTO THEM. We did it. We were the culprits, the instigators of the poisoning by . . . air . . . WAVES.

So, Milton Klonsky—who first detected a devious illustration of this kind of infection, which operated massively—located a single case in his Flea essay, "Art & Life: A Menippean Paean to the Flea; or, Did Dostoevsky Kill Trotsky?" Describing there how the gist of the murder of Raskolnikov in Dostoevsky's *Crime and Punishment* was picked up like a cloak by a killer a continent away.

As if the dreaded instrument that killed Trotsky was not the axe or ice pick but behind that the idea, wrapped up in finished, masterful form in a book.

But we never intended fictional characters to be pushed into life by our energetic response. Is that part of our modern world? An effect of technology, just as splitting the atom led to the bomb? Well, now, just look at what this next intrusion into nature has wrought. At the same time, we discounted nature—so that we had not even the slow-reaction patterns of nature to protect us. To shield us from these antinature units of action, these Air Wave-traveling responses all packaged for us.

So if you watched a TV program, occasionally the situation would resonate; you would "receive" not just a thought or insight but the *ordered picture* in action, set up, emoted—kinetically ready as it played into the right brain and got "replicated." Already unconsciously APPLIED in a situation the next day. You unconsciously "decided" to *paste* that situation onto a scene—just as the Initiator was pasting energy fields with great care, in great light. I will come back to this with more examples.

Time is sequential to our rational selves, but outside that it can be analog-oriented. Matching by pattern attraction.

Even to take terrorist suicide bombers, who want to go to paradise. Already during the Zurich Initiation the field of *Home* was being set up. But *going Home* meant returning to a consciousness. It was an archetype, a project: Earth was en route Home. But sometimes the intent would be literalized. Receiving the drive toward home from the symbolic level, the "lower," nonsymbolic mind was not told that it was an energy field *of going home to our planetary consciousness*—even as it received the intensity from the symbolic, archetypical mind infected with the pattern of making it literal.

Further, this energy field would be called "the end of the world." Hey, it was not meant to be played out physically.

The energy field of the End of the Old World—the passing away of the consciousness that came to an end in the twentieth century—meant transformation, reconceiving our consciousness (reoriented toward groups), accessing the Universal Mind where we were One.

I hope someone gets the joke and from there understands why I had often been told to lighten up. It was this sort of territory that ultimately made my life interesting. I could fly here. I believed it.

Your energy field is Now

In the initiation, sometimes I would intentionally be guided wrong. When I resisted, in spite of his commands to the contrary, I learned to listen to myself.

A test came when he took over my "big book," *Love in Transition*. He raced through editing, planting changes in my head at such speed he would have finished in three days. I didn't like the result.

It did not match the lucid dream of my life (described in the Prologue), in which my writing opened, at the end, into paintings—unknown self-portraits in a museum of great art. I would throw away a lifetask if I thought *his* opinion trumped my inner voice.

I stopped the editing. Applauding, he gave me a dream of a small boy being hurled—feet tied—into the water. Bound by instructions to obey him. The boy would have drowned had he not undone the rope and discovered in that instant he could swim.

I was to take from this a lesson, often called on, that no one knew my own needs better than I. This despite the fact that others did often know better. I did not need the outer message in those instances. On the outside he might misguide. On the inside, never.

— 17 —

Comparison—Intention to Heat

Emotional Energy to Physical Energy, the Principles of Dilution or Concentration:

Why Cooling Down with Doubt Is Like Putting a Cooler Water into a Heated One; Also How Gravity Works on this level—between patterns and other forms or systems of order: their outlines

A Little Lecture on How to Get Things Done, or Not to

A Beginning Lecture on/Discovery of Another Dimension of Gravity

Back to Contours of Energy

If I start with a lot of energy, believing/intending to do something, and I insert/encounter/feel even for a fraction of a second doubt, it's like when you put hot tea into a cup; some of the heat in the tea leaves it and enters the cup.

    The power of intent, the life force energy dissipates, diminishes; it loses (or shares) its original power. The sole, concentrated intent is met by doubt; the doubt takes away from—subtracts from—the intent. The energy of doubt spills over into the intent, even a tiny bit. The heat of concentration cools, even a bit. Even a bit is a quantum jump, from certainty to less than certain. Certainty has no room for doubt. Making room for even a modicum of it changes the structure. From one-pointed focus. To something else.

Now that our scientists understand energy so much better, we are perhaps ready to extend those principles into areas we don't think of as operating by the same laws, such as emotion and other intangibles.

Arnold Mindell points out in *The Process Mind* that "Freud seems to have borrowed the term *complex* from chemistry." Therefore, he says, "complexes and drives in psychology are indirectly linked to electrostatic chemistry fields and forces."[107]

A thousand eurekas! So "complex" was borrowed from chemistry. His statement backs up unintentionally what I experienced and am proposing generally.

I've speculated that electricity is where we sometimes pick up patterns. We do this in an unconscious attraction to patterns we pick up ready-made—invisible to us, "distant" from us; harmless patterns, we suppose, in every way. Never suspecting electricity might figure in. Or that as photons carry light, patterns might be conveyed on the quantum level; that is, patterns we experience. Patterns without expression, but that have perhaps been expressed countless times. So, particles respond to archetypes? Is that it? All by themselves? No. This is not to say that particles choose. They come right up to our noses, as it were, with opportunity—or temptation. With choice. Prepackaged. Tried out. Taken often on test drives.

— 18 —

NEWTON & ALCHEMY

In the mid-twentieth century, papers resurfaced that painted a new (to us) picture of one of the world's greatest scientists. In *Isaac Newton: The Last Sorcerer*, Michael White highlights a passage from the papers, in which Newton's assistant (for five years beginning in 1683) recorded the hours the great scientist kept. He wrote: Newton's concentration was so focused that "when he sometimes took a turn or two [in his garden], he made a sudden stand, turned himself about, ran up the stairs like another Archimedes, with an 'eureka!' fell to write on his desk standing, without giving himself the leisure to draw a chair to sit down on."[108]

Newton almost never "went to bed, till 2 or 3 of the clock, sometimes not till 5 or 6, lying about 4 or 5 hours, especially at spring & fall of the leaf." In those seasons he spent "about 6 weeks in his laboratory, the fire scarce going out night or day, he sitting up one night, as I did another until he had finished his chemical experiments. . . . What his aim might be I was not able to penetrate into."[109] A million-plus words by Newton on the subject having recently come to light, the answer, we now know, was alchemy.

D. W. Hauck reported, "As a practicing alchemist, Newton spent days locked up in his laboratory, and not a few have suggested that he finally succeeded in transmuting lead into gold."[110]

Secretively, Newton wrote, "For alchemy does not trade with metals as ignorant vulgars think."[111]

C. G. Jung and Alchemy

In Knittlingen, Germany, Dr. Johannes Faustus's original home, a museum plaque corrects a derogatory impression. Alchemy, it states, was not fired by the intent to transmute base metals into precious metals, lead into gold, but had, more deeply, a spiritual goal: psychological transformation.

Stephan A. Hoeller notes the degree to which—largely due to Jung—the reputation of alchemy has been restored. Jung was perplexed as to what linked us back to the gnostic myths and traditions of seventeen hundred or more years earlier. He wrote: "First I had to find evidence for the historical prefiguration of my own inner experiences. That is to say, I had to ask myself, 'Where have my particular premises already occurred in history?'"[112] Jung's early experience included writing a gnostic treatise, *Seven Sermons to the Dead*, privately published for friends in 1916. The three-day period of intense writing was in response to ringing doorbells with no one there and a heavy sense of ghostly presences.

Hoeller describes Jung's 1926 dream of being caught in the seventeenth century. This led him to finally identify the purpose of the unsuspected wing next to his house in still earlier dreams: he would be locked into the study of alchemy.[113]

In 1928 Richard Wilhelm, a German sinologist, sent Jung a translation of an esoteric Taoist meditation treatise. This manuscript, now called *The Secret of the Golden Flower*, interested Jung tremendously. He decided that Chinese alchemists were not really looking for immortality but, as in the Western search for the Philosopher's Stone, were involved in, as Hoeller put it, "the transformational symbolism of the human soul." He contrasted how history links past to present, yet the East-West bridge "might be seen to consist of archetypal rather than historical substance."[114]

In 1937 the British Indian government invited him to India. He went, with a long-standing interest in how India had integrated the concept of evil and the West had not.

While there, he had a significant dream: *Sightseeing in India, he suddenly finds himself with friends on an island off the coast of Britain. He sees a candle-lit castle, the home of the Holy Grail. However, the Grail isn't there. A German professor lectures learnedly as if it's dead. Jung realizes he has to swim in the dark to a house containing the Grail and carry it to its home.*

The dream revealed to him: "India was not my task." It warned that the Grail was desperately needed in the West to avoid—by treating it as dead—the destruction of what centuries had built. This was a turning point. He began to read the sixteenth-century surgeon, professor, master of alchemy Paracelsus on the boat back to England.[115]

But it was not only Jung who plunged into alchemy; it was also Pauli. Pauli believed that in its hermetic form, based in symmetry, it related to the archetype behind quantum mechanics. And we shall see how, coming up.

PART THREE

Jung, Pauli, the Meta4

If the unconscious can contain everything that is known to be a function of consciousness, then we are faced with the possibility that it too, like consciousness, possesses a subject, a sort of ego.

—Jung

— 19 —

In Search of a "Psychophysical Theory"

It's time to bring in the centerpiece conversations of Jung and Pauli that illuminate and add vocabulary, plowing into the territory of coincidence.

The book of Bipod Metallics in Jung's study inside his museum

There was no such book. No such topic. And yet before considering study at the Institute, I was steered toward the topic by a Jung assistant in a dream. Let's take out *Atom and Archetype: The Pauli/Jung Letters 1932–1958*. Suppose "atom"/"archetype" are two pods (matter/psyche).

Where do matter/psyche overlap? Pauli wrote Jung that this must be the Self.

What did *meaning*, they asked, have to do with the fact that an event occurred? Did it play a role in *cause*? Jung used the term "synchronicity" for meaningful acausal coincidences. Pauli was bothered. He accepted "meaning as an ordering factor." But asked, "*So what is the connection, then, between meaning and time?*" The term "synchronicity" seemed to imply a synchronous occurrence, but in his view, meaning-connection was the "primary agent"; time was secondary.[116] He preferred to say "meaning-correspondence."[117]

Speaking of acausal in terms of the discontinuities (the invisible quantum jumps) of microphysics, where nothing prior to the particular lab test can predict the result of that test, Pauli said to Jung, in today's nuclear physics "every observation is basically an intervention that interrupts the causal connection."[118]

In Search of a "Psychophysical Theory"   149

So how did the part of me who had secrets and the other, who wanted to broadcast my secrets—introvert/extrovert—relate to psyche and its interface with the world: the unconscious and consciousness? And wait a minute: don't forget the inner extrovert, or provocateur?

Pauli was known for his psychokinetic (PK) effect on matter. Computers malfunctioned around him—or exploded: "the Pauli effect."

In a famous instance in the 1920s in a physics lab at the University of Göttingen (Germany), complex atomic measuring equipment stopped working inexplicably. Professor James Franck, ordinarius professor of experimental physics and Director of the Second Institute for Experimental Physics, sighed, thinking that at least this time it wasn't the fault of Pauli—he being out of the country. Franck wrote Pauli the story and got a letter back from Pauli from Denmark, saying he'd been en route to Copenhagen when the crash occurred and at that exact time his train had been stopped a few moments in the Göttingen station.[119]

Once, the three people at lunch with Pauli in New York, including art historian Erwin Panofsky, stood up and found themselves sitting in whipped cream—but his chair was unaffected.[120]

Again, sitting in the Café/Bar Odeon (Zurich), at a window, C. A. Meier recorded, Pauli was thinking of his inferior function. Staring at a large unoccupied red car outside, he could not avert his eyes. Red associated with the feeling function. While Pauli looked, flames shot up out of the car; it began to burn. Since his inferior function was his anima, how was "she" involved?

In what *Obsession* calls "a supreme example," three of his physicist friends after dining together at a teetotal dinner went separately to hear Pauli lecture on Einstein to celebrate the fiftieth anniversary of the discovery of relativity. En route each had a catastrophe. One ran out of gas, went to fill up, and his scooter caught fire; another had two flat tires; the third took a familiar train route and did not notice his stop. All three arrived, however.[121]

But the particular Pauli effect of interest to *Keep This Quiet! Initiations* occurred at the opening of the Jung Institute in Küsnacht (April 24, 1948).

Pauli had fled Nazi Europe in World War II, in 1940, to work at Princeton University for six years, playing no role in building the atomic bomb. Returned to Zurich, he resumed his chair in theoretical physics in 1946, having received the Nobel Prize. He right away contacted Jung, who—with a history of heart disease—a scant week later became ill. It was Jung's second heart illness while working on *Mysterium Coniunctionis* (*The Sacred Marriage*). Fellow psychotherapist Barbara Hannah explained, "It required at least two actual physical illnesses and the near neighborhood of death before [Jung] could understand enough to go on with this book."[122]

Writing Jung in 1946, Pauli described a dream that revived his interest in early-seventeenth-century astronomer/mathematician Johannes Kepler (1571–1630), whose discovery of the three laws of planetary motion, helped pave the way for Newton.[123] Though giving us the Scientific Revolution, scientific thought demoted the *anima*, the inner feminine. The *anima mundi*, the world soul, had been the prescientific explanation (as Pauli put it) of much that *quantitative* science after Newton would explain technically; when science advanced, she fell from her status as an "active principle" in nature.

In ancient times, it was believed there was a connectedness in all things. Long ago, leaves rustling in the wind—for example, on the oak (or beech) trees at the shrine of Dodona, Greece, the earliest Hellenic oracle—might carry messages.

A belief in a vital force in nature—by various names, such as prana, chi, ka, ki, Great Spirit—is found in many traditions, including Hindu, Buddhism, and Taoism, and in the Native American medicine wheel.

Where nature had been thought "magical-animistic," with the rise of science the descriptions became "modern, quantitative-mathematical."[124]

Pauli had an important dream of the unintended consequences. He was reading in an ancient book. It described Inquisition trials of men (Galileo, Giordano Bruno) who adopted Copernicus's theory of a heliocentric universe; it also described Kepler's view of the Trinity. A "blond man" explained the charges: their wives had "objectified rotation."

The scene switched to a courtroom in which Pauli was charged along with the other men; he notified his wife/anima: "Come at once, I am on trial." She came, and "the blond" revealed the judges themselves did not know "what rotation or revolution is." Yet *Pauli* did. Pauli, or his dream self, answered, "Of course! . . . The circulation of the blood and the circulation of light." (He was referring to an ancient Taoist meditation technique; Pauli had, since at least 1940, studied writings of Richard Wilhelm on the *I Ching* and passages from *The Secret of the Golden Flower*.)

After talking with "the blond man," Pauli wept; the blond said, "Now you've got the first key in your hand." Pauli woke disturbed. The dream, he wrote Jung, sent him back to his work on Kepler.[125]

He explained that "From the higher point of view of acquiring consciousness, the accusation relates to the fact that the men did not know where their wives (= anima) were, nor what *their* role was in the process of perception." He speculated: "At that time, apparently (17th cent.), a projection of the mandala and rotation symbolism had occurred externally."

In outspoken contrast to Kepler (not in the dream) was his contemporary—"that remarkable fellow," as Pauli described him to Jung—the physician Robert Fludd (1574–1637). Pauli praised Fludd's connection to his anima, who, he said, "did not objectify rotation for him"; she "did not respond to the archetype that modern natural science had produced." Fludd's Rosicrucianism was antithetical to Kepler and other scientists, whose anima left her location in matter to enter "the perceiving subject."[126]

Pauli goes on in comments that will bear fruit in the rest of his dialogue with Jung. We will pick them back up later.

Favoring a hermetic-alchemy perspective, Fludd viewed nature in terms of "as above, so below; as within, so without." Pauli thought that in building the bomb in 1945, which he had no part in, science overstepped (landing in its dark side); it lacked a fourth aspect, the unknown—the irrational.

Jungian Remo Roth, whom we will get to in a moment, quotes many letters of Pauli to Marie-Louise von Franz, translating them from the German. In a letter to her in 1951, Pauli applauds the fact that the path of the (hermetic) alchemists "begins with a descent into the physical world." To Meier in 1950: "For [Fludd], matter participates *also* in the bright principle and the soul of man *also* in the dark principle."[127]

Pauli further clarified: "I am definitely in favor of the symmetrical interpretation of the spirit/matter pair of opposites, and I was fascinated with Fludd's pictures that let the 'sun child' [offspring of the sun king/moon queen Marriage] develop in the *middle*."[128] (In an intermediate area between them.)

For Fludd, the spirit/matter split was not into one good pole, one bad, with the intention to rid spirit (the good) of matter.

Maybe matter, like psyche, Pauli thought, was rooted in the collective unconscious. Look at how it had contained the energy of the wildly destructive bomb. Look at how scientists, when not exercising wholeness, built the bomb.[129]

F. David Peat summarizes: "The discovery of the collective unconscious probably stands as Jung's most original contribution to psychology; indeed, he referred to it as his 'personal myth.'"

Peat, physicist and author, recounts how "with the advent of quantum theory, it now appeared that the observation of nature also contained a subjective element—the irreducible link between observer and observed." Similarly, in the discovery of the collective unconscious, "the personal nature of mind had now been shown to contain an objective, impersonal level. Pauli believed that this dualism between objective and subjective was particularly significant and indicated that a much deeper unification existed between matter and mind."

Peat goes on: In the quantum world "observer and observed are intimately linked. Below this level, Heisenberg and others have hinted, there may no longer exist a fundamental ground of matter but, rather, fundamental symmetries and ordering principles. In a complementary way, when the first layers of mind are probed, the subjective realm of personal repressions is reached, but at deeper levels lie the objective contents that can no longer be observed directly but are hidden in symbolic forms."[130]

In Search of a "Psychophysical Theory"

Though some of these thoughts were put on paper later, this is the background of Pauli's appearance at the Jung Institute's launching in Küsnacht. He was a scientific patron. As he entered the reception a large Chinese vase fell down off its perch on a table, onto the floor.

Pauli associated the resulting "flood" with Fludd (a pun by the unconscious).

He felt both Kepler and Fludd lived on in *him*, a clash of opposites: Kepler in science; Fludd, hermetic alchemy, where the anima, or World Soul, had been integrated into a world view.*

Pauli also noted the association of number three (with Kepler) and four (with Fludd). More on that later.[131] Did the Fludd-Kepler tension psychokinetically provoke the Institute "flood"?

Pauli wrote to Jung from Zollikon on June 16, 1948, about his reaction to "that amusing 'Pauli effect.'" He said, "I had the immediate and vivid impression that I should 'pour out water inside' ('*innen Wasser ausgiessen*')—to use the symbolic language that I have acquired from you. Then when the connection between psychology and physics took up a relatively large part of your talk, it became even more clear to me what I was to do."[132]

---

* The hermetic alchemist Fludd, a wealthy English physician (with an Oxford degree), used Paracelsian chemistry and a horoscope in his medical practice and defended the Rosicrucians.

— 20 —

Gate *Eau*, Water Gate

I cannot help but digress upon reading "pour out water inside." I get a needle-sharp spike in attention.

A vivid sense of pouring out—what is that but to DECANT? We'll see later on how that emphatic pun figured in my active imagination in a telling dream interpretation in 1981. (The numinous emotional charge in "decant" denoted hidden energy.)

Newton in the countryside in the seventeenth century . . . three dimensionally, the London inhabitants dying off in the plague . . . But the mediator of the unconscious untouched . . . to give birth to—in hermetic alchemical terms—the sun child in the *middle*.

The child of what Pauli calls "Fludd's polar reality," or the symmetrical "spirit/matter pair of opposites."[133]

Pauli adds, "Only the future will show us whether a sun child will develop—by a true 'coniunctio'—out of this collision between psychology and physics."[134]

In his letter to Jung addressing the Institute-vase flood, Pauli enclosed his unpublished essay "Modern Examples of 'Background Physics'" (1948), which gave illustrations of quasi-physics language found in his dreams.

He added: "I attempt to show that in this [type of representation] it is very easy for the unconscious to replace *the alchemistic oven* with a modern spectrograph" (my italics).[135]

A few exclamation points.

I got another adrenalin shot, seeing in this oven an amazing clue to the poetry below, which likewise developed out of the moment I began *Love in Transition* in Paris, on seeing a beggar's head bouncing across a window in front of me (the pertinence of which keeps growing):

> So if we see the world as a Thought Form
> the Fourth Dimension is a
> meta4
>
> The oven where the cooking, the cake, was timed a
> FOUR[136]

Four = "**oven**" in French. The cake is the gâteau (see pages 54, 116).

In the next stanzas, I was talking about a *clé*—(pronounced "clay" = "key" in French)—oven. *En haut* (pronounced "O") = "on high"/ Above. Though I knew no alchemy, just look how I plunged into it in the puns below:

> Cook-key
> *clé*
> clay OVen
> ready to come out in the op-
> N
> The GOT TOW
>
> Now what could be cooking
> in a meta
> FOUR, TURNED ON HIGH
> *EN HAUT*
>
> IN O
> the *HAUT* in the END
> the N-O now
> *EN HAUT*
> a turned-around spelling coming in
> in

a
META-

4

So there it was.

Enantiodromia,* and all the rest. It appears that this oven, *this four*, is (and has been) cooking up a *gâteau*, or gravitational pull—a Got Tow. In a metaphor. Or metaFOUR (oven) or 4. Our missing FOUR.

Peering over the text as down into a cauldron, I try to figure it out. Secrets, a clay oven; a clé, or key. How the unifying symbol holds it together, compacts. Makes a nano map.

But how could a metaphor pull? Help the planet swerve? Like gravity? What are we into here? Whoa, just a minute. Old Newton might think he'd found the key itself, and had he? The transformation formula, just now when we needed it? And if he could wrap it into a theory of gravity? That would do nicely.

Bringing back out physicist David Bohm's implicate order, we might find a lead provided when the beggar, as if explicating this implicated puzzle piece—though in his world he was merely desperate for a cigarette—mimed a message to dig there.

It's often hard to follow the punning twists of the unconscious. But look. This is perfectly rational, given the references.

However, the pieces are spread out—acted on by a "radioactive nucleus," or spinning elliptical anima, or oscillation process.

Unlike the men on trial in Pauli's dream and unlike Kepler, Fludd understood rotation. In his view the world still had a soul. A wholeness, now symbolized by number 4. And being cooked up high above, *en haut*, in our master oven, or *meta*4.

---

* Jung got the idea of "enantiodromia" (anything, at a certain extreme, reverses into its opposite) from Heraclites.

Where does this take us? How could Fludd confront the science-portending Kepler *in the present-day physicist* Pauli?

What kind of comment did that, *could that*, make to enlighten the dream-term door, which would open into the enigmatic topic: bipod metallics?

In the tension of the seventeenth century that Pauli recognized—captured in Fludd/Kepler—was there a statement of the job of consciousness?

A major part of it to go back and see what, in the seventeenth-century path of science, we got short-circuited out of—lost?—that remained as answers down in the unconscious? A direction of ideas we never looked at and now desperately needed?

In *The Meeting of Two Great Minds*, Lindorff says there is so much mystery and synchronicity in him that "it is possible to view Pauli's life as a meaningful coincidence on a grand scale. . . . During all his adult years Pauli was confronted by pairs of opposites."[137]

— 21 —

More to Ponder

Turning to Remo Roth, a Jungian researcher in psychophysical reality (with a PhD in operations research from the University of Zurich) and his two books, in 2011 and 2012, we find the puzzle deepening.

Commenting on the outpouring of water at the Institute launching, Roth, a twenty-year analysand of and longtime collaborator with Jung's famous assistant and colleague Marie-Louise von Franz, notes in *The Return of the World Soul: Wolfgang Pauli, C. G. Jung and the Challenge of Psychophysical Reality* that in a letter Jung mentioned that the astrological sign of the new age of Aquarius "is a man who pours water out of a vase."[138]

Roth wades in. He considered how Jung and Pauli believed in a psychophysical reality "beyond the split into the outer world of physics and the inner world of C. G. Jung's depth psychology."[139]

In *137: Jung, Pauli, and the Pursuit of a Scientific Obsession*, Arthur I. Miller put it: Pauli "was eager to go back to the moment when mysticism and alchemy clashed with the new rational scientific thinking. He suspected that this collision still went on in 'a higher level in the unconscious of modern man.'"[140]

We remember that Pauli added a *fourth quantum number* (spin) to the electron, which had earlier been assigned three numbers (n, l, m). Also, he discovered the *exclusion principle*, which, succinctly put, prohibited any two electrons in an atom from having the same four quantum numbers (n, l, m and s). The exclusion principle was later extended to all fermions (quarks, leptons, and other matter particles). Fermions have half-integer spin, $\pm\frac{1}{2}$; the *force-carrying* particles, bosons, have integer spin and do not obey the exclusion principle. For this principle he was awarded the Nobel Prize. Another major Pauli contribution resolved a problem involving beta decay of an atomic nucleus.

At issue was a violation of the law of conservation of energy; that is, energy went missing when electrons were emitted (during the radioactive decay). To reconcile this deficit, Pauli hypothesized the existence of an unknown particle. His idea, expressed to Lise Meitner in a letter in 1930, was that emitted with the electron, there must be another, postulated particle that held the missing energy.[141] This was later verified, and the ghost particle was named the *neutrino*.

As it happened, Pauli's dreams took his interest in radioactivity into psychology, and Jung picked up the clue. For most readers, radioactivity is an unlikely topic in a book on initiations.

I associated radioactive substances with atomic bombs, poisoning, or the famous thought experiment involving "Schrödinger's cat," where—thinking about entangled quantum states—the Austrian physicist Erwin Schrödinger asked in 1935 whether if a cat was put in a steel chamber with a tiny amount of radioactive substance (of which *perhaps* one atom would decay in an hour, triggering the release of a lethal acid), after an hour was it dead or alive? Since no one could have any idea of the state of the radioactive substance, one had to say the cat was both—dead/alive. Of course, the answer is illogical.

I was quite surprised to find this highly scientific topic leaping into my book. But Pauli hauled it in.

In fact, Pauli had begun to outline the connection of radioactivity to the Self as far back as 1935 while at Princeton. In sending Jung his dreams at that time, he precipitated a correspondence on some scientific terms, including "radioactive nucleus"—which Pauli paired with "Self" (in a "psychological interpretation"). Under "Self," he noted, the "radioactive nucleus" as a psychological process involved both a "gradual *transformation* of the center, and . . . an effect radiating *outwards* (rays)."[142]

By 1949, in the ongoing discussion, Pauli comments on Jung's synchronicity manuscript. In illustrating, "background physics" (his name for the quasi-physics terms that popped up in his dreams), Pauli posits a thought experiment.

He asks Jung to recall a particular early example of synchronicity in which the psychiatrist had been counseling an overly rational patient in his office. The analysis got stuck. The woman was "possessed" by her animus. As she recounted the preceding night's dream about gold jewelry that had the shape of a scarab, a tapping sounded on the window. When Jung opened it, in flew a green-gold scarabaeid beetle. Pauli tells Jung to suppose that a stranger visited him the next evening and said, "Congratulations, doctor, on having finally succeeded in producing a *radioactive* substance."

He says that for years this kind of intellectual game has been forced on him by his unconscious. And it's useless for him to protest that there's no radioactivity anywhere in the house.[143]

Pauli compared synchronicity to radioactive gas: just as radioactivity contaminates a lab, synchronicity spreads.[144] The Stranger, he said, represented "the archetypal background constellated by the system of scientific concepts of our time"[145]; he was an antiscientist vis-à-vis the scientific approach and was something like the "spirit Mercurius" or a magician, combining superior knowledge with attributes of the chthonic (underworld, earth-based) natural spirit. Also, said Pauli, the Stranger used synchronicity, calling it "radioactivity," to compel attention.

Pauli is clear that if scientific methods reach a cul de sac, then material "pushed out of time consciousness in the 17th century" can rise up in such a figure as the Stranger—"the archetype of the 'mana personality'"; though not science's enemy, he needs redemption in our culture if to be understood. Like the wizard of the Arthurian legend, that "fair-dark form," Merlin—"'half Christian-human,' 'half devilish-pagan,'" he writes Emma Jung, quoting her book, *The Grail Legend*.[146]

A few days later, in the *Atom and Archetype* letters, Pauli is still critiquing Jung's synchronicity manuscript. What distinguishes radioactivity, he said, is the "chemical transmutation of the radioactive nucleus."[147] Rays emitted in nuclear decay transport energy; reaching matter, they "produce chemical and physical action."[148] Along with this process, Pauli stresses the "self-duplicating ('multiplying') and expanding phenomena, associated with further transmutations that are brought about through an invisible reality."

Does this match—in neutral language—anything in psychology? Yes, he exclaims. The "active nucleus" of his dreams compares to the alchemists' lapis; thus, he told Jung, "in your terminology is a symbol of the Self."[149]

This is, in one sense, what he already surmised in 1935, when saying that in psychological terms the comparison "seems to indicate a gradual *transformation* of the center, and on the other hand an effect radiating *outwards* (rays)."[150]

Pauli notes that the Self then passes through "a transition . . . into a more conscious state." He can now state simply, "The transformation process is the missing item in your [Jung's] letter when you talk of the psychological correspondence to radioactivity"; the symbolism today is more developed than with the alchemists, he says, but holds.[151]

Another Pauli dream revealed, in 1954, that a hidden laboratory in Sweden had isolated a radioactive isotope. (Pauli said: "What occurred to me at once is that the unconscious is a laboratory in which the individuation process takes place." He thought the dream was urging him to be more conscious.)[152]

By 1956, Remo Roth states, both Jung and Pauli—unfortunately, in his opinion—had decided that radioactivity and synchronicity were, in the Niels Bohr sense, complementary. Pauli's reason was "that synchronicity leads to a spontaneous spreading (i.e., the 'radiation') of new ideas in different people at about the same time (*kairos*)."[153]

Jung had mused back in 1929: "So far as I can grasp the nature of the collective unconscious, it seems to me like an omnipresent continuum, an unextended Everywhere. That is to say, when something happens here at point A which touches upon or affects the collective unconscious, it happens everywhere."[154]

But what else was that illuminating but "the universal nature of each soul" that Lama Sing had mentioned (see page 15)? Wasn't Jung describing virtually the same—if a point relating to the collective unconscious (a point involving you or me—our experience—) is all places at once?

Googling the topic today, I find a text, "Walking into the Consciousness of the Absolute," by the yogi Swami Krishnananda, who writes: "As things are not in one place, they are not just in front of you. Not only are they also behind you, they are to your right, to your left, above and below. . . . Never look at an object as you generally look at it, because it is not in front of you. The pervasiveness of the location of every object necessitates the acceptance of its presence everywhere. So you are actually looking, so-called, at an object which is pervading you from all sides."[155]

I find these speculations fascinating, especially those about the spreading (radioactivity) of events and ideas. This Self, this "radioactive nucleus" of Pauli, with its ideas nonlocally *spread in synchronicity*.

Was synchronicity dispersing our private ideas like pollination in a flower: carrying them around the globe in an invisible "internet"? Producing even the beggar image that caught my attention because it was part of the idea on fire? That is, when something in the unconscious is constellated—wanting us to notice, wanting to speak to us, to create a new balance—a new awareness. Wanting to help us see what the time calls for.-

As this was quite enough of a brainstorm, Pauli and Jung went no further than considering the two acausal instances—radioactivity and synchronicity—complementary. All of which will bear down on the quest of this *Initiations* book.

Returning to matter/psyche, *Obsession* tells us that to Pauli, physics and psychology being complementary, "the prevalence of these symbols seemed to provide firm evidence that the symbols of atomic physics derived from archetypes."[156] As Jung put it, they come out of the same matrix, expressed "psychically-subjectively" (inside) and "physically-objectively" (outside).[157]

Roth reminds us that in the hermetic alchemy of Fludd, the world soul bound together spirit and matter. He deduces "that a *third meaning* of Pauli's [overturned vase] synchronicity is . . . the goal of finding a new synthesis of the divine male and female principle."[158]

Using this synchronicity, Roth itemized the elements and processes that belong in a new psychophysical theory. Notably, an *exchange of attributes*, symbolically demonstrated in hermetic alchemy in the king-queen marriage (*coniunctio*), in which the divine masculine principle (that Roth calls "spirit-psyche") becomes the divine feminine ("matter-psyche"), and conversely.[159]

We remember that this magical-animistic energetic matter-psyche principle was "repressed in the 17th century, when mathematics reduced natural science to causal science."

In a very complex way, Roth insists on the necessity that a psychophysical theory include a bipolar energy term. That is, it must also involve—unlike physics and depth psychology—matter-psyche (paranormal, magical energy). Must reintegrate the feminine energetic principle. But if psyche and physics were complementary, this would be impossible: the two could never exchange places. Not reaching this conclusion held Pauli back, Roth asserts.[160]

At the moment Pauli dreamed of being on trial with those who did not understand revolution or rotation (see page 151), he was told, "*But you know what rotation is!*" He answered, "Of course, the circulation of the blood and the circulation of light"—thus, referring to the Taoist meditation technique of circulating the light (chi) described in *The Secret of the Golden Flower*. This should have been his cue, Roth believes, to assert: *Yes, I discovered (physical) spin. But there's a second sort of spin (rotation), an inner one. That's what the dream Pauli is getting at.*[161]

In the Taoist technique of circulating the light (breath, life force) inside, the effect also goes outside, through the universe. (*The Secret of the Golden Flower* says, "The Light is not in the body alone, nor is it only outside the body. . . . Therefore, as the Light is circulating, so heaven and earth, mountain and rivers, are all circulating with it at the same time.")[162] Roth hits doggedly on this point, and the reason it keeps lassoing me is my dream of "bipod metalism."

What else is he hammering on but the explication of that term?

Roth points out how central the "feminine energetic principle" (the hidden, pervasive world soul) is to hermetic alchemy and Taoism. Believing in this *inner* principle in nature led Fludd (translated by Pauli) to conclude: "He [Johannes Kepler] has hold of the tail, I grasp the head; I perceive the first cause, he its effects."[163]

When Pope Pius XII in 1950 declared the ascension of the Virgin Mary into heaven alongside the male Trinity, Jung applauded (in *Answer to Job*).

Pauli objected vehemently: "As long as quaternities are 'projected into heaven' at a great distance from people . . . no fish will be caught, the hieros gamos [*coniunctio*] is absent, and the psychophysical problem remains unsolved."[164]

He mentions that "only a *chthonic*, instinctive wisdom can save mankind from the dangers of the atom bomb . . . Down in the depths of the Earth an *assumptio* of the woman is required, and not far away from humans in the Heaven."[165]

Digesting Pauli's vision, Roth concludes, would require—but Pauli never went this far—a bipolar, yin-yang energy term. *Bipolar*, like the Tao and hermetic alchemy—in contrast to Neoplatonic alchemy.

Roth finds the Pauli/Jung interpretations good but only up to a point.[166] They take a big step. He wants to go further.

But so far so good for 1956, which is after all, over fifty years ago!

This clue will be addressed later. While Roth's is not a widely known and widely accepted extension—his research has been just recently published in two books by Pari Publishing and he has a substantial following—it has been highly useful for my purposes, offering the hermetic counterpoint as well as being, unlike Jung's, based in feeling-intuition.

Roth adds that for Jung, the union of opposites in the *coniunctio* meant "the integration of the Anima, i.e., symbolic thinking," but for Pauli, master of Pauli effects, it "leads to the observation of singular magical processes, be it in the outside . . . or in one's inside."[167]

Obsession pictures Kepler "straddling two worlds." Fludd was in the Middle Ages. "The forces of mysticism were at the time still overwhelming while science as we know it today was still in its infancy—but a beacon of light."[168]

Roth further postulated that with the discovery of radioactive decay by French scientist Henri Becquerel in 1896, when experimenting with phosphorescent materials (glowing in the dark), the hermetic myth, in which radioactive decay is a psychophysical process, was again constellated, to balance it. What hermetic myth? The Sacred Marriage (*coniunctio*) and its offspring, the *homunculus*, or sun-child.[169]

As was made clear above, Jung believed the Self archetype was symbolized by the quaternity. Roth believes that unconsciously, the Seal of Solomon was constellated in Pauli (the six-sided double triangle of the Above and the Below)—as indicated in dreams and in his dislike of placing the feminine far away in heaven.

Both men saw physics and psyche as complementary, whereas Roth objects that in comparing synchronicity to radioactivity—which incurs transformation—Pauli already had the clue from the unconscious that the two were interchanging.

It is this clue, it seems to me, that—from out of the same collective unconscious—my dream citing bipod metalism as a topic for Jung study may have supported. And there will be more in support of the Seal of Solomon in a cave I visit in the '90s in Romania. And my dream of a Chinese couple, whose long-postponed marriage finally occurred. The two had been separated; then the bride arrived—in a spectacular, shimmering emerald-green dress.

This makes an obvious partner to Pauli's dream of the dancing Chinese woman who, mounting and descending steps, induced the floors to merge—and rotation to ensue—implying that the single act had "multiplied" into the cosmos. But let's save that for up ahead, in the next volume.

The theme of "rotation" will also return us to the mysterious invisible "puff of smoke" mimed by the clown beggar at Montparnasse as his head oscillated up and down—getting my attention, drawing me into my subject, showing me that entry point. And his miming of cigarette smoke took us to Klonsky's poem "The End Pocket," which asked the Master to "light our cigarette with yours."

What better implication that Jung's point A can become universal, which perhaps the collective unconscious has been trying to say in all these ways these many years.

Roth further believed that this hunch about the importance of the Seal of Solomon to Pauli was demonstrated in the "missing energy" Pauli attributed (wrongly, in Roth's view) to the neutrino. Rather than hypothesizing the ghost particle, he affirms, Pauli had the chance at that point to dig further into the unconscious and emerge with a theory of bipolar energetics.[170]

Are we back in my Jung-study dream, the suggestion to look into bipod metalism? *Metalism*, short for *alchemy*, would represent transformation, just as bipod was shorthand for the Eastern Tao approach, the yin-yang (feminine/masculine) of the *I Ching*.

Regarding the radioactive beta decay, discovered in phosphorescent materials by Becquerel, I can't help but be reminded of the moment—at Delphi—when I watched phosphorescent birds swooping across the night sky, lit up, *in pairs*. I found no explanation of the meaning of the numinous moment. Until this minute.

To Roth a key opportunity was missed when Pauli substituted complementarity for a *bipolar* energy concept, like yin-yang—as "presented to him by the preconscious knowledge of the Self with the Fludd/flood synchronicity."[171]

He speculates that the fact that Pauli didn't understand (but insisted on a *unipolar* energy process) precipitated inner "quantum leaps"; that outwardly these were expressed negatively on matter—in the psychokinetic Pauli Effect, or PK.[172]

To mention another Pauli effect: he was at Princeton in February 1950 when the cyclotron burned. Markus Fierz, a close colleague, reported that Pauli, who believed in his PK effect, told him "that he senses the mischief already before as a disagreeable tension, and when the anticipated misfortune then actually hits—another one!—he feels strangely liberated and lightened."[173]

Pauli was highly interested in Taoism. Hence, the fifth meaning of the Chinese-vase synchronicity for Roth: "*the inclusion of the yin/yang bipolarity* of energy into a revised philosophy of nature and scientific worldview."[174]

Well, this sounds pretty much as if "background physics" was displaying itself in my Jung study/museum dream of *bipod metallics*. Could this ultra-slender clue be a significant piece of the puzzle, tiny as it is? Or just an addendum?

The split between science and faith that developed from the seventeenth century, in personality types, made scientists thinkers who repressed their feeling and had extraverted sensation. This inferior feeling allowed them to experiment on animals, which horrified those with strong feeling functions. In the online "Psychovision: Unus Mundus" forum moderated by Roger Faglin, Roth elaborates:

> With the help of Carl Jung's typology we can also understand what happened during the first scientific revolution in the seventeenth century. Up until then the philosophers of nature (as one calls these "prescientific scientists") looked at nature with the help of their feeling and intuition function, and thinking was based on these two. In the language of today's science we would say that they [fantacized]. They did not see the concrete world as we percept [*sic*] it today with the help of our five senses.
>
> A good example for such a worldview is Robert Fludd, the physician, alchemist, and Rosicrucian. His counterpart was Johannes Kepler who began to introduce mathematics into science and like this found the motion laws of the planets. He found them with the help of the observations of [astronomer] Tycho Brahe. The latter noted thousands of positions of the planets, and Kepler had the idea to describe these motions in a general way with the help of math. Thus, we see here the great leap that happened then. Math and like this abstract thinking entered science. Since according to Carl Jung thinking and feeling are opposites, the feeling function was more and more repressed in science. The thinking replaced the feeling, and because of the repression of the feeling function a new type of consciousness developed. It was based on thinking, (extraverted) sensation, and intuition. I call it the Logos ego. Robert Fludd, however, was and stayed in what I call today the Eros ego, based on the feeling, the (introverted) sensation and intuition functions.[175]

— 22 —

Why I thought "this" and . . .

Why I thought "this" and then spotted the plastic container top still out on the counter

The "sensation function" is <u>organizing</u> while my hand moves, redecorating, rearranging—as I put flowers into a vase, deciding where the colors go. The sensation function is shaping, backed by the intuition. Translating, acting out through juxtapositions, selection, focus.

My hands moving, my thoughts accounting for, aligning, paralleling—<u>those</u> are my thoughts' acts, in awareness of connections to meaning not read by me. Not seen. Not interpreted.

The future hides there. Going ahead. Not intending to. Just invisible to my brain and me because we never get the clue.

The intuition is "thinking," moving my hands to reflect *connections*. So the dreamy intuition, by giving the sensation function information, is in fact influencing it or even directing it as it acts.

— 23 —

Doubling Time: Greece

Greek has two words for time, two for place: *chronos* (linear, clock time) and *kairos* (nonlinear). Likewise, for place: *topos* (map location) and *chora* (energy sense of a place). Peter Merry described how Jim Garrison, president of the global Wisdom University, organized an intensive in Chartres, France, around, in part, the theme "Nature likes to hide," meaning—in a translation of the Greek—from the mind.[176]

Kairos is qualitative—relating to "when the moment is right." Its etymology is in weaving and archery—in both, involving an opening that one creates and/or goes through, perhaps forcefully.[177]

On Moving from A to B in Structure: that is, from Start to Middle, or Start to Finish

How Gravity enters in, recognizing not just the bumps and warps of mass in space, the dips and cavities, the Black Holes, and so forth, but that it also—I began to understand this about a decade ago—recognizes shape in more depth.

That is, for instance, the shape of beginning/end. The approach to that goal. The pull of *finishing*.

In Newton's law of universal gravitation every point mass—in this case, beginning/end, Alpha/Omega—"attracts every other point mass with a force that is directly proportional to the product of their masses and inversely proportional to the square of the distance between them."[178] We are adding the influence/effect of the content—the intent/emotional weight—of these separated masses, that is, the beginning/end.

Why does subjective time speed up as you approach a goal? Does the energy linkage between the intent and the goal, in the pattern of beginning–end, make the energy *at the location* of the end increase as it is neared? As if some energy was exchanged, perhaps in the form of intention/intensity?

— 24 —

Rounding Out Zurich, 1986–87

In my Zurich Initiation, I'd received rudimentary glimpses of energy laws. I was aware I might look like a "primitive"—or neurotic!—*on the surface*. Inside, I never felt the need to cry for help or "wish it would stop." I was being shown how energy masters work, not how to work in energy myself. I knew that to go into these fields was not dangerous, with mastery. But the Initiator cast aside protections and walked naked, it seemed, into the fields he set up, sure that his energy would dominate.

In that, he seemed to me like Don Quixote. Harnessing human potential, he had a conviction that people's unconscious, their inner knowing, would choose this level of consciousness if forced to select or given the chance to. I saw that as the way *this level* of consciousness thought.

Because the Initiator worked in magnetism, everything he did had huge intensity and precision. *If he was the magnet (the nucleus), then of course everything was magnetic to him.* He was banking on the unconscious synchronicity he lined up not being wiped out by a mimicking physically based one. He was banking on the deeper source.

I knew I would be all right. However, I had only the inklings, a glimpse inside the Door. I felt no torturous doubt. And in this context, my ability to merge was a benefit.

Milton Christ, I felt, was putting himself in danger for the sake of the world. Groups were. Great teachers risking their emotional heritage, the storehouse of personal memories, setting them into the most unconscious settings, releasing their consciousness into areas where, on the surface, there was unpreparedness. That's how I saw it. Willingly, I threw myself in. I also knew that my fear for the Initiator in going unprotected into the energy fields (fear for his memories and other intangibles that were the "bait") looked superstitious.

I learned about electrical chains: vibrations remaining on objects, therefore attractions between them, which—if unconscious—made events recur, like pushing a button that said "repeat this."

I knew about "microcosm" scenarios: miniatures that—seemingly harmless—could (as patterns) do gigantic damage or good. And that these secrets of obscure great Eastern teachers were part of the tools, unwise to let out, yet here they were.

I felt the electricity in my hands as it connected to someone. I knew it operated in scales, so a tiny replica could not literally cause anything to happen. No object could. Spirit was always stronger than matter. But I did not have the skills. I only had the awareness.

It looked downright compulsive when I threw away Snoep's yellow blanket because it had become a link—yellow had, everything yellow. *Throw away yellow. Never touch yellow.* I just didn't know the way out of the maze of laws I hadn't been taught, which were the *map not the reality*, operating mechanically—just like humanity in many relationship to the unconscious.

I knew enough to be afraid regarding the events "caused" by what was *information* on the most minor primitive levels.

I knew that micro-event structures could chain-link. For instance, I was shown that if I put a dirty fork into the drawer beside a clean one, I set up vibrational "memories" of "where" the object had been. More, as I've implied, when I choose the closest cup of yogurt in the refrigerator instead of the furthest, to the unconscious did I register a slight hesitation, an unwillingness to do anything that required effort?

For how long? If so, had I set up a routine for the day of always, in choice after choice, *inclining* toward the least effort? Or with the opposite choice of the furthest-away cup, had my sleepy self set up a "conditioning" that unless I pushed "reset," I'd decided on a day in which I would choose the *non*easy option: reach to the far out and atypical? The unconscious read my "body language," as it were, my unconscious tipping of the scales. Read *me*, and not just a statistic.

If someone sensed this underlying system but was entirely unconscious, the result might be obsessive-compulsive or a hint of it.

Take this further—to the theory that information is energy. Mass and energy are interchangeable: $E = mc^2$.

This very subtle information above is based on connections, meanings so miniscule as to seem manufactured. That may be true. It depends on how much meaning/energy is invested. If no energy is attached, no unconscious meaning. But which is it? Which was it when *I* did an action?

So analogical thinking by the unconscious applies a kind of math—a projection of probabilities: if a = b, then b = c. A string of situational comparisons. It has "understood" our underlying intent.

It can hold up charts of *when* it made a certain choice for us, whether at the TV, watching a situation that it lifted out as a module, a gestalt we had an opinion on. Or some other place, where, comparatively, tiny Situation A mapped out in advance how we would respond to Situation B.

To us there had not been the same stakes, *the same degree of reality*, in the tiny scale or the screen of imagination. We knew of nothing at all going on. It was below the surface. In a consciousness we left on its own, calling it "the unconscious." Where none of our secrets pass unnoticed.

It was busy "reading" our motives, which might have stunned us, had we connected all those dots as the unconscious did—when it chose "unintended consequences" we would never have let past our censors.

The above relates to why if one single person breaks a pattern, a karmic lesson, it is potentially for the whole Earth.

That break in the pattern is *available*. For a long time no one may know. *A path is open.* That, I was to realize, appeared to be my deeper self's work. I didn't know how to operate on these levels. I was in some in-between location. I chose to see where it led, awkward as some of it was.

Perhaps the Initiator had no real intent to set up a couple, the times the attempt failed. Once, eventually, it would take.

Early on, having heard a rumor, my former analyst sent word to come by her apartment. I arrived, a shocking specter: gaunt, in baggy white overalls with suspenders. Deciding I was having a bona fide initiation, she held out a rock from Jung's Bollingen Tower.

Unsure whether it would be "good" or "bad" in the *chains* of effect, I refused it! I would think this absurd now. But at the time, I couldn't risk accepting anything that held a modicum of uncertainty about it—anything at all outside the known quantity in my apartment. Even a rock from Jung himself.

To turn inward the second half of life fit the *individuation* pattern. At forty-five I was on track. Would this be as exciting as a life turned outward?

Earth was changing—receiving a new consciousness. How would the planet, or people one by one, meet its/their fate, its/their Day of Judgment? How would this sort of Apocalypse of symbolic Death—of "the old," the decrepit, the learned lesson—occur?

For with the archetype of "saving Earth" in play (the archetype of Home), people were being called to be authentic. To "spin" *themselves,* not information, *on a higher frequency*. Incarnate their truth.

Energy fields had no predetermined outcome except what was in the nature of those in them. When push came to shove—given the archetype of *Choose which?*—most people would choose well. *For instance, choose Christ or Barabbas?* The name changes. Choose Hanuman. Choose Lord Shiva. Chose *myself.* This was all that had to be done. Listen WITHIN. BELIEVE. Be centered. BELIEVE THE HEARTBEAT OF EARTH. Hear it. Believe in this Change.

Otherwise, this much energy unleashed, this much breaking of old boundaries and sturdy restrictive laws, would create a chaos so great it would lead to Debauchery. Not knowing *what was what* as events spiraled out of control, the intensity of spiritually resonating inner potential given over to outer fear.

But it was no risk. Humanity would learn to express this about itself. On this level I could assist. I could even start right now. And this time when I said it was *now or never* and tomorrow would be too late, I would be right.

So Bamboy, the horse I'd seen hidden away in a dream, ran in secret around the track, absorbing determination.

How was I ever going to put context to my life from here on in and to the books we worked on, including the now-revised *Love in Transition*? I felt the book he'd dictated—*The Christ State*—was sacred. For it was coincident with his preoccupations with Earth—little as I was, compared to all that.

The plan to make a pattern couple based in spiritual attraction (that underlay physical attraction) of his energy and mine had not worked fabulously, to understate it.

Much that he challenged me to do was outside the bounds of what I'd conceived possible. I knew that Milton was no longer in a single form and imagined him being blown and exploded into bits all over the universe. I imagined the vivid moment itself; how he/I/anyone would, as an entity or consciousness, step up to the instant of choosing to spread oneself in ways so as no longer consciously to remember—unless you somehow rewoke.

I imagined that maybe my deeper self was preparing for such a moment, my soul grouping, and they were leaving this legacy. Blasting into Oneness. I did not know if it was an accurate supposition. But I did not want them to go through that, supposing they did, without me.

I did not know exactly how to imagine what was going on. I was assigned to make him fall in love with me inside some form of "him" that had no conscious knowledge of him—some Young Personality with the exterior typing of the clowning Mozart. This new personality—in the instances we met mostly being younger than me by about ten years—was often handsome, dashing, physically attractive.

On top of that, if I *chose* "him" *on any level, the highest to the least advanced, he said, he could make the relationship work*: bring all the forms, *the totality and individuality of them all*, to back up a single choice.

On a few occasions I "overheard" in my mind what appeared to be fragments of a group spirit-discussion.

One snatched phrase was "After Christ died he was sacrificed." Who? What? I was against it and wanted to prevent it, whatever it meant. It continued, "Christ would be born in his memory."

Another: "They will be together in *old age*." I thought that one involved me. *Who would I be together with?*

Waking from a dream, I heard the song "Why do fools fall in love?" It seemed to refer to the future end of *two* relationships of mine *at once*.

But there was a frightful, horrid prophecy I overheard: "was reduced and relegated . . . became like a well dried up . . . who had been a diamond." It was as frightening as the worst nightmare.

I vowed to hold this gruesome prediction in front of me as an antifuture. Overreacting at the slightest brush with the possibility, I would later flinch at the hint of it, taking it as a fearsome, dreaded, gruesome horror. Knowing, I could surmount it, watching for signs of it rearing its head—to walk in the opposite direction.

Enter René Pascal, a dark-eyed, brown-haired Swiss former model all over Europe. I thought he looked like a cross between the French actor Jean-Paul Belmondo and Zorba the Greek.

A few months into 1987, I again had the occasional social drink— as a consequence of a few train trips to Belgium to lend support to my ailing alcoholic ex-husband (this is so significant that it has its own section just ahead)—and it happened that early one evening I stopped into a bar in Zurich. At this point the Initiator was gone; his influence remained and the idea of looking deep inside every person. There I might encounter the level of energy I'd been initiated in.

Now we make an abrupt about-turn in this book to let stories and characters, strong ones—and with them a fragrant waft of life—come in.

— 25 —

Bridge: Who Am I?

As I read this I think, naturally, how far out some of it sounds.

Well, OK. Let's ask Jung about it. Noting the numinous charge of archetypes—expressed as affects, emotion—he says that with the resulting weakened ego comes an *abaissement du niveau mental* (lowering of the mental state). Energy is removed from consciousness, thereby opening the door for the unconscious.[179]

In his monograph on synchronicity in 1952, Jung speaks of the Tao and its founder, Lao-tzu, who wrote the classic *Tao-te ching* (sixth century BC). Jung points out that Chinese philosophical thought is acausal, holistic.

Lao-tzu explains, "We put thirty spokes together and call it a wheel; / But it is on the space where there is nothing that the utility of the wheel depends."[180] Similar statements led Richard Wilhelm, then Jung, to ask what Tao is.

Jung praised the inkling about the *I Ching* planted by Wilhelm on European soil, saying, at Wilhelm's memorial service (Munich 1930): "Human instinct knows that all great truth is simple. The man whose instincts are atrophied therefore supposes that it is found in cheap simplifications and platitudes; or, as a result of his disappointment, he falls into the opposite error of thinking that it must be as obscure and complicated as possible."[181]

In 1935 in London he identified synchronicity with the Tao as a principle because of which "things happen together somehow and behave as if they were the same, and yet for us they are not."[182]

He would later say, "Reality, thinks Wilhelm, is conceptually

Bridge: Who Am I?

knowable because according to the Chinese view there is in all things a latent 'rationality.'" On this idea rests the idea of meaningful coincidence.[183]

Tao says, "The soul can become empty and absorb the whole world," Jung explains. "It "is, whenever possible, "*a thinking in terms of the whole*"; the microcosm is present in large-scale, macrocosmic events.

Similarly, with the Greek physician Hippocrates (460–370 BC) and the medieval mind: "The universal principle is found even in the smallest particle, which therefore corresponds to the whole."[184]

With this emotional situation, I was in a propitious position to encounter the unconscious and let its information and depth flow through. The point was not to drown in it. And I didn't feel in danger of that. I thought I was learning valuable things—without answers. Answers would appear along the way if I kept going.

But like you, I was cultivating the question of *who is who? Where does one person end, if not at his or her physical borders? Were there conscious energies operating inside us that were larger than we were—of course—invested in us as holding their energy, as emanations/expressions /consequences of that emotion and energy, that consciousness? And if so, then, again, who was who?*

At bottom, I was me. I knew that. But from that A, how to get to XYZ, where Oneness operated? Had I known more at the time, this question would not have sounded so simplistic. But I didn't. So I withheld judgment as life itself took me by the hand and bade me follow accordingly.

I felt a reality in the spirit marriage on the soul level, not sure how it could play out but thinking he knew better. That is, so long as it was the former *I* in question.

This is where we pick up in the next section.

My soul was intent on "freeing the mind." Later I will meet Shri Dhyanyogi, who will teach me without physical contact.

The initiation was through a nonlocal, global consciousness imbued in the implications of connectedness. But life is also about what it looks like from the other end, called "personality."

So now I have written, up to 1986, how I discovered and was taught, through half a lifetime of experiences, to remember that underneath it all was the UNIVERSALITY OF HUMANITY.

But how to say this simply, believably, when a lot of us, quite rightly, are used to pinching ourselves to know if we're dreaming?

PART FOUR

Meeting Willy and Cast, The Bell

"He was propelled into this lifetime to pay you back."
—Chris Van de Velde

"To me there is no liberation a tout prix. I cannot be liberated from anything that I do not possess, have not done or experienced. Real liberation becomes possible for me only when I have done all that."
—Jung, *MDR*

— 26 —

In the Hospital

The next important part of the story is Willy, who comes in in 1987.

The Initiator left some indeterminate time in 1986. However, something else was determining what happened next: the dollar.

Where my rent had been $600 (1,506 Swiss francs) in October 1984, it was steadily rising: 1,506 SF was $900 and climbing by October 1986 as the dollar took a deep dive. I had felt flush before. The high dollar made normally unaffordable things affordable. But not anymore. Now, instead of 2.51 SF equaling $1.00, only 1.63 SF did and falling. I had to move.

I was living off $29,000 accident insurance from my mother's death, paid by the at-fault highway patrol officer's insurance, and the $10,000 she left me, plus a little trust money (not given me outright only because of my marriage to Jan Mensaert).

I could stretch it if careful. I had heard Willard Trask tell me, at the MacDowell Colony, how he inherited money from his parents and lived all over Europe ten years; then it was gone, and he became a translator, winning a National Book Award.

Lots of countries were cheaper, even half as expensive. France and Italy were magic spots to me. Could I move there? A few weekends I did trial runs into Paris, hanging out in the Left Bank: the Latin Quarter— Boulevard St.-Michel, Boulevard St.-Germain (Les Deux Magots café), Shakespeare & Company bookstore, Notre-Dame. Artistic spots. I happened to fall for a Parisian but not too hard. So I shuttled back and forth on the train. But that relationship was not serious.

In October, I received an urgent letter from my ex (technically we were estranged), Jan Mensaert, in Belgium. We exchanged infrequent letters—maybe once every six months or whenever a letter happened to pop in. In particular, I knew how much he wanted news of our mini-dachshund Snoep. However, this time he wrote: please come right away.

13/10 [October 13]

Dearest Margaret,

The end is <u>very</u> near. These last days there has been a whole series of big and small events pointing that way. This Wednesday or Thursday will be crucial. I beg you to come to Tienen. I feel that is of the uttermost importance not only to me but just as much to you. We must meet one last time in this life. I have some last things I <u>must</u> communicate to you. And you may have some for me. No. The telephone won't do. Margaret, <u>please</u>, there is great urgency behind this. Love,

Jan

I wasn't sure whether he was luring me there or was direly ill, which was likewise possible if his wild life had caught up with him.

Jan had come to Zurich once, the year before, surprising me. I didn't answer the door—thankfully not hearing the bell. I'd just seen a movie where a guy drinks, separates from his wife, she almost loses the farm in foreclosure, then she works hard and gets it back, and then he comes knocking. I connected the two situations. Also, I had the unlikely experience of discovering I'd forgotten a Tampax inside me, and pulling it out, with the old blood, I again thought it was a synchronicity—a picture of rotten, discolored stuff that I forgot about and got rid of.

Nevertheless, I phoned.

If the reader is wondering how I could jump from the Zurich Initiation back into what appears to be normal life, I'm wondering myself. Not yet coming across notes for this period, it's hard to find the transition. The Zurich Initiation planted seeds. Was experiential.

More experiences would be needed to digest it. It was not something I could read about in a book or wanted to. I felt I was carrying the seeds within.

So shortly before Christmas 1986, I went to Tienen, Belgium. As the story unfolds, this is synchronistic right to the death of both Willy and Jan (ten days apart).

Why not go to Tienen over the break? I thought.

After all, the Initiator had taught me to look at the inner person, not the outer—look to where *his* energy might be.

Later I would hear of Hindu gurus who taught their pupils to look for *them* in any face, look for God everywhere, even in criminals. And my energy teacher in Belgium would say to denounce a deed but not the actor. Turn your back on a pattern, but separate that from the person in it.

I was worried (in fact, afraid) to tell Jan of our little paralyzed dachshund's death. I felt partly responsible. I knew Jan would hold me accountable.

Beautiful Snoep died alone in the kennel during my Zurich Initiation, which had made me quite angry with the Initiator for not alerting me or protecting Snoep, though in fact two dreams warned me, but I didn't understand. One took place in my studio apartment (a foyer and living room). The foyer was not the "inner room," the dream said; some people wanted to be there. In a little panel, Snoep spoke up: "*I among them.*" He would have liked to remain with me during the rest of the initiation, which he'd earlier taken part in; for instance, his diet changed to rice and a plum on top.

I had often taken him in his shoulder carrier to Institute classes, workshops, and ballet. I sat him on the floor. And he didn't make a sound. No one knew that before getting on a tram (he had no bladder control), I had to empty his bladder somehow. On the flight from JFK to Zurich, the stewardesses boarded him and me first, just like with a human in a wheelchair.

But I couldn't possibly have kept him through the initiation. So I thought. I meant to leave him two weeks but postponed the pickup,

In the Hospital

thinking no harm done. In fact, he was put in double diapers, which he hated, perking up a bit when they sat him on the grass a few hours a day (I later learned). He'd been depressed when I first flew from Charlottesville to Belgium to get him from Jan, but with a lot of massages by me to his paw pads, and swims together in the Charlottesville-motel pool, he'd seemed happy.

The kennel left a message at the Institute. I never got it. His heart gave out in his sleep. In the second dream his rear end was backed into a hole in the wall; he told me he was stuck. I took it symbolically.

The Initiator had explained that Snoep held his heart emotions. So I hadn't imagined he would callously let him die. I thought he'd wake me in alarm. Had I thought otherwise, I'd have in a flash, racing with my heart in my throat, gone to pick Snoep up.

Who knows if that had anything whatsoever to do with my not turning my back on Jan?

Perhaps we'd enjoy seeing each other, without ties or attachments. Okay, okay, I get that it's farfetched. Was this another *uh-oh*, bad choice? Not as it turned out.

As we move into a whole new section, here is a little chronology: I learned of Milton's death July 1982 (he died in November 1981). This set in motion the process of leaving Jan; I left definitively in March 1983; I spent August 1983–October 5, 1984, in Charlottesville, Virginia, and moved to Küsnacht in October 1984. The initiation began in September 1985 and ended around one year later, which is where we pick up.

I was dramatically changed inside: how I thought, what I wished for.

I wanted to enter a romance again but with someone who fit into my path, in other words, was—perhaps in secret—accessibly carrying this energy. But how to detect that? I wasn't sure I could.

I asked how would I "know"? The Initiator had told me, as Milton, to look for him *outside* his physical form, which, of course, was "dead."

Years later, when I visited my Hungarian shaman teacher in a retirement home, knowing it would be the first and last time, I said, in leaving, "I'll look for you in your [Tibetan] bowls." I meant the sounds when I played the instrument he had mastered and was known for. He said, "*No, look for me—in the universe.*"

I didn't ask what he meant. He spoke to the part of me that understood and would someday explain it to me.

Anyway, in 1986 it was of great importance to me to "find"— look for—the Initiator, after all signs of his presence had vanished. Look for him in people, as he had taught me to. I don't believe at that point I was looking for his presence in myself.

I thought I'd been given an initiation by my soul, that it was highly important to me, in ways I could not fathom, to live the opportunity of this spirit tie, this, if you will, spirit marriage, with Milton Christ Mozart. I also thought it made me the oddest person on earth, who could not say a word about this situation but walked into a room, carrying the tie, which perhaps was creating all kinds of energy collisions, important in ways beyond my understanding, related to memories I didn't have. I completely believed this.

Now I was on my own to figure out how to stay on this path. I remembered my father's advice to my middle sister, Lee. At three she was diagnosed with very weak eyesight, made to wear strong glasses, do exercises so one eye wouldn't droop. He sought out the best medical advice at McPherson Hospital (Durham, North Carolina).

World War II had only just ended a year earlier. The car industry was booming. My father took time off work, which he never did—not day or night. But he had to help out his little daughter. Driving to Durham, he told her, just as if she were an adult, that they would listen and if the doctor thought there was a good chance an operation would help, they would try it. But if McPherson's recommended against it and the odds were against it, they would never speak of it again.

At McPherson's they said the operation held a high risk of blindness.

Going home, my father said words she kept in her heart always. He told her stories of people who had risen through adversity. He named names. He told her, "Adversity builds character." Not that anyone wanted adversity, but it could be turned into a positive and you could still come out okay.

I knew the type in whom I'd encountered the Initiator's energy so far, though again being transpersonal it was everywhere, depending—I would now put it—on being resonant with. But to me, even where unconscious in people, it was conscious. That's how I saw it and even today am still figuring out the metaphysics of personal/transpersonal, how far we can follow where our energy goes, in resonance, and how to see our human dimension in light of these other dimensions.

So the Initiator left. I wish I could remember exactly the moment.

It had been self-evident from the start, 1965, that my relationship with Jan would be in heavy waters. For a time, I thought I was responsible for keeping him alive, not as a theory but as a step-by-step situation I found myself in. Even blackmailed in, to the point of shielding him from discovering his own inner strength. I allowed projections. On the other hand, he was, as a reader of my memoir speculated to me, "a hummingbird." And what I drew from the marriage was a piece of myself.

Jan had lived in Thailand in his twenties on a hitchhiking trip to the Orient that led him eventually to Morocco. In Thailand he'd had a male-prostitute lover, Pong, whom he told me (later), lying, was female, making up a mystique about her—as about the tragic Aziza, another lover, who, likewise I eventually learned, was male. Jan explained to me with these confessions—which surfaced in self-examination in writing *The Suicide Mozart* in 1980—that it was an accident (of a childhood wound) that made him gay, he'd dropped the practice in marrying me. That was a half-truth, if that, and the orientation was too deep in him psychologically, whether practiced or not. Anyway, he'd wanted me to stay, and knowing his powers of persuasion, I slipped away in March 1983.

I did wonder, in 1986, how, with his widely read philosophical, even metaphysical mind, his marijuana journeys, his intent in

Morocco to "write a book about God," he would see my initiation.

I took it as an encounter with the Self, which I'd been led to by my soul, the one I'd glimpsed twice in rare out-of-body moments. Seen once looking like a Big Dot that radiated such love and understanding that, hands down, I abandoned my body (below) and saw myself fly off with her, to who knew where. My first out-of-body experience, or OBE.

I took from that the memory of her sheer determination—about what, I didn't know. But I wanted that determination now. Could I turn this experience into something worthwhile, or would it just brush off me because I didn't care enough, wasn't brave enough to live it, no matter what?

Also, if I look hard inside, I can find the little girl about twelve who was bullied and (I believe) once thrown into a ravine and who was derogatively every day called "Bugger" by the most popular female classmates, and who once, having walked down the hallway to her school locker, was accosted by a young boy who, while everyone watched, caressed one of her breasts, holding it out to the crowd for applause while I froze, and he did it again the next day; the boy who at the beach on a group outing came by and said something about peanut butter (I forget the sentence but remember he was laughing at me)—*because I was different*. I was different. In this book, I'm, in my mind, presenting myself as "different." Though, in the way I think now, that statement is too self-centered. If I get out of the way and let "the universe" flow through, the question will take care of itself.

On the other hand, it's a risk. It was a risk in *Keep THIS Quiet Too!* I could lose everything, everyone, and become just a punch line for jokes.

I was to one reviewer. But *just one* publicly. So that's my vulnerability. I combat it by calling on my higher awareness, that comforts the little girl (*my feelings*) and turns the fear into deep surrender and peace of mind. I have to do this, I remind her. So it's going to be all right.

And then she transforms into the little-girl me at the top of the stairs who couldn't be stopped from tiptoeing and crawling down to

In the Hospital

see what was going on. What were the adults doing, the men doing? Playing cards. Would they reject me? Maybe yes. Spank me? Maybe yes. But I didn't think so. I was a squirming, determined bundle of curiosity at that moment, who thought, with stars in my eyes, *let's go see what the action is, let's go see if they like me.* And they did!

I sat in on the game. I saw one hand *before* it was played. This was an expression of my personal myth. I was back in that myth. It was part of psyche's world. Was it part of the "real" world? Let's find out as events from one weave into the other. Anyway, life would probably knock me down if I got too far ahead of or behind the curve. Life being an even more predictable teacher than the Initiator, who wasn't around. My biggest hope was to carry on through the doorway he'd opened, wherever it led.

Who knew where?

So this brings us to Willy, who just walked right in around September 1987. Here's the story.

The Zurich Initiation had wound down. At first, not knowing how to adjust, having withdrawal symptoms, I went to bed about 8:30, got up at sunrise. I was somewhat at loose ends. On the other hand, I was inspired—deeply seeped in what I'd just been through, still greatly involved in what it had opened up. When Jan wrote, I phoned.

Had he been coming to Zurich, I would have felt it invasive. But this was on his turf. As he was ill, I didn't expect him to follow me back.

Jan was deliriously happy to get my call, upbeat. He promised if I'd visit we'd go to parks—a first. Stay out of Tienen cafés.

I remembered how the Initiator had taken me into what he said was Jan's Third Eye—a very high energy. Maybe I could interact with that part of him. I got into the narrow seat in the train for the eight-hour trip during the Christmas break.

He met me at the station, then led me across the street to—where else?—a small brick café on the corner, with knotted pine walls inside and a sprinkling of males at small tables. He dropped coins into the jukebox, and "Don't Cry for Me, Argentina" floated into the room.

Followed by Willie Nelson's "Always on My Mind." Behind his tinted glasses he looked piercingly at me, expecting the answer he wanted. It was touching. His eyes glistened ("Tell me / Tell me that your sweet love hasn't died"). However, I wasn't there to make up.

In spite of his fervent promises he herded me (straight from my Zurich-purification lifestyle: no alcohol, coffee, meat, sugar) to the Market Square. Moving between cafés, we spent ten-plus hours. The first day. And the second.

I ordered nonalcoholic beverages and a few snacks. Belgian pub-cafés serve the famous locally brewed beers, wine, individually brewed coffees, bottled waters, Coke, and light meals. The bustling Tienen Market Square is Belgium's second largest. Especially at Christmas with carols and pop music piped through the streets and shoppers dropping in for a spa or snack (maybe an *américaine*: raw ground beef mixed with mayonnaise and capers on toast), it was festive—as much family- as alcohol-oriented. However, after midnight Jan steered us back to the station area for the late-night cafés frequented by shift workers huddled over beer with chasers.

Drinking twenty draft Stellas—slowly, quietly, steadily—he smoked two packs of dark-tobacco Gauloises Caporal (filterless). He longed for a restaurant, which was outside his meager budget (consumed by the beer and cigarettes). I felt concern and pity and a few times treated him to a fancy restaurant, remembering what a connoisseur he was and chef.

Jan would never eat or cook in his two-room apartment provided by the state, as it had a combo bathroom-kitchen. To cook beside a toilet? He turned up his nose. Rather starve. No talking him out of it. He'd tried to get a job, I knew, but had no luck at almost fifty, with his résumé of teaching/writing poetry in Morocco.

Polite in the café, he drew little attention but was intense. He'd never expected to live this long. Be sure, he kept urging me, to get his novel *The Suicide Mozart* published. It was his soul's message. A Flemish press would publish it if he commercialized it; he refused. I believed in the book.

He dwelled on his happy memories of Morocco, adding flavorful enchantment to fact. Somehow, I always felt under the spell of his intense or wistful emotion. His needs seemed important, possible. His world worth rescuing though incredibly frustrating. A week passed—inside cafés.

Restless over Christmas (1986)—with all pubs closed except for five-course holiday menus—he popped a valium to sleep round the clock; I shared his barren apartment (even the double bed—on a strictly-to-sleep basis). Christmas Eve, I went for Greek takeout for one.

I didn't know what kept him going. His new-grown wrinkles replacing the boyish smooth face and twinkling eyes came with a look of agony. In the presences of the anguish now etched into his face—despite the reality that his choices had been his own—I felt a pull.

I still believed that the unpublished novel should find its way out to the world, not be lost in time. We had different starts in life, made different choices. I preferred mine. Yet here was the *puer*, the "eternal child" part of the artist, which he had in abundance. That, to some extent, still unlived part of me—who leaped into life unafraid with both guns roaring, maybe fell into the mud, didn't care. I was still feeling some pity for the artist, the man, who had, in a sense, made a mess of his life. But not entirely his art.

Some of his work was known only to me. He gave me instructions for his legacy. I took his copy of *The Suicide Mozart*. To protect his most recent English poetry cycle, which I was afraid would get lost, I stole the text and later got it published. I remembered how once in Morocco he set fire to a pile of papers, telling me it was the novel. Writing with an Olivetti typewriter, he had only one copy. I had watched him stab two paintings in a fit of emotion.

I couldn't imagine that this work we'd invested so much in would dribble into the sands, just because no one took care. As it turned out, by coincidence, it would be in delivering those poems to the Leuven Poetry Center for publication that I got a break myself—invited to read at the international poetry festival in Romania, through which door my own books found publication. I would be thinking I was helping him, but the tables turned. Through the Poetry Center, I would then be hired by the Museum het Toreke, from which more ensued. That's far ahead.

For now, I made a couple of brief trips. On the second, I drank Stella but popped back into the nonalcoholic style in Zurich. It had served me well in learning attentiveness at Institute functions, finding I could go into a high frequency—in conversations.

I hoped Jan would be interested in hearing about the initiation. He wasn't.

But when I put it in terms of being forward-thinking and bold, he said, "Genius always goes first." This comment I lit on, being such an introvert about public speaking, furthermore having to struggle against a desire to please; this reminder, with steel-blade directness, shot into me. I wanted the courage to go first whenever my path led there. I thought it had now. Fearlessly, not caring about rebuff and ridicule.

He said this, sitting in his baggy pants, having given up all the niceties of life in pursuit of his art. But the sheer energy of his look carried credibility.

Soon my teetotaling ended and one night I slipped into the café/bar Odeon in Zurich.

Enter René Pascal. Forty-six years old. Former model. Painter. Gorgeous. His name excited visions of the mathematician/physicist (child prodigy) Blaise Pascal. He was standing in the crowded Café/Bar Odeon.

Though marked indelibly by the initiation, with the autumn-1985 fasting a distant memory, I didn't draw attention due to thinness. I had turned a page and was trying to absorb the learning and aftereffects.

René was a virile, robust Swiss force of nature. His pan-Europe modeling career having timed out, he retained his dark good looks. He was now a painter. In the elegant downtown bar at Limmatquai—which had been frequented by artist exiles and intellectuals, from

Joyce to Einstein—we hit it off. The high-ceilinged Odeon, with its dim light and marble columns, provided a romantic, glittering setting for cocktails—a little cup of roasted almonds on the side. A young girlfriend at his side, René heard me speak English and being his gregarious self started a lively conversation.

I got home to a ringing phone. René. Come right over? He'd been gloomy and taken medication on top of the alcohol. He could see himself outside himself. He thought it was dangerous to be alone.

Florence Nightingale to the rescue, I hopped a tram to a rambling basement apartment. His huge canvases of planets and gigantic black-and-white photos of Sri Lanka hung on the walls. All by him. He wanted me to stay the night on a floor mattress, to be on hand in case. I was glad to. René, I sensed, was in the Initiator's energy.

At one moment suddenly, tossing, he erupted with "You came." It seemed to me *that* was the Initiator. Another memorable thing he said, out of the blue, was "If my heart explodes, I'll just go to another planet."

By the weirdest coincidence, for the first time in Zurich, I'd been telling tales of Hunter Thompson to a stranger the night before I met René.

I instantly liked René. Dawn broke and he was fine. I liked his huge, raw energy, Life Force, monumental sensitivity, looks. Upbeatness. How large-scale he was and his paintings. An artist whose big brush strokes supplanted a modeling career, no small task. Though the vibes between us had roots in simpatico, the electrical, tingling physical pull was undeniable, at least to me.

The sprawling basement did double duty as his studio. He told me that his landlord formerly used it for storage. Angry over this, René rolled the clutter out into the superhighway; he could have been jailed for traffic mayhem—having passed where a warning sign said *Stop*! (like the one I went past at Chartres Cathedral: GO FURTHER AT YOUR OWN RISK). Instead, he had the pleasure of seeing his landlord clear out the basement.

We ran into each other—alone—at the fancy bar a few times. To see him was the reason I went. He immediately asked me to join him. Once, a gorgeous model with chic hair and makeup came over to our table: *Hi, René!* He said his girlfriends were mostly runway models. "From the old days." But their beauty didn't sway him.

A passing seller hawked flowers and he impulsively bought a bouquet, swirled to face me. Then he uttered these words: "I would *never* go down on my hands and knees to them. I *might* to you." I gulped to take the message in.

Though not an overt romance, the relationship seemed to me to qualify as that type underneath which, said the Initiator, lay another possibility.

René moved to a hotel; I arranged to place a down payment on a painting. As I approached his door, gushes of blood from my period suddenly trickled down my legs. I dashed into a hallway WC to repair the damage. I felt the cause of the blood rush was the intensity of the attraction.

When I entered his room, he was sitting on the bed; he'd just dozed into a nap in which he saw a book, *Love*, beside a planet. (*Love* was the painting I was putting a down payment on. It was also in my book title.) He said, "I'll like having you at my patrons' evenings" (he relished the contrast I'd make with some of his rich, pretentious buyers). Would I carry canvases to a nearby gallery for his upcoming show? Also, he startled me by asking if I'd manage a gallery he hoped to open.

I was exhilarated and—carefully holding the paintings—took the train.

But to even contemplate a relationship with this flashy, dashing masculine Artist Personified seemed to me much too complicated, improbable. I don't suppose I ever believed it would develop.

I just had a real, valued friendship with René, as with the two close-buddy males mentioned earlier. The lusty physical attraction, the Initiator had said, could be brought alive under the surface. But we didn't test the hypothesis. I was entirely unconvinced.

However, this would not be the case soon. Not with Willy. He was too simple for such slow-dance maneuvers or friendship with women. Willy would be all in or out. I chose Willy—of various men

In the Hospital

I thought I'd detected to be in the Initiator's energy. There, that is, on an unconscious level, personal and collective. (From my point of view, however bizarre that seemed to me and sometimes confusing, as I wasn't always by any means 100% sure I'd correctly identified who was in his energy—or that level of energy—or not.)

Actually, I don't think that with anyone other than Willy in this period, it was remotely possible to slide into intimacy, despite the fact that the Initiator had, in 1986, for instance, given me a dream in which his face replaced one of these above males'. And then a similar scene played itself out just afterwards in life. He said always talk to the inner, not the outer person—look for *him*.

By fall 1987, Jan was hospitalized—with a mild Korsakoff syndrome or threat of it—in danger of liver cirrhosis. His mother wrote that he was very ill, which made me again visit, causing the next page to turn, the next shoe to drop. Korsakoff syndrome, originating in alcoholism and/or severe malnutrition, was not apparent to me at that point, except in some long-term memory distortion, which there were only hints of, if at all. (His health had checked out well when he returned from Morocco.)

Into the TV room walked a thirty-three-year-old dusty-blond-haired truck driver hunk, Willy Van Luyten. Recovering from an accident, he looked cute—like a life guard, on the one hand, a blue-collar factory worker on the other. Thirteen years my junior! He asked to move into Jan's room out of a private room (which Belgian single-payer insurance didn't cover). Jan said sure.

Exchanging pleasantries with Jan, who appeared in every way a creature of a different species, this muscular truck driver ferreted out that Jan briefly taught French in tiny Al Attafs, *Algeria*. In that same very remote, miniscule village—wonder of wonders—Willy had worked (he had a certificate to prove it, which I later saw). Pointing to a steel pin, Willy held up one leg. Jan had a steel pin in the *same* leg.

Crosshatching through time, this coincidence recalled, I thought, the moment—in Al Attafs—when Jan first proposed to me by letter. But now he seemed to be saying stubbornly, *I am at the end of the road. I have no hope. My heart is shut.*

I'd had a dream in Morocco in which a man was "in his physical self wounded beyond despair." And maybe—I think of this for the first time—it was Jan I'd heard the prophecy about in the Zurich Initiation: "Was reduced and relegated. Became like a well dried up." He fit.

The psychic Al Miner, channel of Lama Sing, had told me Jan had *not* learned the lesson of the "karmic bond" I had broken. Willy, on the other hand, was fiercely sure his life was going uphill.

The accident, he said, was a turning point. That year, mourning his marriage breakup and a restraining order against seeing his eight-year-old daughter, he'd shot up cocaine, as did his friends—but daily in his case. Though he was not faulted for the wreck, finding coke in his body, the police expunged the report on the condition that he rehabilitate.

I wondered why once again I had a boyfriend who (like Jan) was a daily pot smoker (though just one a day) and—in Willy's case—was temporarily a coke addict.

But let's turn to a *High Times* interview September 1977 with Hunter Thompson. After reading the galleys, he almost had smoke coming from his nostrils. There, in print, were his off-the-record comments that, he told friend (and later memoirist) Jay Cowan, "could bring down the president."

Hunter called his confidential remarks "fucking nitroglycerine." He said, "If this runs, they'll lynch Carter on the front steps of the White House, and that'll be after his people have me killed or thrown in some unlisted dungeon somewhere . . . Do they think that ugly little magazine will last more than twenty-four hours after something like this comes out?" *Something like this* was his not-for-print revelation that prominent Carter-administration staffers had snorted coke with him "in the Oval Office."

The news article was reworded to locate all such anecdotes off White House grounds. President Carter, Hunter added, would, in a second, imprison him if he did drugs in front of him but wouldn't pursue him into the bathroom to set a trap.[185] Actually, a Gallop Poll puts it better, headlined: IN U.S., 38% HAVE TRIED MARIJUANA.[186] But then I guess the answer lies somewhere in the vein that I was more unconventional than I looked to myself, from the inside. At least, up to this point.

Willy was strapped for funds. Jan liked him. Now in a parallel bed, Willy told me that every day he shut himself in the bathroom to meditate, as I'd taught him. There, he "felt" my approach to the room.

I thought that this strong intuitive sense and our obvious attraction—both physical and subtle—indicated that inside him his higher-awareness energy must be trying to steer this wild, life-surging man out of his most damning habits.

In an unconscious part of him sat this energy, I thought. That's how I saw it. It was odd.

Still in the hospital—he invited me to move into his apartment. That was before any romantic physical contact. Neither of us would overtly, in front of Jan, start a romance. We were getting to know each other, talking in the hall, also down in the lobby. Sharing lots of moments that—added to the *uuumph* factor—made me want to know more, to be with him. Maybe it was love at first sight. Anyway, I was falling in love.

To speed up the process, he took the discharge endurance test early. Afterwards, he was told no one in his condition (half his bones had been broken in seven truck and motorcycle accidents) should be able to perform such demanding exercises. But he never let pain be an influence. He was, his family doctor later said, "riding with death."

Could his potential emerge? He was determined to shake the coke habit and brought an iron will to bear, also determined to have a woman to live with—and he was going to find her this year—he told me. I didn't want that to be someone else. Besides, sex hormones were raging. Willy was about to fill the hole in the relationship with Jan. Having not been doted on in the way I expected sexually— though put on a pedestal in other ways, relied on, valued—with Jan, I loved the life force exuberance in Willy. I didn't mind his lack of book education. I liked how he looked at me. I was quite beside myself with imagining that we'd soon be sharing a bed, and that he wanted this just as much as I.

The doctor gave Willy heart pills because to go cold turkey off coke could endanger his heart.

So, I left Jan's apartment (Jan was still in the hospital). A child of the '60s, I had no qualms about moving in with a guy on so little notice, though I had done this only once before, in New York. (Not on such short notice.) I had my heart set on it. I had instant attractions, and if I liked a guy, knew it right away. Also, it wasn't so important to me how long a relationship lasted, provided it lasted at all—one hour, one day, one year, a lifetime. With Willy it was to last three years.

I'd have rather moved to Paris. But Willy was in Tienen. And now that's where my heart was. A week after he left the hospital he stopped taking the heart pills but avoided old friends and continued to kick the habit. The next month was secluded. It was fun. We didn't bore each other. I asked, "Why did you use a needle?" He said, "For the rush." He still smoked a joint every day. I asked why. He said, "It helps me think."

His subsidized, roomy low-income-housing apartment, three floors up, was in a building with no elevator—on a tree-dotted property at the edge of town. There was a harvested wheat field in front, where he sometimes rode his dirt bike. He also had a Harley. He had disability income, but with a mechanic buddy intended to set up shop rebuilding crashed cars (they went to a lot in Holland to pick up parts).

In the fall, I returned to Zurich a few times to ship suitcases by train and see friends, including René. Also, I probably attended one of Jyoti's breathwork workshops. (More on those ahead.) The first time I left, Willy was somewhat cavalier—not sure what to expect.

I moved in permanently in November. In January, René sent a letter signed with a clown drawing. I replied. Knowing he was broke, I—without being asked—enclosed a *four-hundred* Swiss Franc eurocheque installment on my painting; I said, "I wish space were different, so I could walk out into the evening into Zurich. I'm in a time different from all times I've had before, but that's par for the last 3 years. . . . My bouquet is in my writing room. Love, Margaret."

The letter returned unopened—4.2.88 (February 4), stamped *Gestorben, Décédé, Decesso.* Dead.

Dumbfounded, grief-stricken, I phoned. His girlfriend, Sandra, told me he'd felt Death "stalking him" for a month. Living in a hotel, laden with expenses, he was "too tired to fight," which recalled to me how, when we met, he passed through that night of sensing himself outside himself. Safely, however.

After cutting his wrist, when he was sure it was too late, he phoned her to say goodbye. The paramedics got him to the hospital. When the medical team assured her he was out of danger, she left. Then he had a fatal heart attack, thus indeed bringing alive his image of being "stalked by Death," or "If my heart explodes, I'll just go to another planet."

She would not honor my down-payment receipt. I mourned both him and the painting.

He was forty-six. I lived (with Willy) at 46 Lunevillelaan. René's phone number had two 46s. Some synchronicity was afoot. This Belmondo rugged style and robust, unconventional charm, this Anthony Quinn energy—was it in only forty-six years exhausted?

Soon one afternoon in the Tienen field outside our apartment—a grocery bag in each hand—I thought I felt him above me, freed and happy, expanded.

Superbly physical, Willy lifted his heavy barbell over his head with one hand in the apartment. Lacking backing, he'd foregone his ambition to be a Formula One driver—or boxer. Now, to get their wings, young men tried to provoke him into fights. He had a kind of masculinity I wasn't used to.

After his father died in a motorcycle accident, he'd left school, at fourteen. Financially, his mother needed him. When I first walked into his apartment he was at the sink, washing plastic grocery sacks. I asked why. He said to reuse them.

Though no one suspected it, he didn't know the alphabet (he spelled by ear). He spoke excellent English—learned from pop music and TV-film subtitles. On TV we watched every kind of sport: dart tournaments (he played darts in bars), snooker, soccer, Wimbledon matches, Formula One racing. We attended dirt bike competitions. I loved watching the riders go airborne over mounds. The way I'd loved slalom waterskiing.

Willy often stood before his tape deck, volume full blast—light on his feet, dancing in double time, 8/8, whereas my tempo was 4/4.

Willy was on an extra-fast track. I see him listening to Joe Cocker, which he pronounced "coke-r" ("I just wanna be the one you run to" or "If you want a partner for a ride . . . I'm your man"). Willy was grainy, passionate, muscular but not knottily lumpy (unlike a professional bodybuilder). He played Dire Straits tapes and oldies, "Get Ready" with a long sax solo. Saxophonist was another career choice he'd have liked. Or swimmer. He'd have been lost in the car without his music.

Often battling a dead battery, he pushed the auto downhill in front of the apartment. With the engine sputtering, we hopped in. Later he had a charger in the kitchen.

He coasted to the last drop of gas—perhaps, miscalculating, hitting empty. He carried a gas can in the trunk and would walk or hitchhike down the road a ways to fill it. Once, while he was tinkering underneath, his jacked-up auto fell on his chest. The next door neighbor's eyes bulged as Willy lifted it and continued tinkering. He was occasionally a bouncer at a disco.

Willy seemed to work the world like a room. He connected people. No matter what, if the doorbell rang he answered. He loved nature. And took me on picnics where—with cows in the distance—we lay in the grass to feel the blades. Or wearing a bright orange workout jacket, he drove us to woods to jog together down a trail.

We'd bicycle forty kilometers, then drink water from a natural spring. I'd not known such things were masculine, but with ultra-male Willy they were. He might find a private outdoor nook near a lake to make love in after the bike ride, or in the ocean. He was all in all a breed I was glad to hook up with. We could not marry, because in Catholic Belgium without paying a lot of money for a divorce you had to wait out five years' separation.

Willy always wore his cross. It was "the Man," he said, adding enigmatically—no explanation—that if he ever lost it, our relationship was over. He also said that after one accident (not his fault) he woke from a coma with amnesia. He'd let on to no one; finally his memory returned.

However, the amnesia left him a budding psychic. He demonstrated how he could use a pendulum. I challenged him and he asked it if I had ever had children. The pendulum said *yes*, and he remained horrified when I explained I held a "yes" in mind, thinking of my manuscripts. So, he thought, I was overriding his will. That didn't go down well, but I found it amusing. I reveled in how freeing it was to relate like this, where I could express any emotion, in fact was encouraged to. Willy was up for it. The meeting between us was significant, dramatic, downright odd if you put the experience into its beginning and end.

Willy's ex, whom I considered a classy, stand-up person, had—in the past—filed a restraining order against him so that he could not see his little daughter. He agonized about this in the hospital and had earlier violated the order, at which point he got charged for disobeying it. To that complaint—before we met—had come a second one: he'd been reeled in in a marijuana stakeout. In Belgium, cases hung in limbo. After we were together eighteen months, he was tried. Sentenced to four months, he was jailed in May 1989. (Ironically, his ex was by then ready to drop charges—and, very importantly to Willy—regularly let their daughter sleep over.)

To jail Willy went. While incarcerated, he had a private daytime construction job, returning to prison to sleep. However, on his first day in prison, a guard made a derogatory remark. To silence his quick temper, Willy hit his fist into the wall. His fist broke, turned black.

He concealed the break in a cloth and went to his gig. I found it hard to imagine the stoicism of breaking your hand, then doing construction work. But if he'd reported to the infirmary, he'd have lost the job. This added more broken bones.

I wrote him how different it would be to communicate by letters, "especially since I'm more used to movements—speaking with your hands and body—from you. Your face. The way of sitting on a motorcycle. Or dancing. Not very often real speech. Write me anything or draw pictures or tell stories. I'll be waiting." It was while in jail Willy told me he didn't know the alphabet, and I sent a list of the ABCs.

As I've mentioned, the channel Al Miner is considered by many to be the successor to the sleeping prophet, Edgar Cayce. I trusted him, to the point of being willing to cough up the stiff price of $400 for a reading, which I did May 10, a few days after Willy went to jail.

I put the tape he sent back into the player.

June 23, '89. Silence. Soft music. Time shifts. The music takes me back. I knew Al had made the reading sitting in a room where he, as he describes it, feels his body "walk off Earth"; he has done this thousands of times; inside him Lama Sing takes over, begins to speak.

Al read my question. It concerned "the decisions I've made and am newly faced with long range." About Willy, I wrote: "when I had gone the most extreme distance inward, I remet, because I feel we have known each other before, Willy Van Luyten, born April 27, 1955." I felt the relationship had "enormous challenge and I believe blessing."

My first question went right to that challenge; Al Miner had no difficulty picking up on it. But what he also did, as I listen, in 2013, was to outline the consciousness I would get to a decade or so later. In the meantime, he had many insights. What I could I expect with Willy, why I was with him.

He used my questions to communicate that—as I see it today—I was in danger of falling again into a pattern of giving to depletion, and there were severe consequences.

He warned that the similarities between Jan and Willy indicated qualities that "tend to call out to you and to inspire the urging of service, ofttimes to a fault. By that, we meant to a point of self-sacrifice for the gain of another . . . Do you see?"

In fact, no, I saw Jan as manipulative; Willy wasn't. But Al suggested that discarded patterns could reappear in disguise.

"With regard to the potential for Willy, of course as you know the choices he faces are important ones for his soul."

If I stayed, he predicted "a significant testing of your ability to forgive and forget."

Al distinguished between "bountiful and enduring fruit" (produced in harmony with others) and that creating personal gain, where one wins, the other loses, as in Willy's case. Then, he "must bear the responsibility and ultimately the end karmic relationship with that tainted fruit. . . . It is not a question of right and wrong in the spiritual sense. It is a question of which is the greater in terms of joy . . . yes, in many respects, this is the next step or the next lesson."

Now I'd been told, in the strongest language, that if I stayed, Willy and I had a rough road ahead. He even predicted "highly energized events." Was it worth it to me to go on with him? Yes, I was in love. Willy too, which he showed me all the time.

I seized on the comment that if Willy hurt me or anyone, it wasn't intentional.

Further, there was an ornery side to me. A close friend wrote, in 1983, after my mother died suddenly. Regarding Jan,

> Well—as you know, most people just daydream their fantasies, whereas you have the ability to live them and to live them out in the "ironic mode." That is, Margaret Ann the artist. Maybe the only thing wrong is your timing, and that may be controlled by the opposite side of the coin, the more conservative you. What matter if you were a housewife in San Diego! Oh—but I'm leaving out the need and desire to feel—to feel pain that comes with not being able to close doors quite soon enough. And yet I think that Jan can close them quicker than you can. Now, look—I certainly am not saying that he does not feel—I believe that he very "smartly" faces

what is to be in a necessary, fortified fashion. He dilutes his pain and, therefore, can pursue the irresistible. I'm glad it's over and I liked it while it was. So easy for me to say. . . .

Margaret Ann, I was horrified at the idea of Milton's death. . . .

Willy was asked in Brussels to *instruct the police to drive in chases*. He replied wryly that he was afraid he didn't qualify, it was illegal to teach policemen if you've been arrested! Nonetheless, he had in his wallet a license to transport explosives.

His reputation spread far and wide locally. He'd park cars by lifting one end with his hands (calculating tight fits). While he was in jail, his mechanic friend finished Willy's turbo-charged Renault diesel, rebuilt from crashed parts. Back home, he poured over investment bulletins, deciding how to use his accident money.

Willy was proud of a letter to me from the author Herbert Tarr. After Random House, I'd worked with Herb in a freelance editing capacity. Intent on building me up in every way, including his belief in my writing, which he'd not read, Willy carried Herb's letter in his wallet even after it got frayed. He also hung my glamorous New York City modeling-shoot photos; I'd been too shy to display them.

I signed up for a weekly Inner Landscaping class in Brussels with Chris Van de Velde. It would begin September 14, 1989, just after Willy was released. The course focused on psychodynamics (aura healing, neuro-linguistic programming, etc.). I was very excited to have this opportunity. Now I had an English-speaking support group (and fun group), a tight-knit bunch of women, translators and secretaries at the European Commission.

Chris was Willy's age—lanky, tall, brilliant, innovative, naturally entertaining, funny. He led us in eye-opening exercises in guided meditations. He would one day pass on to me those notecards he held in class.

In a few months, I traveled to his home for a psychic reading. Brushing aside my questions about people, he had nothing whatsoever to say. Then I mentioned Willy. He stopped, settled in.

In the Hospital

He saw, he said, Willy and me in a castle in the Middle Ages. I was in charge of the workers, hired by the castle. Willy was a hotheaded leader, like the Pole Lech Walęsca (Chris had never met Willy). His impetuousness got him into trouble, sometimes in recklessness unsupported by the other workers. When rebellion would be pointless folly—at peril of being flayed—I calmed him.

Everything else Chris said about Willy, I thought was accurate: that he *externalized*; he's a "master of transforming others but not himself, a chameleon."

"He was propelled into this lifetime to pay you back," Chris said. I was very touched, though I assumed he must have multiple goals. I told Willy and he was amused at having had me as a father figure and would sometimes mention wryly his "biographical age" (younger than me) and his *other* age.

Chris later told me he imagined the attraction as in *The Prince of Tides* (the film featuring New York City therapist Barbra Streisand and teacher/football coach Nick Nolte).

Willy was to heal what got broken in my marriage. He taught me to hurl myself through the stages of an emotion *with him*, till both of us collapsed in gales of laughter. That I didn't have to freeze up but could race after an intense emotion, like anger, till it climaxed. It would wind up in a good place. Things worked if you confronted them.

He also said, "Be smarter than I am"—that I could be confident, even if he stayed out late alone: "I will always come back." He required emotional strength—sometimes forgiving and forgetting, as Lama Sing had indicated—which I was determined to be up for.

I went deep inside. I searched out the strength I needed. It was there.

I suppose this will raise a lot of questions. I had a choice. Willy was thirty-two when we met. I was forty-six. I see now that before I could learn nonattachment and emotional flow and ease of manifesting—which I did later—I had to cross this bridge of bringing out my emotions. That, I learned with Willy. I loved the feeling when—he was still hot headed—he said something I greatly objected to and I unthinkingly balled up my fists and started pounding him in the chest. He was surprised. And thought it quite funny. Instantly, the argument stopped. To think I could imagine those little punches would hurt him—that was far more interesting. Willy, being a sensation type, was easy to reach with touch. It dispelled the other topic.

After finishing Inner Landscaping with Chris, I took his Enneagram course. This is an alternate system of personality typing to Jung's. I found it helpful in describing Willy. He was number eight: a man of action, acting from his gut: "Eights are self-confident, strong, and assertive. Protective, resourceful, straight-talking, and decisive, but can also be egocentric and domineering. Eights feel they must control their environment, especially people, sometimes becoming confrontational and intimidating. Eights typically have problems with their tempers and with allowing themselves to be vulnerable. *At their Best*: self-mastering, they use their strength to improve others' lives, becoming heroic, magnanimous, and inspiring."[187]

As an eight, "your greatest strength is your sense of justice and desire to protect the weak, vulnerable, downtrodden and under-represented." In that he'd grown up so poor, protecting the weak was certainly important to Willy. He once told me, "Don't take that away from me."[188]

I was in many ways his opposite, with strong elements of nine, the peacemaker, who is likely to say: Who, me? I'm not angry?

So it startled me when I let some of his confrontationalness rub off, as he had in reverse picked up, on rare occasions, my meditation practice. The moment I brought myself to pummel Willy in the chest was a great freeing: Ah-ha, I felt. A thrill went through me. Ohhhh, so I release my feelings of frustration without words, and he doesn't fight anymore. Neither of us wins. The argument is just over. We think it's funny. All my words might be to no avail, but to meet him in kind, with action, that was magic.

He loved to eat my Flemish meals, such as carbonnade flamande (beef-and-onion stew) or sausage with spinach stumpf (potatoes mashed with spinach), or baked Belgian endive with ham. Also, my chicken sautéed with carrots in a white wine sauce. He had a healthy appetite.

In the Hospital

When he was out with a couple of his friends, they might get hungry. There were no cell phones. If he had the chance, he'd phone to say he wanted to bring them. If not, they might show up. And since I knew this, I wasn't caught unawares.

I was thrilled they all loved what I prepared. Imagine if it had been the other way round. Anyway, Willy's life was unorthodox. I didn't make a fuss if he stayed out late sometimes, even occasionally slipping into bed at 7:00 a.m. I knew that in return he'd take me on a lot of evenings out, the kind I'd enjoy, such as in Leuven.

I liked it that Willy noticed how I looked and cared that we looked close in age. He paid a lot of attention to such details, and it was flattering. So I didn't expect him to be traditional if his actions didn't upset or greatly inconvenience me.

I knew I had often preferred to do what I wanted, not ask for permission. Once I slipped away to Zurich, to Jyoti's breathwork workshop, without telling Willy. Every day I planned to, but the last night came and daybreak. I still hadn't gotten up the nerve, so I crept out of bed, leaving a note.

But confrontation was a thing I learned to do much much better with Willy. I had to. I didn't begin to know neutrality and nonattachment. Or how to let the energy of the universe flow through me. But I learned this other very important thing that had been a sanskara, a blind spot, in my personality.

He helped me, being, as I said, a sensation type who lived in his senses. And if a thing wasn't really important to me, instead of "forgiving and forgetting," I might just jump over that stage, go deep inside and feel at peace. I felt loved. It was not so important if sometimes Willy stayed out. What was he doing? I supposed and trusted it was just fun with the guys.

Then it came time to go for a visit to the United States. Besides seeing my author friend Hannah Green and her painter husband Jack Wesley in January 1990, I renewed my relationship with Hunter S. Thompson, and *New York Times* critic/editor Anatole Broyard.

I again phoned Hunter from the New York apartment of my

decades-long friend Jim Mohan, whose career I'd watched as it spanned supervisory field positions for UNICEF in ten countries, including Chile, Afghanistan, India, Sudan, Cuba, and China. I made a stopover en route to North Carolina (to visit my sisters). As I looked out his window onto the East Side, facing south downtown with a view of the Empire State Building, Hunter came on.

We reconnected so simply. He said, "I should have known I'd get into soul searching, talking to you."

In Boston I saw Anatole, whom I'd last seen when visiting in his house in the late 1960s. He being one of the closest friends of Milton Klonsky, if not the closest, I wanted his benediction on my Milton depiction in *Love in Transition*. On the snow-covered ground of the train station no Anatole waited. Twenty minutes . . . I telephoned.

His wife said look in a certain spot. There he stood, handsome, dignified, healthy-looking, approachable, receptive—a scarf wound round his neck. Time swelled, expanded.

Over cheeseburgers, he told me he was collecting Milton stories—for a memoir. "People want to read about the '60s. . . . You were a very important person in Milton's life."

I wished I'd come back to the U.S. to Milton earlier, I said.

"Why?"—he pinned me down.

"To marry him."

"That would have saved him."

I was amazed he was so fast, so frank. Hesitantly, I admitted I felt Milton *was alive*.

He said it was OK: "Your whole relationship with Milton was a fairy tale. With me Milton was an ironist. With you, a romantic."

Before leaving Boston, I phoned again, intending to leave a message. He picked up. He'd been jumping on the trampoline. There was incense in the background, he said. He felt great. His work was going great. "Writing on the '60s, I find myself calling Milton 'Robert,'" he said, *an untoward, outrageous compliment*. "Phone back anytime."

He never mentioned cancer. It was about to return; he'd be dead in October. I also had no idea some people were unaware of his

In the Hospital

Creole background. Never did I bring up race, as it would not remotely occur to me.

His unfinished posthumous '50s memoir, *Kafka Was the Rage*, ends with him pursuing a girl. Milton objects. Yet Milton told me a different story: after Anatole's father died, he (Milton) tried to distract the bereaved son, suggesting they double date.

Reversing the *Kafka* ending, Anatole rudely refused, shut himself away alone—and wrote "What the Cystoscope Said"; Milton told me that Anatole had offered his horribly suffering terminally ill father a way to die, wanting to do anything to remove the father's pain. His father was appalled.

Anatole died *before* finishing the '60s section, and *Kafka* ended in a 180-degree-different position.

I thought that death prevented him from—in the next chapter—using a technique prevalent in *Kafka* whereby a position in one chapter was inverted the next.

When I broached the fact of having a boyfriend fourteen years younger, Anatole said, "You seem to have found the secret to happiness."

He mentioned that at the end of Milton's life they used to speak every day. But he missed him so much now because *"After Milton died no one talked to me as an equal."*

In perfect symmetry, born at the bottom of the socioeconomic ladder, he found inequality at the top. It was a thing to lament. His smile, his healthy handsomeness, his saying "I'm an old man now" but belying it in every way, were reviving. And the fact that he boiled down the point to wanting people to act natural—as if he were neither Creole nor celebrity. Or it made no difference which.

Underneath the postdeath rush in *The New Yorker* to say he should have been a spokesperson for blacks, this point got lost. He had been perhaps lonely at the bottom of the totem pole and definitely so—in ways that mattered to him—at the top.

— 27 —

Jyoti's Workshops, "Willy might not survive," Kundalini, An Event Ball

I returned to Belgium not a moment too soon. It was Willy's last year.

My narrow writing room—rectangular-shaped, large enough to hold my typewriter desk, and a twin bed for Willy's daughter's visits—was to the left of the front door. It overlooked the balcony walkway (flights up, with no elevator) and the large yard with communal clothesline, which was fronted by wheat fields (mown or growing) below.

One day Willy entered my writing room fresh from the bakery. Held up bread to my nose. Funnily, impossibly, he said, "Hello, Mrs. Bell"—no explanation. He did this a few more times in the next months, and I never asked about the nickname, which he used only at such times.

In the Zurich Initiation I'd learned of sacrifice: On certain levels of consciousness one sometimes made a decision within the soul level to die, or as the yogis say, "drop the body," in order to change the energy field, *be it with aware or unaware consent on the human level.* Willy fought the odds. He nearly succeeded? I don't think he came near.

We were barely back from a holiday in Portugal in January 1991 when Death—I say "struck," because the pattern repeated that of René; he felt stalked. But the process would only begin to become transparent to me months later. Let's trace the steps. I was completely oblivious.

I attended Jeneane Prevatt's Maitri Breathwork workshop in Zurich in the summer of 1990. (Soon she would be given the spiritual name Jyoti by the realized Eastern master Dhyanyogi-ji in India.) A "Buddha belly" (kumbhaka) she received in September 1988 made her look five months pregnant, although it changed size with the sun.

Jyoti's Workshops

In a Buddha belly, she explained to me, it was believed that the *prana* and *apana* (the inbreath and outbreath) were in a holding position. This condition is found primarily in the East among gurus—though the "Buddha belly" can be internalized, it's believed, she said.

A few years earlier, in Charlottesville, Virginia, I'd had monthly Holotropic Breathwork in a group; this technique, developed by Christina and Stan Grof, helps access nonordinary states of consciousness, allowing us to move out of the personal into the transpersonal.

While living with Willy, I'd participated a few times in Jyoti's Maitri Breathwork seminars in Zurich, which she led with her fiancé, psychologist Russell Park. Maitri is a mediumistic, healing breathwork using a strong sense of prayer as medicine.

Jyoti was later to be Director of the Spiritual Emergence Network (SEN), founded by a vision of Christina Grof; SEN became a grassroots effort to assist individuals undergoing tumultuous transformative processes. It sensitized mental-health professionals to psychospiritual issues and helped educate globally on the issues surrounding such crises. Spiritual emergencies would eventually be included in the diagnostic manual DSM-4, in a section that distinguished them from psychotic episodes. (The DSM sets standards for the medical profession and insurance companies.) During that time Jyoti would earn a PhD in psychology, and later she became, with her husband Russell, a founder/Spiritual Director of the Kayumari community and the Center for Sacred Studies. She would also be one of the original conveners of the International Council of the Thirteen Indigenous Grandmothers, now a global movement for peace and unity amongst all people. But this says nothing of her incredible intuitive touch—using an eagle feather—that I experienced in her workshops. Back to Zurich in the late '80s.

Some of my experiences in her workshops were phenomenal. Eventually, during Maitri Breathwork, I entered a couple of "magnetic memories" from lifetimes in history. I entered *only* a fraction of a second, isolated like a bubble. Critical moments. Pure energy. No past or present, only the awareness, the significant split second, stretched out, lengthened. Though I cannot say *which* experience occurred in *which* workshop, I am sure that in this particular summer of '90, I had the following.

I was met by my "clan," as Jyoti called them. For she could see with her inner eye some of what I saw. The leader (whom Jyoti "saw" as a tall man) showed me a series of faces. In each face he highlighted the same features. For instance, I watched the nose from one transform in the next. And the next. The "tall man" was illustrating the physical connections between some of the males I had known who related to him. He showed me how in conjunction with his Light, they began to darken. That is, become unbalanced as his light hit their energy and thoughts. I watched their forms become unstable, visibly disintegrate.

He showed Jan waiting a long time (for me) with his leashed boxer at the Tienen train station until he began to fall apart, turn dark, his features crumbling. It appeared, according to the vision, that this disintegration only occurred after he went back to Belgium and that at first, symbolically waiting with the dog, he was all right. By now it was too late, definitively.

The last was Willy. Being uncomplicated, with a simple faith, he was at an advantage—still innocently bright. The tall man told me to *take himself* out of my heart and "put Willy there."

"Or," he said, "Willy might not survive."

A single silver drop of mercury slid out of my heart. Astoundingly, I thought, he was saying that he, the tall man, was my mercurialness. Mercury got me unstuck, made me not twiddle my fingers. Let me "go down," because it found a way up. Mercurialness made me suddenly reverse course, not take *no* as a conclusion.

The tall man said that if I took *him* out, I would find *him* again on the level Willy would move to. Like saying to let go of a brass ring with nothing to hold onto and something solid would magically take its place—soon enough.

It was the idea of transformation again, as in the Barcelona dream, where I was on a high plateau with Milton (he was dead, in a hole), and looking down, wobbly, I saw how far I could fall onto the concrete. Then, leaving the insecure plateau for a lower level, I was given a "monster" to hold under a fountain—till it transformed into a little fish.

But in the present case, I could not comply. My instinct was to follow the tall man. Lying on the mat in the workshop, I raised my arms, climbing, as if to haul myself upward on a rope. Not be left behind. I could not give "him" up, him being a drop of mercury, he said, that personified as a part of living beings.

But I did not even consider it. It was like the longest shot I'd ever heard of. And it was my very heart itself I would have to overpower.

Instead of immediately coming out of the breathwork I tried to climb the rope. A young part of me did "come back," and said aloud, "*I live in a world all lavender, where it's always snowing in my father's heart.*"

I was aware of saying this but was not really back. Jyoti spoke to *that* me, calling her a star baby. She assured her, "I was a star baby too" and coaxed her "*not to believe you can walk on ceilings and don't need any food*" but let Margaret return. So I did but was not willing to take *him* out of my heart.

Willy was certainly uncomplexed and courageous enough to risk everything to get to his higher consciousness if he made a decision to.

This assignment, if accepted, would be carrying even further the lesson I had so recently learned—not to divide a human being up into physical/spiritual.

The tall man, whom I took to be the Initiator, was sure he could activate a drop of himself, as mercurialness, in Willy—triggered by my need. In this way and this way only, he, the tall man, would be able to put his light more strongly in Willy without blasting him out of commission, he indicated.

If the tall man could not put his light more strongly in Willy, the deal was—though I did not think this through—that Willy must "leave," to raise the energy field.

Vacationing for a week in September with Willy and friends, as the lone female—romping around the Costa Blanca resort of

Willy and Margaret—Spain

Alicante, Spain, on the Mediterranean Sea, where palm trees shaded clear sand—provided a highlight of the last months of Willy's life. We battled valiantly—in fun. For instance, in the apartment in the evening his friends played poker. He didn't want me to join in. It was all males. When I did, he left the game in a huff. I stayed and won some hands. He relented.

He didn't want me to jet ski, but loving to water ski I was undeterred. When I drove my miniature car with the guys at an amusement park, Willy and a friend—in distraction—collided; the heavy-set truck driver broke his leg. As always, when he slept, Willy flung his arms and legs around me, which, besides being romantic, from my point of view made the energy flow between us. And I slept like a baby.

In November, as Willy's time wound down, I spent five days with my EU Inner Landscaping friend Helen Titchen in her birthtown: Bath, England. Helen drove us around, showing me Stonehenge and Glastonbury (Avalon). We arrived back in Tienen at 2:30 a.m. I asked if she wanted to come in to meet Willy, whom I guessed would be waiting up. She said no, she still had to drive to Brussels, then work the next day. But she had a premonition, she later told me, that "it was now or never." She didn't know why.

Beginning the last week of November, I had a kundalini episode once a week. Intense discharges of blocked energy, these episodes took the form of involuntary shaking called kriyas, focused on an arm or a leg. I think these kriyas served to shift my consciousness (breaking up blocks) without the shock of a full-blown kundalini awakening. According to the Hindu system, which I did not yet know well, they operated on *sanskaras*: conditioned reactions (or past mental impressions).

In me, they created a much heightened state of awareness, as if I were electrified with energy that caused the shaking while I stood otherwise still.

Willy knew nothing about this. Upon returning from the previously mentioned workshop in Zurich, I had an incident that began on the Tienen train-station platform. I was about to catch the 5:45 to Inner Landscaping. I decided not to turn back.

As I recorded at the time, "I entered the class in Brussels, where meditation was about to begin. I sat down and was trembling all over. The teacher had an assistant stand behind me to balance the energy, but it didn't help. After half an hour the meditation ended and half the room reported that their minds had blanked out, in one case causing fear."

Putting his assistant in charge, Chris Van de Velde pulled me aside. Standing with me near the counter where we had tea breaks, he said rather sternly, "This is *my* class. *I'm* responsible." He lifted his hands to read my energy (saying, "I want to be sure this isn't harmful").

Then he began moving his fingers through my aura. In a first-of-its-kind for me, "a stream of lifetimes flashed before my eyes; some, known people. As they floated by, each one changed my energy. Though I was aghast, if kriyas were breaking down "mental impressions" from the past, this would make sense.

The last was of my father, John Henry Harrell. With his wry wit, he said, "Well, I'll be *John Brown*." In surprise to find himself in the roster.

Another image-experience was of being alone in bed, dying.

In my father's case, his presence in my energy made it dense-feeling and solid—uncomfortable. I hoped surely I didn't have to stay like that. And Chris shifted me back. He explained that those were some of my incarnations; in the past I'd helped others, but this lifetime *I* was being helped; it was all OK. He said, "*Your heart is opening.*"

I suspected that not all of these were specifically my memories but was not quite sure how to explain them.

So this is the background to what would occur January 6, Old Christmas, 1991. It is eerily the exact anniversary of the only telegram to me from Milton (signed "Mohan"), January 6, 1967—where he wrote: GIRDER OF O, GIRDLE OF I, IMMACULATE, UNBREAKABLE. Later titled "X^2."

After several once-a-week kundalini episodes, I consulted psychic Mariah Martin, as I had off and on by phone since 1983. She confirmed that Milton was changing form, perhaps "going home." I'd witnessed, I thought, perhaps a transfer of *his* memories in some of the overwhelming kundalini incidents.

I did not think: *Maybe it's the soul grouping, collectively.* But more accustomed to kundalini literature today, I would say the important thing was the breakup of the sanskaras, or "mental impressions."

A Jung Institute lecturer told a mythical story in May 1985 about the snake Kaliya. One day in 200 AD the young god Krishna, about six years old, fought the snake and danced for a whole day on its head(s). The snake finally yielded, becoming kundalini. That was Shiva in the crown chakra.

This idea of "going home," I'd dreaded in Zurich, first wondering if it meant total loss of memory—thinking of consciously standing on the brink of forgetting, even being shattered all across Earth (and further), with bits of memory and potential falling far and wide as energy—conscious energy. I imagined it like that. Anyway, whatever was going on, I was sharing it. As it turned out, it would sweep up Willy—in one level of this multidimensional event, which, I was learning, all events are; some more than most.

Jyoti's Workshops

Here the shape of an enfolded Event Ball began to occur to me. That is, Willy's death seemed foreshadowed, I thought, in Milton's ten years earlier, just as if it were bound up inside the enfolded Count Down, as, at least, *a probability*.

Just before Milton's *November 1981* death—in the *shadow* of its approach (a term Carl Jung used to describe the events, dreams, etc., that might portend a death, such as had forecast René Pascal's)—I'd dreamed of a car accident.

I had assumed it symbolically anticipated Milton's death, which it probably did.

In that 1981 prototype the willowy male driver, as if taking the initiative, *stepped away from a group*. He was glassy-eyed, his body elastically stretched as if on *remote control*. In the next scene there was a drop of blood on the glove compartment of his now-empty car, which was parked outside Greek temple-like steps; I inferred it was the now-dead driver's blood, indicating (to my mind) suffering on a human level in some heroic fatal gesture.

In 1981, I had taken it that Milton was the "driver" in his death (that is, in charge behind the wheel).

But that dream *redepicted itself in November 1990*—now no longer a symbol.

Flying over ten years, it plopped down again—this time in our Tienen apartment. Jyoti and her husband Russell D. Park, both with PhDs in transpersonal psychology, in their first visit, were asleep in our bed, where Russell dreamed of an impending, realistic car crash. Associating it with Willy, they were so troubled they considered hiring a taxi to the airport (thereby avoiding having the high-speed Willy drive them). Deciding to say nothing, they got into the car.

In several instances in December—the last month of Willy's life—as he drove home late from a Leuven café, he "saw" a head-on crash into his windshield. He flinched at this premonition. Taking it seriously, he hoped to avoid it. New Year's resolutions, he thought, were called for.

Willy resolved to stop smoking. He wasn't rational about it. He didn't say, "I'm being punished, I need to reform," or try to figure

New Year's Eve—Portugal

it out. But he intuited he needed to change. He must outwit death.

In December, with our timeshare, we vacationed in Albufeira, Portugal. The timeshare, only partially paid for, allowed us a week in the popular southern Algarve. Typically, Willy rented a car and drove us to out-of-the-way towns, beaches, and restaurants. I dreamed (but made nothing of it), "He was trying to tell her goodbye."

During our absence Jan committed suicide, December 27.

The day *Willy was to die* was heavily laden with warnings—the death occurring, as it did, in the wee hours of Old Christmas, January 6, 1991. There was an eleventh-hour effort to stop it: the last of the seven kundalini kriya episodes.

Our flight from Portugal having just touched down, we were in the Brussels airport. In only two days he would die. The episode began right there. In such incidents, as I said, blocks break up.

While Willy looked for a cart I trembled in a chair. By the focus that took over my mind, I identified the pattern in the kundalini: two events clashed like dueling knights. In one event, Jesus on Palm

Sunday rode through the crowds. *Another archetype was trying to intercept it*—that of Mary looking for a place to give birth.

I wrote not long afterwards, "They were what we call archetypes, but they were real memories, in intensity, and applied to real situations. Willy was to die on a Sunday morning. There had to be a way to stop it. There was if the birth memory could be so strong that we together found a place for the feelings that would, in being realized, prevent the Palm Sunday, or crowd, experience. But this wasn't to be the case."

This crossbred model was trying to waylay the tragedy: to amalgamate the events, just as we genetically modify seeds. By combining historical peak moments, it would try to create a new event, or work in an archetype, push from its shape a new option.

But I didn't get it—didn't suspect that it related to Willy's approaching death.

For observation, with a light rib injury acquired in Portugal, I stayed one night in the local hospital—back in the very building where Willy and I first met. The next day I was free to go but opted to stay one more night.

With Willy in my room that second afternoon I tried to hold his attention. But couldn't, for once. The elderly woman in the other bed—*who reminded him of his mother!*—got him to focus on her. The wrong level of the kundalini took—intensely. Willy said he could hear a voice, "in the back of my head," telling him to focus toward me.

Usually, I soothed him. This time I watched helplessly, sensing its urgency. But I didn't for a moment believe he would walk out of the room, and my life, forever. In leaving, he looked over, said, "I'll be back, even if I have to bang on the door—at 2:00 a.m."

I saw him drive out of the parking lot, the last time—waiting long inside the car before starting it (thinking over what?).

As Willy left to die, warnings were aflutter. Literally. In Portugal once, physical distance hadn't stopped us from communicating. Alone on the beach, he was approached by a coke dealer. At a distance I felt an electrical current in my right hand. I knew a deep energy contact was taking place between us.

He came back in from the beach. And said he'd been tempted but *remembering me* said no—that he'd drawn on the strength of our tie. I knew that it wasn't just remembering. It was communication.

That communication was trying to happen again, this night—but I didn't realize it.

Now in the hospital room the slow tick tock of the clock begins. The motherly woman on the other bed recited something impossibly uncanny, but the energy field to prevent his dying was so high that the synchronicity could be precise. She, who had usurped the Divine Mother energy that was trying to reach Willy, now recited how she lost *two husbands by age 50. Yikes! I was fifty!*

Further, she said she might have warned the last one.

I tried to phone Willy. Something was *really* not right. No answer. In a bar, he was telling a friend, a blonde, that he was "here *again*, having lived *before* to [such-and-such an age]" (he never talked about reincarnation), "and this time would live to"—he wrote down a figure on a piece of paper and handed it to her—"*if I don't die in a car accident.*"

She protested. He insisted. Asleep that night, I dreamed I flew through the sky in panic, trying to get a male's attention—to warn him. To no avail. In fact, that was the exact dream situation I'd found myself in two nights before Milton's death—attempting to sound an alarm, say the situation was ultra-serious, in a message that wasn't received.

Photos from Portugal went down with the car as—in the head-on crash to his windshield, as he'd foreseen—Willy's car struck a tree and dove into a canal. The beach photographs showing off his physique—a lifeguard's lifeguard—were unharmed. He'd broken bones in seven auto/motorcycle accidents (such as when the brakes on his international delivery truck failed); none his fault, though in one wreck the blame was equally divided. One occurred *exactly where* his father died on a motorcycle. Willy prophesied that the eighth accident would be his last. Now was number eight.

The psychic/teacher Mariah Martin said afterwards Willy had died "out of his body in an unconscious suicide." That is, he unconsciously *consented to the sacrifice but not the time*, which was unknown.

What did that mean, unconsciously consented?

It meant to me that his soul grouping or soul, "canceled him" out—thought he'd absorbed too much shadow. Consciously, he had zero knowledge of this, but his premonition of an accident plowing into his windshield showed *he did know* and was trying his hardest to turn the story around, avoid the advancing moment of truth.

Given not only my 1981 prototype accident dream (of an El Greco-like driver with a stretched body *as if on remote control*) but especially Willy's tire tracks, that explanation makes sense. In that foggy 4:00 a.m. no-visibility winter hour on an empty road he rounded a curve; the tire tracks witness that the car, in a flat field, went for the only tree in it—in a line as straight as if drawn with a precision ruler. A tree he had no way of seeing. My European Commission friend Helen Titchen, who saw the tracks with me, said, "That accident couldn't have happened. This"—pointing to the tracks—"is *for us*." She told me he was out of his body before the car left the road.

His friends asked, "Why didn't he use the hand brake?" Even if he'd been drinking, which he had, I'd have trusted him to drive me home above anyone else. As to reaction time, he was the person after all who taught me to dance in double beat, his chemistry was so fast.

I also knew nothing was definitively predetermined—which could not be changed with enough energy, *electricity*, or other depth.

He has to be loved with a whole heart . . . take out the mercury . . . I did not make the connection.

And making it, probably still could not have managed such a step. But who knows?

Anyway, this is not in regret. Because of what was coming next, there was no time for anything but attention to it—the future from which the energy field he was not supporting was removing him, so as to step it up. Step in. Take over. Settle down into our apartment.

I now entered an amazing period that lasted ten years—only after which I would leave this hermitage, rub my eyes to see the light outside, having been almost exclusively in the inner light all of the 1990s up till 9/11. But first, something else would work itself in, which involved—Hunter. However, let me introduce the new energy field that helped Willy, in the shock of sudden death at just under thirty-five, and that operated more widely in the consciousness of the multidimensionality of events and life.

Willy had consented, rightly or wrongly, unconsciously—consented before whom? The fact was he had *not utterly refused*. A refusal, if he'd been aware enough to refuse, would have aroused such strength, such determination, shown such resolve from the personality level that his soul would have known he had merged with *it*.

With that strength, there would be no need to leave. But who of us gets such things as mortals? How can we believe we are "invincible gods" if we accept our immortal allegiances, our divinity, aligned with our highest potential, *this minute*, in this *split* instant? Who can convince us it is possible, except that *Knowing it is* shows itself in resolve?

But this was a soul level (or higher), that was used to, in connection with its energy in individuals who held it on Earth, causing a degree of consternation and false steps—the intensity being too high, the complexity, the scope, the light, the frequency too intense, blinding. And not risking a project too far. Or let us say, who, using universal energy (as shown me in Zurich, which I now understood better), had this dynamics. For we are getting into a discussion of Oneness.

I believe Willy entered this lifetime, attempting to transmit from one level of himself to another that he could do this—transform as much as need be—which would have made him a Master teacher. But it was a long jump across buildings. Yet he was not out of the picture. And we will see to what extent.

It was January 1991 when I was told he was "gone"; in the same breath I was told that in addition Jan had died ten days before.

"Two husbands at fifty," the woman in the room with me said.

I was in a daze or shock. Or both.

In waking from a Zurich Initiation dream, hearing the song "Why do fools fall in love?"—thinking it involved a double relationship ending—was I foreseeing the *potential* for these two deaths?

Jan had written me from the clinic—a few short letters saying to publish *The Suicide Mozart*. And summoned me a few times between 1987 and 1990 to remind me.

He was institutionalized because—if he didn't have anyone to live with and he didn't—alcoholism made him "a danger to himself." His mother committed him. I would not have. I did not see how he endured the droning emptiness, the static repetition, the noises (of insane people and people who had given up, never lived). But he sat it out in mostly steely silence; he did not even numb himself with TV. At last, he'd become the picture of my Moroccan dream phrase "wounded beyond despair." But he clung to that Higher Self he was so proud of, who had given him the semiautobiographical novel, *The Suicide Mozart*, he wanted posthumously published.

Part of his long-term memory having succumbed to alcohol, he finally firmly believed that in Morocco I left him "on a bed of typhus." But he sent me one or two sentences now and then, begging for a visit. Being unsuccessful now in prodding him into positiveness, I could barely bear the bleakness, except he did appreciate my gift of corduroy trousers to replace his baggy pants (no one else seemed to have thought of this) and a new shirt.

Sometimes Jan told me he dreamed he was writing a glorious "book about God." But that was impossible, I knew, although perhaps not in some other dimension or time he was peeking into. I felt he was really aware of such a book *somewhere*, but that it wouldn't physically be written by him.

He'd earlier sent me a letter in Zurich that he said to destroy. In it he informed me that he was not resisting damaging his brain, because he felt he was meant to learn something through his heart. I had a physical revulsion to destruction. Yet it was a major part of his playing with freedom.

And then one day, choosing among the many implausible attempts he'd made or thought of—turn a screwdriver into his head, jump off a wall, cut his wrists in a tub, swallow all the pills in sight and go out to a bar as Popeye the Drunken Sailor Man, or pretend to take arsenic day by day—having sombered into merely the position of outgrowing his life (other things calling him: things this side of himself heard and said to the child that he was, yes you are done here), he died.

He committed suicide (having hoped, in a poem about a skinned fish in a frying pan, to be "pure in the last hour"). But I thought of it as suicide only if one contextualizes to this extent. Moreover—can one say it?—he considered it not an act against God or the lifetime he'd been given.

In fact, once in a failed suicide he'd left a note describing himself as "happy, as I have never been." He was, we remind ourselves, by now a nonparticipator. He left to become, one can speculate—not quite in the snap of a finger; there would be healing first—the self he had given up in the first place, when coming here "on a mission, the work of Divine Sin." (I had dreamed that too.) He left to do the next work of his soul.

Can all this be true?

I wrote some of the above reflections in an e-book for the retrospective of his life launched by Museum het Toreke, in Tienen, Belgium, in 2001. I would hope that if I leave anything behind, it is the habit of wider thinking, the habit of stretch, of the solution beyond the boundary of solution, the explanation beyond the last boundary of explanation, where the known truth is exhausted, where resides the truth *coming into being*—for which lives are paid, by bringing us to that border.

It may be the border where knowing something doesn't fit, we go on and become—in universal contexts—individual. Then we say what is left out, what no one else can. Then we stand shining in the only light we have. Then we talk to each other in what Kierkegaard called "poetic infinity." Then we are unreproducible and uncopyable, though we can be stood on top of.

This poet, concealed from all others, in his younger days drew freehand cathedral after cathedral interspersed into pages of poetry and novels—for whom the tall, straight lines of the past held so much significance that the bombing of towns like Dresden was as if all he stood for—or was?—had been bombed. But he kept that relationship to cathedrals private, just like the boxes of music composition (concertos, etc), some of which no one but he played—till in a concert after he died.

For the Eastern Orthodox Christians, Jan's death date—December 27—celebrates the feast day of St. Stephen, stoned for blasphemy just outside Jerusalem; on that date the Catholic Church celebrates John the Baptist. The 26, 27, or 28 is variously the celebration date of the Massacre of the Innocents by Herod, who ordered male babies slaughtered right and left to try to nip in the bud the authentic Christ. All these symbols swirling around, put into the box (Pandora's?) of anti-self in the final Jan Mensaert work.

A theme in *The Suicide Mozart* was that evolved artists, teachers, etc., wait on Vega Fünf to "go to the next level." Before leaving Earth, they must find a replacement. In the case of Mozart, he had to guide the semi-autobiographical protagonist Fiss into that role—as the suicide Mozart—through suffering. But never destroy his will.

Jan Mensaert always wanted things to be taken to the genius level—that is, say the thing no one else had! From that, perhaps—without having lived it in a sense, in that it was too unconsciously located—to make his genius survive. For it would be beaten into plowshares of its own planting. Curiously as well, the death date came full circle; it was on December 27, 1969, that the envelope of his Greek suicide letter to me was stamped. A letter that motivated me to fly from the United States to Belgium to see him for the first time in four years. I had met him in Morocco four years earlier.

That decision, December 27, 1969, made the story continue, eerily punctuated by his death twenty-one years later to the day. And that means—BUT WE HAVE TO STOP SOMEWHERE.

Afternote:

As the lifework of Gopi Krishna was inside the evolution of the human race, and pursued some of these personal-myth checkpoints, is this also a story about pathways into the unconscious evolutionary future? That is, the real pathways, those that no one knows until being on them? And figuring out where they are? Is it an unconscious message? No, in the end, no longer unconscious.

Immediately after learning of Willy's death (and Jan's), I went home and got on the phone. When I told Christine, a member of Inner Landscaping, she said—suddenly feeling Willy—"I think he's going down the phone wires." When I called Jyoti, she said, "Hold on. All the lights on my switchboard are coming on at the same time."

To get me back on my feet, Helen Titchen (now Beeth) left her European Commission headquarters job, where she had the highly coveted, well-paid position of translator, for a week and rushed over. Helen is a Brit and studied Modern Languages at the University of Bradford. I called her the day Willy died; she too felt him coming down the phone wires.

She says now that when she got to my apartment, I was quite calm—trying to make some sense of the situation already, talking about the bigger meaning of it, linking it to Milton and soul groupings, and she thinks now I was probably in shock. "Back in those days," she says, "you were talking very personally about how things fitted into the cosmos, seeing meaning in connections that most people would see as random. But that was the artistry."

She went on (in 2013), "Now I see you as something of a pioneer, but in many ways you were living without a support system.

I would say that you're held so strongly by the thread of your own storyline. You've woven this thread of connection that goes beyond the veil between life and death. It's like these men really become real for you after they're dead."

I asked what she meant. It didn't sound good. Of course, in one way, they were the most real to me when they could interact physically, touchable, in person. Beyond the control (or need) of my imagination and subtle sensing. She explained philosophically and poetically, "I think we die twice: once when we die and again when the last person alive on Earth stops remembering us."

She went on about the effect of death: "Once they're gone, you bring them into yourself in a different way because you're breathing life into them. So the act of remembering is almost an act of creation. It's the art of keeping them present on Earth."

I observed that "I could experience more dimensions of a person after death." How did she think I was a pioneer?

"Because you pay attention to signals so subtle that other people wouldn't register them. Most people would say they were hallucinating. But you let signals like that take you over . . . You were on the trail of every imaginable clue that you could weave into the story of his death. You weren't doing an awful lot of crying." She remembered—and I don't—that I "wanted to find him some nice clothes for his coffin, but it took you so long to get round to it the mortuary was closed, and when they reopened, they told you his body was no longer in a state it could handle putting clothes on it, and so basically he stayed in his mortuary gown. He was quite beaten up."

I would say I was being helped with specific energy in order not to fall apart. Seeing the bigger picture kept me from feeling a void, of the wrong sort. The whole accumulation of Zurich was now coming back to fall down onto me in this second death, and the many synchronicities or psychic things were keeping me busy so that I didn't succumb to torrents of grief.

She slept in my bed, on Willy's side. Well able to sense him.

Waking up the first morning, she saw the window on her side

cast a shadow on the wall; she woke feeling really frightened and alone and knew those weren't her emotions; she was picking up on his, she told me.

At 6:30 a.m., in bed, she showed him an Inner Landscaping "Energy Exchange Exercise," telling him to keep his energy over there, leave hers with her—especially because when I stood up she was *seeing through* my cotton gown, as if it were transparent, as if he was looking through her eyes. High-functioning, enormously intelligent, with a strong, rational left brain, she did not usually have experiences with "a ghost" but immersed herself. Further making her Willy's type, she was incredibly beautiful, with rich long brown hair, high cheekbones, and sexual/spiritual/intellectual appeal.

I compared the developments to the 1990 film *Ghost*, unknown to me in January 1991. The names would be shuffled. In the film Sam Wheat (Patrick Swayze), happily in love with Molly Jensen (Demi Moore), is murdered by a thief (named Willy), on instructions from Sam's money-laundering banking partner. Refusing to go into the Light, Sam makes Molly aware of him. In a similar way to Sam, *my* Willy made a number of people—not just me—feel he was hanging around. Both he and Sam died suddenly, violently; as in the film, Willy appeared to be trying to make his presence felt, testing to see who could sense him.

"The bell" arrived in the first week after his death, while Helen was still there.

When we were talking together about him, suddenly we both heard an electronic beep. "The sense was that we were saying something and he was confirming it," she recently recalled. "We went looking around the house for anything that might have made the noise and there was nothing."

Reviving Willy's enigmatic comment "Hello, Mrs. Bell," it was to be yet one more "impossible"—this time day-to-day—occurrence the death left in its wake.

Multiple times every day the bell was audible in the apartment—sounding something like the then-new watches that beeped on the

Jyoti's Workshops

hour. Only, there was no such watch in the apartment and not many in Belgium. Often it punctuated a thought or statement by me or something on TV. In those cases I felt it was "rung"—who knew how?—by Willy. Helen, who had a highly developed sense of "knowing," never doubted it.

After we missed one class, I returned to Inner Landscaping. By then Helen was back in Brussels. As I walked in, she said: "Willy's already here." Seated in a circle, as Chris led us in meditation, the group tried to send Light to Willy, and we each sought to receive a communication. I heard (in my head) Willy singing, "Fiddely-dee, fiddely-dum, look out, baby, 'cause here I come . . . Oh, oh, oh, oh, oh, oh, Get ready, 'cause here I come."

I bought my first computer, and it began to act strangely—in conjunction with the bell. Sometimes when I was about to print, the bell would ring, which I quickly detected to be a signal not to give up and turn the computer off if blank pages spilled out. Then, in the printing, a single line from my manuscript (a book I'd working on since 1965!)—of which a page was on screen—would be lifted to the top left. After a large space, more lines would follow lower on the same printed page. In such instances, isolated beside a few words of text, an annotation was inserted by the computer itself, as in "p815X," or "*p815X."

I sensed the annotations were keyed to the Thompson Bible concordance—not yet used—I bought at Paradeplatz, Zurich, with the Initiator. As earlier mentioned, the morning of—around the time of—Milton's death in New York, I'd seen a numinous *parade* in Blankenberge, Belgium. *Parade*platz and this experience with the "computer-PK," as I began to call it, seemed a hop, skip and jump—or an abracadabra—from it.

I recalled that back in 1983 in my first reading with Mariah Martin, she said she thought my soul grouping was working on a project in "mind *through* matter."

Al Miner, channel of Lama Sing, had said that from several dimensions in consciousness beyond Earth, this soul group tried to *spread its consciousness*. And that its current project was "the illumination of the universal nature of each soul."

That is, as reported by the most revered Hindus, such as Yogananda and Babaji. The Christ I'd been introduced to, like theirs, was cosmic, not confined to any church.

I did not have vivid dreams of Willy after death. Instead, there was the bell and what I took to be spirit committees. I had to talk to someone and could not think of anyone I'd rather share a bit with than Hunter Thompson. That's ahead.

Willy died on Old Christmas, in a car accident as depicted literally in a dream I had during the approach (shadow) of Milton's death *ten years before*—Willy's death now, in 1991, coinciding with Milton's changing form (a form change I'd surmised during my seven kundalini episodes, once a week). As mentioned, the death of Willy coincided exactly with the anniversary of Milton's only telegram to me, January 6, 1967, a poem called X^2—which said: GIRDLE OF O, GIRDER OF I. INVIOLABLE. UNBREAKABLE.

January 6 is the Feast of Epiphany. In Eastern practice, it represented originally a general celebration of Jesus's life, including his birth, the visit of the Magi, and his baptism by John—but the celebrations became divided up on different days. However, in essence, Old Christmas, January 6, is "the manifestation of Christ to the world (whether as an infant or in the Jordan), and the Mystery of the Incarnation."[189]

Old Christmas, Epiphany, a day so laden with significance it is as if a multileveled Time building hung over this point. Or one point of time hung in layers. A slice of time. A Cross section around a point. Which? Did time take such forms?

But I had no days to grieve, swept into another action-packed development in which Willy, from my point of view, participated.

In four months, I was to be in Owl Farm with Hunter.

But there are reasons for *this tight knot of associations and events*. On another level I was following an evolution from the initiation in Zurich, itself on the heels of Milton's death.

From his death (November 1981) to Willy's, January 1991, when Hunter was barely months off the horizon—ten scant years—my consciousness shifted. So many emotions were set in motion, *such a trial was endured,* that the techniques of computer-PK and other psychic "condolences" made sense to me.

Death was/is a loss, a separation. It was a stab in the heart. But it was possible, I felt, at least in this case, to follow to other levels, which also opened up—go to this School of Consciousness, now that I had every inducement.

The bell would help work through lingering issues, such as that despite Willy's insisting how proud he was of his fidelity, one of his friends revealed (after he died) that they'd been to a prostitute together—more than once!—during our relationship. I couldn't believe it but eventually was convinced. I turned all his photos face down. Paced the floor of the living room, telling his spirit that I knew was watching *he was in deep water. I was finished with him.* Why had he done this? I began to imagine reasons. The bell seemed to follow my thoughts.

Curiosity, I thought; he *wanted to compare.* It rang. Not a good answer by half, especially in view of the insincerity, in that he'd insisted so much to the contrary.

But I also realized he was "dead," and look where he was. *Here.* And wasn't that the ultimate statement?

Life with Jan had made me vow never to split the soul from the physical in a male again. Willy helped me fulfill that. In our three years together, I toughened. I learned to spit things out.

Nevertheless, on another level, of vision and impossibility made possible, I could hear the song about fools falling in love (from a dream in the Zurich Initiation) and believe that to some states of awareness such an ending was foolishness. Yet it had been contrived and facilitated, I firmly believed, by Willy's soul grouping, or if not that exactly, an even more transcendental soul grouping, and that it had been foreshadowed in the dream before Milton died, thus in some way predetermined but at the same time avoidable.

Just like his own vision of the accident that met him head on through his window as he drove home several times preceding the wreck—that stalked him even as René Pascal felt stalked—avoidable, difficult to avoid, possible, yet not avoided. And not for lack of trying. So, Willy was killed, at just under thirty-five years old, Earth-time.

— 28 —

Hunter Reintroduced in 1991

I wouldn't say that Willy died and the next day I called Hunter. But not so far off.

In 2013, I found an unexpected note—dated January 25, 1992. It tells me: "I had taken Hunter as confidante, sensing I had to communicate with someone in the beginning [after the death], and he was there, familiar with terror and such—with edges and motorcycle speed. And secrecy. For we had slipped me into California [during the *Hell's Angels* book tour in 1967] right under the noses of my publishing house bosses."

What on earth did I tell him? How much about these exploits? I'm pretty sure I didn't mention Willy's death. Not yet. If I could be a fly on the wall, I'd like to listen in.

In January 1991, with Willy barely buried under a tall tombstone, I gave Hunter's number a try. I now had a sense that on a soul level—not only this level—he was formidable.

Hunter's editor Jim Silberman had sent me a copy of the just-published *Songs of the Doomed*. Hunter filled me in. He'd been embroiled in and won a legal battle. Allegation: that he tweaked the breast of a woman who'd gone to Owl Farm wanting his consent to produce an art porn film from one of his books. He didn't like the idea. When she stayed to party, becoming rowdy, he forcibly made her leave.

Cops roamed Owl Farm. Brandishing a warrant from a nonlocal judge, they instigated a fourteen-hour search. With advance warning, the ranch was mostly clean. But in addition to assault, he was charged with possession of dynamite and traces of coke, as well as some long-lost LSD and pot the search turned up. Then the porn producer flirted with him in open court . . . Case dismissed. Somersaults on the grass.

When I called again in January, he said his (live-in) lover, Terry Sabonis-Chafee, was that minute walking out. He was mightily upset, a bit brusque. It was astonishing he even picked up.

But the hole she left I filled. We were a telephone twosome again. I adjusted my sleep. He prowled nights. The timing worked.

Once he was making tomato soup. "Can you cook?" I asked. I began to associate him with tomatoes.

About the present, we knew little.

He asked my advice on buying kitchen equipment. We roamed. He read the opening of *Songs of the Doomed*. Did I think it was funny? (*Hilarious*.)

It was the Editor's Note, which begins: "Shortly before this book went to press, we were stunned and profoundly demoralized by a news bulletin out of Aspen—along with murky AP wire-photos—saying that Dr. Thompson had been inexplicably seized, searched, and arrested on nine felony counts and three bizarre misdemeanor charges of brutal sex and violence. Initial reports from the Pitkin County Sheriff's Department were hazy and incoherent, but Thompson's alleged attorney told reporters that 'The Doctor is probably guilty of these crimes and many others, which means he could go to state prison for at least sixteen years.'"

However, according to the Editor's Note, he parted with bail and "flew out to California on a private Learjet to deliver a series of lectures on 'Journalism and the Law.'" Avoiding an ankle bracelet, he disappeared with "a key female witness, and remained incommunicado for many days until he was finally tracked down in a bungalow at the Beverly Hills Hotel by his old friend and colleague Raoul Duke, who flew in from Shanghai on a U.S. military jet to head the search for Thompson and force him to deliver his book manuscript on schedule." Duke took over "the Operations wing of Thompson's legal defense and also compel[ed] delivery of the doomed and desperate writer's final chapter. . . . Duke told reporters [at a press conference] to 'stand back. This is victory or death.'"

Then, quoting John Keats's "Ode on a Grecian Urn": "That is all ye know and all ye need to know."[190]

We had to feel our way through the missing time segments. When I mentioned having experienced psychic incidents and asked if he had, he said, he preferred the word "intuition." Exactly what I told him escapes my memory. It must have been here he interjected: "You talk the craziest of anyone I know."

"I'm not crazier than you." I was aghast.

"No, but you *talk* crazier. . . . I feel like I'm talking to a naked child." I felt warmed.

He explained that to handle such fine lines, he invented Duke, then Doc could observe.

"I can't figure out why we didn't [meet] before," he mused aloud. Did I know? No, I said (though I had some pretty good ideas). He was speaking from the heart; I was profoundly moved, hoping our feelings would stand still long enough to bring us to a physical spot finally, unimaginably, lyrically, wildly.

In May, I was to visit in North Carolina and also with Jyoti and her husband Russell in California. Hunter suggested we meet flamboyantly—off Key West in his boat. Or at his log cabin home ("fortified compound," as it went by).

Owl Farm, it was. To meet off the Florida coast—a dashing idea—involved too much travel for him. I didn't care which place. Maybe first one, then the other. I'd last seen him in New York City in 1969, last had a letter in '73, with off-and-on phone calls since.

Of course, there'd been occasional vivid dreams. But lifetimes had been lived in between hands-on touch sight. *Was this the meaning of " They will be together in old age"?*

— 29 —

Hit Pause

Well, not in the strictest sense.
    The meeting came and went. I've written about it elsewhere. But never fear. I will tell a version. Just not right here.

— 30 —

Looking Ahead

Right now with a bell in the apartment, an interactive computer receiving energy from another dimension operating by a law I did not know (although by 2013, NASA would be using a quantum D-Wave Two computer that set up a superposition of answers hovering over questions before the wave function collapse)—and with Hunter on the horizon—this book is almost at the end. While I was conversing with Hunter, the afterdeath phenomena were going on—taking me by surprise.

Also, not only I but also some of Willy's friends had the sense that he was hanging around. One truck driver mentioned pulling over to the roadside once, when he was too tired, thinking Willy told him to. I went knowingly into the Unknown, the Unconscious, the Guided. In fear and trembling but elation. It was the prelude to the '90s.

The channeled writings I was receiving from what I took to be a "spirit committee," whose energy was evident throughout the apartment, included "Invocation to Masters of the Past," plus a title, "The Bedtime Tales of Jesus." Were these texts meant somehow to fit into the book I'd been writing since 1965, *Love in Transition*? In Zurich I had thought we finished the book.

Now it took off again, adding a new top layer of the spiritual. One well-respected light body teacher in Belgium told me this spirit committee was "the energy Jesus was in in his teaching." *What? What energy was he in? This was news to me.* I felt the energy throughout my apartment, my cells, nourished in manna. But what could I possibly do with a sometime *novel* invaded by writings focused metaphysically—or by poetry—speaking about Earth?

Wanting something to ground this situation, I had Chris Van de Velde do a "timeline reading" for me. That was supposed to be a reading of past lives of my soul on my timeline. I took the train to his apartment in Ghent. Standing in front of me to begin, he immediately said he could not "find my soul." I was watching a face enveloped in purple/indigo in front of mine. I said: "Look here."

He said, well, yes that was Jesus—"Somehow your soul is related to him. But not the one in the Bible."

The Jesus my soul related to, he said, was "the one who took his whip against the hypocrites."

At times—watching TV with me—the bell concurred with a line of dialogue. For example, an actor told a joke based on a famous Jack Benny line: a mugger says, "Your money or your life." In the version Willy knew (which I heard on TV), the victim coughs up the money. The thief shoots him anyway.

Willy had often told that joke. Now he rang the bell, to refer, I felt, to having undertaken at symbolic gunpoint a rigorous program of change. I see him in Portugal New Year's Eve, making a resolution not to smoke.

But nothing altered the course of events. He was "killed anyway." On the soul level it probably counted a lot.

In another instance, an actor was chased right to the edge of a cliff; he could not stop. The bell rang. I interpreted it to be Willy saying that his shadow (when he was out of body) got him to the point of hitting the tree; he could not step back in. Too late. But then, we have said Willy gave unconscious consent.

Meanwhile, Hunter and I continued phone conversations; I felt he was open, available, amusing, interesting, grounding, though I restricted what I said.

A sketch of the 1991 meeting between Hunter and me, which did take place, is in *Keep THIS Quiet Too!* Now that *Initiations* shows

Looking Ahead

the buildup, the back story, it may seem a shock that we managed to come together.

Hunter might as well have been the beggar whose eyes I stared into in 1965, with the life-gnarled face. However, I had my own life notches by now. Could our hearts overpower our opposite paths? We plunged in, no test too great. No fun too out of reach. Could his "old softie" side accept my mystical bent? Would that side even come out? I could keep it at bay, couldn't I? In his house. And if not, how would he handle it? How indeed?

As I left for the U.S. and Owl Farm, I was not sure if the bell would come along. And if not, would it be in Tienen when I returned. If it did go audibly with me, what then? **To Be Continued.**

Preview

Volume IV

A "Naked Child" in the 1990s: Divine Child & the "Hieros gamos"

The 1990s stood out radically in my life: a solid, unbroken initiation for ten years, once Willy "left the body" and the bell came. But not only that. Spirit committees in succession helped me organize *Love in Transition*; they intercepted that still-unpublished manuscript begun in Paris. They gave me "Jesus" materials that did not fit—in a novel, which I'd intended the book to be!

Nevertheless, I tried to make them fit.

Meanwhile, across the ocean, Hunter would one day call himself "a roadman for the lords of karma." Only a year and a half had passed since I went to Owl Farm at Woody Creek. But now not even perhaps a "naked child," as he'd called me, could express it. Perhaps even, it would be too challenging for someone who said it "never got too weird."

I know no answer to the question of whether the karma of my past lives is the outcome of my past lives, or whether it is not rather the achievement of my ancestors, whose heritage comes together in me. Am I a combination of the lives of these ancestors and do I embody these lives again? Have I lived before in the past as a specific personality, and did I progress so far in that life that I am now able to seek a solution? I do not know. Buddha left the question open, and I like to assume that he himself did not know with certainty. . . . In the meantime, it is important to ensure that I do not stand at the end with empty hands.

—Jung

APPENDIX I

Meditations & Exercises

Margaret and Chris, 2012

Of Chris Van de Velde

From Inner Landscaping

Chris Van de Velde offered his Inner Landscaping course in Brussels, Belgium, 1989 to '91.* As readers of this memoir know, I was fortunate enough to take it. Below are a few meditations he opened the two-year course with. Though they have not yet been published, he gave me permission to reproduce the ones below in his own words. I've taught these meditations in my courses in the United States—with great success. Following Chris's exercises are Author Exercises you might want to try after reading this book.

Imaginative Thinking

Chris began with an introduction to Imaginative Thinking (I.T.), which most children employ spontaneously before being gradually forced into verbal-linear thinking. Typically, he explained, in storing an experience, we make an *inner representation* of it that we replay when the right button is pressed. "Our representation system relies on all five senses: Visual, Kinesthetic, Auditory, Gustatory (taste), Olfactory (smell)—V.A.K. + G.O . . . But mostly we emphasize one. . . . There's something holographic about our representation system; by remembering, for instance, the visual component, one starts to remember the K. (feel) of it and so forth."

Below is a meditation to explore which I.T. sense you use most:

> Close your eyes and find a spot inside that you call your inner home . . . make yourself comfortable . . . imagine a very fa-

---

* Based on a work co-created with Douwe Nutterts at the Institute of Human Development in Ghent; that institute has since evolved, under Douwe, into the School for Psychospiritual Work; Chris's path has since led him to train and coach teachers and executives in Belgium, Holland, Turkey, and South Africa.

miliar space, somewhere in your house or apartment . . . and while you get your first impression of this space, start looking around . . . watching the shapes that come to you . . . perhaps noticing the colors . . . maybe you see the whole room or maybe become gradually aware of it . . . and you can also see the floor . . . maybe it's covered with a carpet or you start seeing objects on it . . . a piece of furniture . . . doors—windows—the wall . . . see what you can discover with the eyes of your imagination . . . focus a little more sharply. See if you can change the wall colors . . . and as you give it totally new colors . . . notice if you become aware of a different feeling . . . a different body sensation . . . and which new feeling the color gives you . . . then while you bring back the colors of the wall to how they were, notice a shift, maybe very subtle, in feeling. . . maybe you feel like you always do on a quiet day, alone in that room . . . and imagine walking around . . . your feet stepping on the floor . . . and become aware of the sound of your feet . . . maybe traffic noises . . . or other sounds that are characteristic of this room . . . and while you catch fragments of sound, stretch the hands of your imagination to feel some object . . . touch it, explore the texture and shape . . . notice the feeling that comes through your sensitive hands . . . and when you breathe through your nostrils, catch the smell of that familiar place . . . and with each outbreath make the perceptions smaller . . . and smaller . . . and a whole new situation might appear now to your Imaginative Senses . . . an experience you recently had that gave you joy and delight . . . a pleasant memory . . . allow yourself to become aware and to re-present that pleasant moment . . . notice how it comes to you . . . perhaps you feel your body slowly feeling the same beautiful sensations; maybe there are subtle changes in you . . . or maybe you see the whole situation . . . you re-picture it . . . or perhaps you smell the flavor—or taste the taste . . . and while you are go deeper and deeper, become aware which sense is easiest for you . . . whether you see it, or hear it . . . or feel it . . . or smell it . . . or taste it . . . maybe it's just knowing it is there . . . and see how much of the joy and delight you can bring back into your cells, as if you are filling yourself up with these happy sensations, as if you open up your body's cells to remember that precious moment, to bring it into this very moment, in which you softly and gently open your eyes and look around to see whether you meet other joyful faces.

Grounding Cord Meditation # 1

This is a centering meditation—good preparation for any other exercises. It makes you feel present, gives stability and aliveness to your whole body . . . more affective response-ability, more contact with your feet. It connects to the first chakra and enhances your sense of physical security. It helps you relax, adapt to situations:

> The energy dimension is not a matter of activity/doing. It's more like a process of onion peeling. . . . It has many layers . . . every time you discover new layers, new dimensions. Sitting in a chair, glance around the room and find three images to look at; then close your eyes . . . listen to three sounds present here . . . three different sounds here now . . . and let three thoughts arise in you; whatever they are, listen, and feel two different body sensations . . . that come to you now . . . and while you feel these . . . keeping both feet on the ground, focus your back, the spine . . . stretch your back, put your head straight up, as if pulled by a string . . . continue stretching gently with your attention on the backbone, how it's lining up. . . Look down your spine and imagine there's a line going further down, through the seat of the chair . . . . into the space beneath . . . it goes right through the space underneath the floor . . . down to the ground floor of the

building . . . and beyond, as if down into the brick layers . . . the liquid masses . . . down to the center of the earth . . . When your line reaches the center point of the earth, let your creativity and imagination fix it there . . . Maybe you glue it . . . Maybe you use a nail and hammer it down into the point . . . so it stays fixed. And let your focus now go to the shape of the line . . . perhaps it looks different. Let your creativity change the appearance so you feel closer in contact with it . . . maybe it becomes a pipe . . . or a rope . . . or a string . . . or a root . . . whatever . . . Notice which shape you give it right now and write your full name into the grounding cord . . . Notice if your cord is flexible or tense . . . feel what happens to your body sensation . . . Then maybe put the spinal grounding cord on automatic as you focus your attention on your feet (go through the same process, letting a grounding cord descend from each foot to join the one extending from your spine).

Grounding Cord Meditation # 2

Now let's go further. Let's flush superfluous energy (physical, emotional, mental) down the grounding cords . . . your physical tiredness . . . any negative emotional energy (such as anger, fear) you've picked up in the office, on the street, on the TV . . . mental energy of others . . . the physical, emotional, mental energy you don't want all flushed away . . .

> Again let the grounding cord extend down from the bottom of your spine to the center of the earth, noticing its shape and whether your bodily sensation feels different. Does the shape need changing when you adapt it to the present situation? Feel the center points on the bottom of your feet and let their grounding cords appear. Feel how much energy they give you, how much more present you feel now. Make the

grounding cords into hollow pipes and let them release all the superfluous energy of the week . . . all thoughts that have been occupying you that you don't need now . . . noises that entered your head from outside in public places, media, etc., the business of the day . . . all emotions that you can let go now . . . anger, jealousy, . . . lower-chakra emotions—flushing them down the cords. . . . all physical tensions, which spontaneously flow out down toward the center of the earth . . . and picture your personal sun overhead, the essence of your being . . . get an impression of it, as if your sun became a magnet drawing clear, bright colors toward its center . . . and let these colors flow inward from the top of your head, the crown chakra, down to all the cells of the body that can absorb them.

Adapt your grounding cords to the new situation . . . the higher energy levels.

Partner Exercise

Find a partner. A, Bob, closes his eyes for a minute. B, Louise, just sits, listening . . . and now, Bob, let your grounding cords appear by themself . . . see if you can imagine your grounding cords on automatic and find a color, a shape for conversation level . . . Louise, you will tell a little about yourself, maybe about today, some activity you can share . . . and watching your grounding cords . . . you start talking now . . . STOP . . . Notice if you still have the same grounding cords . . . . pull them back . . . Bob, start telling something . . . STOP . . . Come back into the circle . . . close your eyes and let your sun reappear as a magnet . . . All the energy of the short conversation returns to the magnet . . . fill yourself up with it . . . bow down.

From here it's possible to learn to withdraw energy from past scenes where someone was angry at you, flushing it down the grounding cords, releasing just the right amount and filling those cells back up with energy magnetized by your sun. As Chris puts it, "When the Buddha got enlightened, it is said he had withdrawn all his energy under the Bodhi-tree." This is just the opening curtain on Grounding Cords and Energy Withdrawal. If you remember, with the "ghost" of Willy, Helen, who was staying with me, taught him an Energy Exchange Exercise to withdraw his energy from hers.

Of the Author

Learning to Think in Energy—General Introduction

These exercises, I've found useful in introducing energy awareness. Working in your energy can affect your life dramatically. The first exercise brings together body consciousness (what your body knows) and your rational brain . . . it opens up communication between your five senses and your ability to symbolize. I have found that even people with no prior experience in energy work tend to love this exercise and do it at home.

Energy Ball Exercise

Sitting in a chair, with your palms horizontal—facing each other like two bookends—put your attention on the sensation in the space between the palms . . . keep the palms still till you feel a mass of energy between them. Move them slowly apart—a foot, now less, now further. Now very gently, inch the palms toward each other . . . with your attention still on your energy ball. Then inch the palms away from each other . . . as if you were playing an accordion in slow motion. Sense whether this energy mass—this ball of energy between your palms—feels lightly compact as you slowly bring the palms closer. Or does it begin to feel cramped? Imagine it is actual energy. It needs space and you are deciding how much.

Fixing your attention on the "ball," think of a project and imagine that the energy for it today is isolated there between your palms. See how that space feels. Let your hands tell you whether they need to move further apart or closer together.

Holding your attention between your palms, let your awareness continue to coordinate with the "ball." Let it tell you—as you move your hands apart, then stop and wait for the energy to solidify—is this ball too large? Not large enough? Experiment . . . notice whether it firms up or can't absorb that much energy and needs a smaller space. Remember that this is the energy for your project—that this space represents the project, it is telling you about it . . . that it is a real representation. A real measurement. That the energy is being worked on just as you would draw a floor plan to illustrate the layout of a house. This is the feel of the energy.

The symbolic part of your mind finds this experiment easy. Your hands *feel* this mass, its heaviness, its compactness, and transmit the information to the brain.

In Jungian terms, your intuition and sensation are coordinating. The experiment is providing a coherent information setting. *Coherent energy optimizes potential.* You are setting yourself up for success.

Exercises Keyed to the Book

All of the exercises below should be done in a centered state with a relaxed mind, with perhaps some meditation music in the background.

Prologue

SLIP-OF-THE-TONGUE-LIKE ACTION

Refer back to page 17. I visited my Zurich analyst, and she diagnosed that a particular action ("hiding" my dream notebook between the couch cushions) illustrated contradictory motives: a *me* she called "Little Margaret" wanted to share my secrets; another *me* was intent on concealing them. Now let's see if you can think of a similar instance where you consciously intended one thing but you can detect that your action signaled something else:

> Think of an action that you later realized—or now realize—had an unconscious motive; it was like a slip of the tongue. Take a few minutes. Let something jump into your mind. Where exactly are you? Was it day or night? Do you remember the year? What can you see? hear? Are there any smells? Who else is there? Can you see that person? Can you hear anything being said? Try to hear your own voice if you spoke words. Feel the vibration, the tone, the intent, of what you said.
>
> Did you take any action? "Who" did it? What part of you? Why?
>
> In my case, I insisted the analyst couldn't see the dreambook. But "Little Margaret" had another idea entirely. She wanted to confide in the analyst, not hold anything back;

that is, a part of me I was unconscious of did; the dominant *me* resisted because I had a history of getting under people's influence and trying to please. So, I was completely unaware of letting the dream book slide between the pillows.

Detect this past-action slip you made. Be very honest about this unconscious motive. Let your imagination bring you information about why it happened, what the positive purpose of it might have been to a part of you. What is it?

Just as in the Energy Ball Exercise, you are working above to learn about your unconscious, in which a part of you may have an entirely different motive than the conscious you. Once discovering this subpersonality, I encountered her in many dreams; she often appeared using my middle name.

Part One

"On a Scientific Footing"
EXERCISE IN A COLLAPSED AND A NONCOLLAPSED WAVE

In the Science section beginning on page 32, we spent time on collapsed and uncollapsed waves. It is clear, in quantum physics, that many options hover above a possible event (or laboratory experiment) initially, and this superposition of possibility dissolves into a single outcome when that wave of possibility "collapses." I like to apply this model to choices.

Let's look at two different perspective: one is literal; another is back in time or outside time, where you had other choices.

Beyond the obvious, there is always a higher field (of different options) that you can look for.

To experience this, try the exercise below:

Imagine you are in a relaxed outdoor setting, perhaps sitting

Exercises Keyed to the Book

under a tree enveloped in all the shelter and peace of nature. Think of a situation you'd like to feel better about. We are going to say that, in the energy sense, it exists in a frequency; it's at a point after the wave collapsed. That is, where *once* there were many choices, *now* they appear to be very limited. Picture the participants, the place. Is it an office? A social setting? The ocean? Picture the facial expressions. In your mind there's only one possible outcome—at most two possible outcomes. Again, visualize the scene as it existed this morning . . . as it exists now, *before you try to change it* . . .

Now imagine a new screen in front of your vision, a new atmosphere—new information—around the situation. Painting it differently. Allow this information to begin altering how you feel. Watch the new details begin to change the alternatives. Maybe these details were possible only in the past. That doesn't matter. For now, just try to surround the problem with different people, places, perceptions, colors—a new atmosphere, a new symbol of it. Whatever comes to mind. Latch onto the higher area, of the alive, active information, where the energy is uncollapsed. Suddenly the situation doesn't feel frozen.

Now bring your new emotion back into "everyday reality." Test to see how you feel. Try to believe that in envisaging alternate details around the situation, you've tapped into *the might-have-been before the wave collapsed* and that this may actually cause the literal situation to shift in some way, since you've been working in its energy.

Every day we accept solutions as inevitable, when information is missing. We say hindsight is 20/20 . . . we say: if I had only known . . . *But this hindsight is present with us before it becomes obvious.*

At any moment you can look for this more inclusive level of options: a space where this situation connects to choices, not only in the present-day. This other area is not that. It's nonlocal.

The uncollapsed, nonlocal, timeless wave is available at any moment, like the collapsed one. Who knows what unknown, synchronistic solution—connections—might shake loose from the tree of possibility.

"Pauli and the Piano"

A PILOT WAVE EXERCISE

In the Prologue, Arnold Mindell mentioned that as he looked back at his life, synchronicities seemed to chart his course. James Hillman similarly mentions an "acorn theory" (page 34), by which a personal myth, or pilot wave, seems to run below the surface—strong from the start, though perhaps invisible. Hillman compares the child to an acorn born to be an oak. In the exercise below, let's look for signs of your personal myth that popped up in childhood.

> Think back . . . You are four, six, eight, even fourteen . . . Remember an emotionally charged scene . . . Something you felt very strongly about. Take one incident. How did you react? From hindsight, can you see—in your reactions at that moment—signs of your future?
>
> Along with other factors, might the "call of the future" have played a role in who you are today? Take this compass and see what you can learn about yourself if you test this theory.

In the light body work that I teach, we imagine it possible to "contact" your "future self" and draw energy from that future *you* or, correspondingly, to send healing energy into your past. By doing the above exercise, you can begin to see yourself on a timeline. Entertain the possibility that you might send healing energy back and forth.

"Pauli and the Piano"

ACTIVE IMAGINATION EXERCISE

In the exercise below we will look at a problem or a dream through the free-associations tool called "active imagination." Pauli's "The Piano Lesson" was written this way. I refer to active imagination often in this book. Look back at page 35 for an example. Then try it for yourself below:

> Think of an issue you want insight into or a dream you would like to interpret. In a relaxed, open-minded, centered state, sit with paper or computer. Let your feelings and thoughts flow without censoring. Write down what might even seem to be preposterous feelings, thoughts, images, so that they tell a story or lead somewhere. Follow the associations. Maybe they create word play, maybe you have characters who want to speak. Let all this happen. Take a half hour—maybe longer. Let the development unfold.
>
> Now set that aside. Revisit the problem. Perhaps the active imagination has already clarified the dream or resolved the issue. If not, do you have more perspective? Did a new vantage point get unblocked? Does it have value for you? Did characters come in? If so, look at one. What does he, she, or it stand for? This process can take time. Through it, you will start to open up unsuspected associations.
>
> You may be surprised to find you are on a hunt—tracking a point you didn't know you were in pursuit of. The language may lead you there. It led me in word play. Often the problematical situation or dream is trying to show you a transforming outcome. Let it continue to speak.

"Ordering Archetypes"

EXERCISE IN THE UNCONSCIOUS

Throughout this book we returned to the topic of how we make choices: "My brain, when on its own—left unsupervised by the conscious thought process—uses an inbuilt frame of comparison" (page 41).

Let's look at how analogies form influences all the time inside me, inside you, in the unconscious—just as the particles inside us are always moving and jostling, and we don't feel a thing. And how you and I might take the upper hand. Below is a description of an actual morning where choices unfolded all by themselves; an exercise follows:

> In the kitchen, brewing coffee and tea, I started cleaning off cabinets. Next I removed objects littering the table in the hall, phoned the water company. The bill had seemed too high; it had sat by the phone for days. I hadn't been motivated to inquire about it. But this morning, after I tidied up the cabinets, each thing led to the next without my thinking about it. I took Step One, and the other steps followed. Now let's do an exercise.
>
> Imagine yourself waking up. Downstairs, suppose that you begin to clear up a to-do list you've put off a long time. Without thinking, you do number one on the list. AN HOUR LATER: imagine yourself at your computer (or any typical location. Do you continue to clean out clutter? Does the straightening-up, organizing impulse carry over from chore to chore, situation to situation?

The above pattern was welcome for me. But others are not. Just by becoming aware, we can avoid *setting in motion* an unwanted repetitive type action—an unconscious emotion or attitude.

"A Pantomiming Archetype"

EXERCISE IN "VIOLENT INTERNAL STATES"

When Freud's bookcase cracked during an animated conversation between Freud and Jung on psychic matters, Jung immediately predicted that a second crack would follow. As described on page 49, he felt a red-hot sensation in his belly. In the guided meditation below, we will explore the relationship between outer and inner states:

> Think of a violent, charged inner state you've felt. A time you've been passionate about something in dispute. Suppose, however, you don't want to get overheated at that moment. Can you withdraw the violence from within? Take deep breaths. Imagine your heart rate slowing. Imagine you are much calmer inside. Feel yourself getting centered. You could even quickly do the grounding-cord meditation.
>
> Now look with your inner eye at your surroundings. Do they seem calmer as well? What happened to the other players? What did you learn? Entertain the possibility that your heightened energy was translating into the environment.
>
> How might you be on the alert for opportunities to quiet an overly dramatic scene by silently calming your inner emotion? This is only one option. At times, you may, like Jung at the bookcase with Freud, not mind at all that your outer circumstances pick up on your intense inner turmoil.

Part Two

"Threshold of the Initiation"

ANIMA/ANIMUS EXERCISE

In the Christ Menu dream, page 78, a very extraverted male personified my inner masculine energy, my animus. For a man, the comparison would be to his inner feminine, or anima. I was an introverted female. My dream male was a performer, a crowd pleaser.

In fact, illustrating the adage "Opposites attract," many people project their animus or anima onto a real person and fall hotly in love until the projection breaks. To integrate that dynamic anima/animus energy is often a challenge of the second half of life. But it can start at any time.

> Imagine this opposite-sex energy that's you. Can you detect its presence in your life? Does it influence your actions? Which? Perhaps you've wondered about a male dream figure who keeps trying to get to know you or another female (if you're a female) or who intrigues you; vice-versa if you're a male. A confident figure, when you're unsure. Or glamorous, when you're a large-glasses, bookish geek. Imagine that when you are in touch with it, you are energized. Things work. Imagine such a time. When was it? What were you doing? How can you better balance this inner/outer male/female you?

Exercises Keyed to the Book

"Newton & Alchemy"

DREAM ADVICE TWO NIGHTS BEFORE HYPNOSIS

Dreams run throughout this book (see, for instance, some of Jung's, pages 142–143). The example below happened September 26–27, 1984. It was in Charlottesville, Virginia. I had an appointment to be hypnotized in the sleep-and-dream lab where I volunteered. Before falling asleep, with a notepad and pen at my bedside, I asked for guidance as to whether to go through with the hypnosis. Below is the dream that followed:

> My mother and I had been playing Ping-Pong in the basement after dark. (In actual fact, there was a Ping-Pong table in my childhood basement.) I thought it was too late to play there and expressed my reluctance. But her mind wasn't on danger. Then I see a giant snake, while we're on one side of the basement, which is divided from the other by a small wall-like area. The floor is concrete.
>
> The snake was monstrously big and long; it came for Little Henry (the name of my father and my nephew) over and over; we could do nothing. Then it left.
>
> I wanted to hurry and get a poison antidote. Mother appeared concerned about something else. Little Henry's face looked wounded. The snake had attacked five times, lunging with its mouth. We wonder if Little Henry was hurt from being bitten or maybe he'd fallen hard. Then I see the doctor closely examining his head.

Would you have gone through with the hypnosis? I did. But it took putting two dreams together to understand the advice.

The second dream indicated I should go *up, not down*. If I went down, I felt, referring back to the first dream, the snake was indicating danger to my young inner-male growth.

I told the hypnotist, Joe Dane, a clinical psychologist in the dream lab at U.V.A. Medical Center.

Under hypnosis, I focused on going "up." All went well. I recorded just afterwards: *I saw a woman with flowing hair on a white horse, and then rode in front of her—grounded by being roped to the whole Earth by a rope behind me. I expanded; then it re-expanded for landing. It's hard to come out of the session. I regain Earth focus by rubbing my eyes, counting three ... two ... one ...*

DREAM INTERPRETATION EXERCISE

Below is a second dream to interpret. After reading through it, take a piece of paper and write down the details of a recent dream or dream fragment of yours. If possible, one in which you asked for advice. Then ask yourself how the dream addressed your question or what question it raised. Here is my dream June 5–6, 1985:

> I broke off a chunk of cake, dark with chocolate drops, and realized I'd taken too little. My father showed me what to do with the second half. I had to cut the cake cleanly and thoroughly. NEXT SCENE: In the train ride home I offered to finish a translating job (if I didn't find a translator). The word I needed to translate was "couple." I needed it spelled out.

I noted: "2nd half of the cake. 2nd half of life. I broke the 1st half to eat, found I wanted more."

QUESTION THE DREAM RAISED: how to make a clear-cut portion of "the cake" for my second half of life. My father demonstrated. REAL LIFE EVENT #1: a Jung Institute lecture on the Absent Father preceded the dream.

REAL LIFE EVENT #2: There was a male I liked whom I wanted to approach. INTERPRETATION: My *unconscious* understanding of "couple" needed to be "translated" into my conscious mind. In the second half of life, I needed to learn things about being a couple, with a clear slice of "the cake"; the Wise Old Man archetype (my evolved animus) could assist.

Part Three

"More to Ponder"

EXERCISE FROM SWAMI KRISHNANANDA

In explaining how, in his view, we are all connected, all One, and that looking at the world purely with the senses creates the perception of being separate, the yogi Swami Krishnananda gives an exercise in universality of being. We remember that Lama Sing (through psychic Al Miner) started me out on a journey by mentioning—in 1984—that my soul grouping was involved in a project to foster "the illumination of the universal nature of each soul," that is, that on some level we are all One.

Swami Krishnananda narrates a Creation story. In it the universe began through a vibration of sound: "In the beginning, there was a tremendous Om [that] . . . broke the barriers of limitation, spread itself continuously through all space and time, and manifested itself in every nook and corner, in every form that you can conceive in your mind."

He imagines the universe as "a concretised form of spatio-temporal objects." And that "the centre is here within you—here just now. There is no distance between the universal centre and your existence here. There is no such thing as distance at all. It does not exist. Everything touches everything else." Below is an exercise Swami Krishnananda proposed, to experience the sense of distance not existing. He said this possibility should be introduced into your mind by a deep chanting of Om . . . Do it every day. Close your doors, sit alone for one hour, chant Om in this manner, and feel that you are melting into the all-pervading force of nature—which is not only your friend, your parent, but your own very, very beloved substance, of which you are made. You will feel you are everywhere at that time, and nothing can give you a greater joy than this kind of feeling by mere[ly] chanting Om properly, once, twice or three times daily.

Reaching this understanding, he promised, will lead to actions and sensations of joy and bliss.[192]

"Bridge: Who Am I?"

EXERCISE IN MICROCOSM/MACROCOSM

In the Tao, the focus is on the whole. See, for example, page 179. As Jung explains the Tao, "The soul can become empty and absorb the whole world." What might this mean in practical terms? The exercise below applies this idea of the macrocosm being in the microcosm:

> Think of a project or issue important to you. Think of yourself as the microcosm, with the magnified issue out there large-scale. Think of it as a group energy. What would be the group shadow of this issue? What would be the group goal? How does the issue affect *your* energy? In what way are you experiencing its shadow? Think of how you felt lately when working on it.

Part Four

"In the Hospital"

EXERCISE IN SYNCHRONICITY

On page 44 the distinction is made between repeatable scientific tests and unique synchronistic events, or meaningful coincidence. Part Four is filled with synchronicities: the meeting in the hospital; the warnings before Willy's death; my dream of flying around, trying to warn him, that last night. As you reflect over recent experiences, let's find some synchronicities:

> Look back over the last few days, weeks, a month. Or further. Think of anything you would call a synchronicity. If possible, choose a strong one. What was the meaning of the coincidence? For it to be a synchronicity, the meaning, or correspondence (between what happened and some coincidental inner event), has to be paramount. Maybe you dreamed of a boat, turned on the TV and the first word you heard was "boat." This is still only a coincidence unless it has a meaning for you.
>
> It might be that you felt goosebumps in your house and the sense of a particular person, and then learned that he or she had just died. Or felt a strong urge to go to a spot and there met your future husband (or wife or partner). If you have thought of a meaningful coincidence, how did it make you feel? Excited? Empowered? Worried? Was it followed by a series of synchronicities? How much impact did it have on you? Is your life more or less filled with synchronicities today than a few years ago? Why?

"In the Hospital"

REMOVING A SANSKARA, A KARMIC BOND

As we saw in Part Four, the Sanskrit word "sanskara" means "past mental impressions," that is, in the yogic belief, relics of past lives that create patterns we carry. To us in the West, regardless of whether we believe in past lives, it's easy to recognize the term's validity.

In a satsang at a Hindu ashram in Belgium a young guru described sifting flour. He was explaining what a sanskara is. He said: imagine something in the flour is too big for the sifter, so big it's like a rock. He said this was like a *sanskara* that was ready to go; when a sanskara got that big, it was a simple matter for him to reach into the flour and lift it out.

But we can do this ourselves. One example in *Initiations* was my inability to be confrontational, which Willy, by his actions, helped me tackle. There is an exercise in lifting away a sanskara below:

Identify a pattern you're tired of. It's not serving you well. Picture yourself breaking it in a single instance. Imagine the scene, the habitual response rearing its head . . . like St. George with the dragon, you halt it right there. The story of St. George and the dragon has many variations. As narrated in *The Golden Legend*, the dragon St. George slew was plague-bearing and required sacrifices, chosen by lot. At one point, the lot drawn was by the king's daughter. But when she went out to the lake to be eaten, St. George stayed with her and boldly charged the rearing dragon, wounding it with his lance, then capturing it and making it do his bidding. See yourself in such an act . . . for instance, at the time to confront, I no longer froze. I spoke up.

Imagine that you break the mold . . . you respond freshly, inhabitually. Watch yourself in a scene as you discover this new strength. Congratulate yourself. But if this is a sanskara, it doesn't end there. You want to lift away the entire "mental impression."

If you have been able to extract yourself from the sanskara *in one instance*, imagine that example streaming over the events in your life lived inside the now-extinct pattern.

Your unconscious needs to be updated—to learn that you are not operating in that pattern any more. You want to tell it how you now deal with such situations, in the way a banner-streaming airplane flies over a football stadium. You need to communicate the new plan to your cells. Imagine that your intent can be received down into your unconscious. Now watch the other instances of this pattern stream away, as if magnetized to leave with the one incident, all lined up like little train cars on a track. That's how a karmic bond is broken—some underlying pattern (sanskara) you are in the grip of, which makes you repeat the same error over and over. Before doing this exercise, decide that you are ready to let this pattern go.

"In the Hospital"

EXERCISE WITH JOSKA SOOS

Joska was one of my teachers in Belgium—a Hungarian master shaman, born into the de Basca shaman clan, an artist and sound master (of Tibetan instruments). He was the teacher who, as I visited him in the Antwerp clinic where he was about to die, said not to look for him in his instruments: "*No, look for me—in the universe.*" His appearance reminded me of a force of nature, his actions the same. Around him he always had antique metal singing bowls, porcelain conchs, drums. When at age sixty he went to the exiled Tibetan lamas in London for discussion and instruction, these red cap monks of the Karmapa Order told him, through reference to a Tibetan horoscope, that he had been in a past incarnation a Tibetan lama, before that a Chinese mandarin and Taoist.

When he almost died at five years old, Joska had an initiation in which he first experienced himself in a timeless energy state: "He felt himself as being vapor, receiving impressions of powers, as if he was going through electromagnetic force fields. The walls were electromagnetic force fields. He enjoyed that very much. He was experiencing himself as timeless, spaceless and as consciousness. He had another consciousness, a consciousness that was more omnipresent."[193]

His book is titled (in Dutch) *I Don't Heal, I Restore the Harmony*, which takes us back to Jung's story of the Tao in the Prologue. I will bring in Joska in the next book. He believed this simple exercise he gave me (below) was protection enough. The thing I like about it is that it's so simple. He had demonstrated it in the first twenty minutes after birth, when his mother was alone; he remained sitting in the placenta, *inside* a caul connected to the umbilical cord until help chanced to come. Joska said that to protect yourself, you need no more than a good intention. Let's try the exercise:

> Feel your good intention. Then imagine the person or situation you need protection from and see what feeling it brings. Say a sound inside that feeling until the sense of harmony is brought to it. You can use whatever inspires you as a sound and image.

For a sound, you might use, for instance, "om," "ah," "huh," even a guttural hsss, or anything vocal. Let your imagination tell you what feels right. It will have a vibration and it will be focusing your intent. Vibration is a very high healing tool. Align the vibration, the sound, with a feeling of harmony, and it moves the pieces of the situation around into harmony, and you can also add an image.

APPENDIX II

Summary of the Major Initiations

Summary of the Major Initiations in *Keep This Quiet!* III

Milton Klonsky's Death "Parade"— November 29, 1981

A numinous parade—November 29, 1981—punctuated the foreshadowings of Milton's death. I later realized it was more or less simultaneous to the event. Carl Jung, in *Man and His Symbols*, called strong anticipatory warnings the "Shadow of the Approach of Death." Precognitive dreams and other precursors figured in my preceding book. In this book I refer to dreams involving Milton after death, which built intensity and readiness for the Zurich Initiation.

Trip to Rome with Jyoti—July 1985

The trip to Rome was another serendipitous preparation for the Zurich Initiation. Anticipating a big shift, which according to my numerology came every nineteen years—and that matched up with my life events—I went to Rome with Jeneane Prevatt; she later received the spiritual name "Jyoti." I hoped she would help prepare me. Already, she had had out-of-body experiences—and was well ahead of me in understanding kundalini.

Zurich Initiation— begins September 1985

Jung experienced a "confrontation with the unconscious," from which he drew the seeds for his lifework. In Jung's prescription for individuation, a person is likely to look inside in the second half of life. At forty-five, one September morning, after meditating several hours (for the first time at any length), I broke through into what appeared to me to be the consciousness of a spirit. Looking up into an empty stadium, he was silently addressing crowds of the future who would read his book. I called him "Milton Christ," and in *Initiations* often say simply "the Initiator." Milton Christ related to Milton Klonsky as a higher being whose consciousness Milton was part of. He was multidimensional and universal, which, Al Miner (the channel of Lama Sing) had told me we all are. The Initiator said he did not occupy a single physical form, he identified with an energetic signature. In other words, his energy was threaded through many people, he said and showed me.

Seven Kundalini Episodes preceding Willy's Death—Fall/Winter 1990 to 1991

"Kundalini" is a Sanskrit term meaning "coiled up." The kundalini energy works inside a system of energy wheels, or chakras, located on or around the spine subtly. At birth, in each person, the kundalini is backwards-facing, coiled at the root chakra. When awakened, it begins to climb to the head, where, in the wisdom traditions, it precipitates self-realization, or unity consciousness. These seven kundalini episodes I had—once a week—were part of the Shadow of the Approach of Death of Willy Van Luyten. The last attempted to avert disaster.

Initiations following Willy's Death— January 6, 1991

After the car-accident fatality a number of dramatic paranormal events occurred. The word "paranormal" is relative to Western vocabulary. In Eastern parlance, they are often explained as a mastery of energy laws inside yogic science. In particular, in my apartment there was, for some time, a bell from a nonphysical source (presumably) and an interactive computer that printed out pages in a reconfigured fashion. These psychic circumstances intensified my consciousness as I wrote the book I'd been working on for thirty years, which I began as a novel in which Klonsky was the thinly veiled protagonist named "Robert." Robert often spoke in Milton's actual past words I'd recorded.

Notes

Abbreviations

Meier, ed., *A & A*—*Atom and Archetype: The Pauli/Jung Letters 1932–1958*
Miller, *Obsession*—*137, Jung, Pauli, and the Pursuit of a Scientific Obsession* (hardcover title: *Deciphering the Cosmic Number*)
Lindorff, *Two Great Minds*—*Pauli and Jung: The Meeting of Two Great Minds*

1. Jung, *Memories, Dreams, Reflections*, 160.
2. Peat, *Synchronicity: The Bridge between Mind and Matter*, 14.
3. Briggs and Peat, *Looking Glass Universe*, 109.
4. A story told by Jung in various forms. This account is based on the version by psychologist Stephen Diamond, "Redefining Reality (Part Two), Psychotherapy, Synchronicity, and the Rainmaker," http://www.psychologytoday.com/blog/evil-deeds/201001/redefining-reality-part-two-psychotherapy-synchronicity-and-the-rainmaker.
5. Ven Sochu, "Turning a Tap in Adelaide, a Downpour in London," http://www.thebuddhistsociety.org/resources/previous_stories/Tap.htm.
6. Thompson, *Kingdom of Fear*, 144.
7. Ibid., 145.
8. Miller, *Obsession*, 143.
9. Woodman interview, "Jungian Analyst Marion Woodman on her approach to therapy," http://www.youtube.com/watch?v=-q9Re6YD22M.
10. Beach, http://www.mainejungcenter.org/index.php/programs.
11. Jung, *Psychology and Alchemy*, 26–27; also see Meier, ed., *A & A*, 46.
12. Sabini, ed., *The Earth Has a Soul*, 14; quoted from Jung, *Letters* II: 540.
13. Ibid., 12; quoted from Jung, *Letters* I: 119.
14. Ibid., 13; quoted from Jung, *Letters* II: 592–93.
15. Ibid., 12; quoted from Jung, *Letters* I: 537.

16. Henderson, Introduction, *The Earth Has a Soul*, x; quoted from von Franz in *Man and His Symbols*, 161.
17. Lindorff, *Two Great Minds*, 149.
18. Ibid., 183–84.
19. Mindell, *Quantum Mind and Healing*, 76.
20. Weber, "The Enfolding-Unfolding Universe," in Wilber, ed., *The Holographic Paradigm*, 103.
21. Weber, "The *Tao of Physics* Revisited," in Wilber, ed., *The Holographic Paradigm*, 226.
22. Wilber, "Physics, Mysticism, and the New Holographic Paradigm" in Wilber, ed, *The Holographic Paradigm*, 172–73.
23. Ibid., 173–74.
24. Peat, *Pathways of Chance*, 40.
25. Hillman, *The Soul's Code*, 16, 13.
26. Meier, ed., *A & A*, 194; cited in http://herbert.vanerkelens.nl/pauli-and-jung/92-commentary-on-the-piano-lesson.
27. van Erkelens, "Commentary on 'The Piano Lesson,'" http://herbert.vanerkelens.nl/pauli-and-jung/92-commentary-on-the-piano-lesson.
28. Yang, "Square Root of Minus One, Complex Phases and Erwin Schrödinger," in Kilmister, C. W. (ed.), *Schrödinger: Centenary Celebration of a Polymath*, 53–64; cited in van Erkelens, http://herbert.vanerkelens.nl/pauli-and-jung/92-commentary-on-the-piano-lesson. Also see Meier, ed., *A & A*, 195.
29. Lindorff, *Two Great Minds*, 185.
30. Hillman, *The Soul's Code*, 36.
31. Meier, ed., *A & A*, 64.
32. Peat, *Synchronicity: The Bridge between Mind and Matter*, 76.
33. Ibid., 94.
34. Norton, "A Peek into Einstein's Zurich Notebook," http://www.pitt.edu/~jdnorton/Goodies/Zurich_Notebook/index.html.
35. Peat, "Divine Contenders and the Symmetry of the World," http://www.fdavidpeat.com/bibliography/essays/divine.htm.
36. Meier, ed., *A & A*, 63.
37. Meier, ed., *A & A*, 63–64.

38. Jung, *Synchronicity: An Acausal Connecting Principle*, 6.
39. Ibid.
40. Wheeler in Buckley and Peat, *A Question of Physics*; quoted in Peat, *Synchronicity: The Bridge between Mind and Matter*, 4.
41. Peat, *Synchronicity: The Bridge between Mind and Matter*, 24; the examples were recounted by Jung in *Memories, Dreams, Reflections*, 178, 215.
42. Meier, ed., *A & A*, 175.
43. Ibid., 21.
44. Ibid.
45. Lindorff, *Two Great Minds*, 57.
46. Meier, ed., *A & A*, 45.
47. Meier, ed., *A & A*, 61; Jung, *Synchronicity: An Acausal Connecting Principle*, 98; also see Pauli, in Meier, ed., *A & A*, 79–80.
48. Meier, ed., *A & A*, 21.
49. Ibid., 27.
50. Jung in Sabini, ed., *The Earth Has a Soul*, 10.
51. Ibid., 11; quoted from Jung, *Letters* II: 81.
52. Meier, ed., *A & A*, 24.
53. Ibid., 19–20.
54. Ibid., 114.
55. Ibid., 115.
56. Ibid., 108–09.
57. Ibid, 115.
58. Ibid., 121–22.
59. Jung, *Memories, Dreams, Reflections*, 232.
60. Jung, *Psychology and Religion*, 80.
61. Meier, ed., Pauli and Jung, *A & A*, 21.
62. Jung, *Psychology and Religion*, 80, 88–-89.
63. Jung, *Psychology and Alchemy*, 205.
64. Lindorff, *Two Great Minds*, 44–45. Also see Jung, *Psychology and Religion*, 99.
65. Lindorff, *Two Great Minds*, 56.
66. Meier, ed., *A & A*, 21.
67. Lindorff, *Two Great Minds*, 57.
68. Meier, ed., *A & A*, 21.

69. Pauli, "The Influence of Archetypal Ideas on the Scientific Theories of Kepler," in Jung and Pauli, *The Interpretation of Nature and the Psyche*, 169.
70. Ibid., 174.
71. Ibid., 176.
72. Ibid., 177.
73. Ibid., 179.
74. Meier, *A & A*, 128n, 129.
75. Chalquist, A Glossary of Jungian Terms, http://www.terrapsych.com/jungdefs.html.
76. Editor, "Mother of Alchemy," *JMag*, http://www.jdate.com/jmag/2011/11/mother-of-alchemy/.
77. Roth I: 56.
78. Jung, *Memories, Dreams, Reflections*, 43.
79. Lindorff, *Two Great Minds*, 184–85.
80. Jung, *Synchronicity: An Acausal Connecting Principle*, 97.
81. Socrates, *Timaeus*, http://classics.mit.edu/Plato/timaeus.html.
82. Jung, *Synchronicity: An Acausal Connecting Principle*, 97.
83. Ibid., 98.
84. Lanza, "A New Theory of the Universe," *The American Scholar, Essays*, Spring 2007, http://theamericanscholar.org/a-new-theory-of-the-universe/. In a slightly revised form it was included in Lanza and Berman's *Biocentrism: How Life and Consciousness Are the Keys to Understanding the True Nature of the Universe*, 12.
85. Small, "The Crisis of Initiation," http://www.eupsychia.com/myst/articles/initiation.html.
86. Jung, *Basic Writings*, 448–49.
87. "Face to Face with Carl Jung—Part I," http://www.youtube.com/.watch?v=eLJsiQ4h3fY&feature=player_embedded#!
88. Corbett, "The Holy Grail of the Unconscious," *New York Times Magazine*, September 16, 2009, http://www.nytimes.com/2009/09/20/magazine/20jung-t.html?pagewanted=all.
89. Jung, *Letters* 1: 377; quoted by Murray Stein in "On the Importance of Numinous Experience in the Alchemy of Individuation," http://www.murraystein.com/articles.html.

90. Book reviews, "Jung and Science," Wordtrade.com, http://www.wordtrade.com/science/psychology/jungscience.htm.
91. "Jung's Model of the Psyche" in *h2g2: The Guide to Life, the Universe, and Everything*, http://h2g2.com/approved_entry/A653438.
92. Jyoti, *An Angel Called My Name*, 37.
93. Ibid., 38.
94. Ibid., 68.
95. Ibid., 72–73.
96. Title unknown, 42.
97. Weber, "The Enfolding-Unenfolding Universe," 46–48.
98. Davies, *Other Worlds*, 14.
99. Ibid., 80.
100. Cayce Reading 5749–14, http://www.edgarcayce.org/are/spiritualGrowth.aspx?id=3253.
101. Roth, *Huffington Post* interview 2012, reprinted in http://www.psychovision.ch/?page_id=329.
102. Jung, *Memories, Dreams, Reflections*, 309.
103. Quispel, DVD: "Remembering Jung (with Gilles Quispel)."
104. Maharshi Facebook site May 15, 2013, https://www.facebook.com/RamanaMaharshi/posts/10151596524564631.
105. Yogananda, *Autobiography of a Yogi*, 347.
106. White, *Newton: The Last Sorcerer*, 85.
107. Mindell, *Process Mind*, 178.
108. White, *The Last Sorcerer*, 215; quoted from KCL (King's College Library Cambridge), John Maynard Keynes MS, 135.
109. White, *The Last Sorcerer*, 213; quoted from KCL, Keynes MS, 135.
110. D. W. Hauck, "Isaac Newton, Newton the Alchemist," http://www.alchemylab.com/isaac_newton.htm.
111. KCL, Keynes MS, 33, fol. 5v.
112. Holler, "C. G. Jung, and the Alchemical Renewal," http://www.gnosis.org/jung_alchemy.htm; quoting Jung, *Memories, Dreams, Reflections*.
113. See Jung, *Memories, Dreams, Reflections* 228–29, 230.
114. Holler, http://www.gnosis.org/jung_alchemy.htm.

115. Jung, *Memories, Dreams, Reflections*, 310–13.
116. Meier, ed., *A & A*, 38–39.
117. Ibid., 44.
118. Ibid., 71.
119. Miller, 18.
120. Ibid., 175.
121. Ibid., 226.
122. Lindorff, 82
123. Meier, ed., *A & A*, 30–32.
124. Pauli, "The Influence of Archetypal Ideas on the Scientific Ideas of Kepler," in Jung and Pauli, *The Interpretation of Nature and the Psyche*, 154.
125. Meier, ed., A & A, 31.
126. Ibid.
127. Roth I: 86–87.
128. Ibid., 88.
129. See Lindorff, *Two Great Minds*, 80, among many references to Pauli's sense of science having a "will to power" and dark side.
130. Peat, *Synchronicity: The Bridge between Mind and Matter*, 103.
131. Miller, *Obsession*, 65.
132. Meier, ed., Pauli and Jung, *A & A*, 33.
133. Roth I: 87, letter to C. A. Meier, 1950; Pauli, *Die Alchemie als nicht geglückter Versuch eines psycho-physischen Monismus* (*Alchemy as an unsuccessful attempt of a psycho-physical monism*), quoted in Roth I: 88.
134. *Die Alchemie als nicht geglückter Versuch eines psycho-physischen Monismus;* quoted in Roth I: 88.
135. Meier, ed., Pauli and Jung, *A & A*, 34.
136. Harrell, *Love in Transition* 1: 29.
137. Lindorff, *Two Great Minds*, 244; quoted from *AA*, 33.
138. Roth I: 19.
139. Ibid., 11.
140. Miller, *Obsession*, 178; partly quoting from Meier, ed., *A & A*, 33.
141. *Oxford Dictionary of Scientists*, "Wolfgang Pauli," http://www.answers.com/topic/wolfgang-pauli#ixzz2JkhCEye0.

142. Meier, ed., *A & A*, 12.
143. Ibid., 39.
144. Ibid., *A & A*, 41.
145. Ibid., 40.
146. Ibid., 49–51, letter to Frau Professor Emma Jung.
147. Ibid., 66.
148. Ibid., 58.
149. Ibid., 66–67.
150. Ibid., 12.
151. Ibid., 67.
152. Meier, *A & A*, 134–35.
153. Roth I: 169.
154. Ibid., 165.
155. Krishnananda, Swami, "Walking into the Consciousness of the Absolute."
156. Miller, *Obsession*, 180.
157. Meier, ed., *A & A*, 126–27.
158. Roth I: 25.
159. Roth II: 52
160. Ibid, 53.
161. Roth I: 13, II: 174ff.
162. Meier, ed. 31; Roth II: 175. Roth quotes from *The Secret of The Golden Flower*. I quoted from http://www.rexresearch.com/goldflwr/goldflwr.htm.
163. Roth II: 53; Pauli, "The Influence of Archetypal Ideas on the Scientific Theories of Kepler," in Jung and Pauli, *The Interpretation of Nature and the* Psyche, 197.
164. Meier, ed., in *A & A*, 95.
165. Roth II: 173.
166. Roth I: 173, 176ff.
167. Roth II: 53.
168. Miller, *Obsession*, 67.
169. Roth, Interview with *Huffington Post* 2012, Section III.
170. Roth I: 176ff.
171. Ibid., 168.

172. Roth II: 88.
173. Roth I: 26.
174. Ibid., 28.
175. Roth, "Psychovision: Unus Mundus" forum, June 26, 2006, http://unus-mundus.fr/viewtopic.php?t=187.
176. Merry, "Sacred Space and Sacred Time beyond the Veil," http://www.petermerry.org/blog/tag/geomancy/.
177. White, *Kaironomia,* n.p.
178. Wikipedia: "Newton's law of universal gravitation."
179. Jung, *Synchronicity: An Acausal Connecting Principle,* 20.
180. Ibid., 71.
181. "Richard Wilhelm: In Memoriam," http://www.jgsparks.net/guides/F/WilhelmAddress.pdf, 91. Later published as *The Spirit in Man, Art, and Literature* (*The Collected Works of C. G. Jung,* vol. 15).
182. Jung, *Analytical Psychology: Its Theory and Practice,* 36, 76; cited in Burns, "Wolfgang Pauli, Carl Jung, and the Acausal Connecting Principle," http://www.metanexus.net/essay/wolfgang-pauli-carl-jung-and-acausal-connecting-principle-case-study-transdisciplinarity.
183. Jung, *Synchronicity: An Acausal Connecting Principle,* 72.
184. Ibid., 73.
185. Cowan, 195–97.
186. http://www.gallup.com/poll/163835/tried-marijuana-little-changed-80s.aspx.
187. Riso and Hudson, "The Challenger: Enneagram Type 8," http://www.enneagraminstitute.com/typeeight.asp#.UZJYT77D9z0.
188. Fauvre and Fauvre, "Enneagram Type 8: Leader, Solution Master, Maverick, Protector or Intimidator," http://www.enneagram.net/type8.html.
189. Epiphany, Wikipedia.
190. Thompson, *Songs of the Doomed,* 11.
191. Krishnananda, Swami, "Summoning Consciousness into Itself," http://www.swami-krishnananda.org/universality/universality_03.html.
192. Gillabel, "Biograpy of Joska Soos," http://www.soul-guidance.com/houseofthesun/biojoska.htm

Works Cited

BOOKS

Briggs, John, and F. David Peat. *Looking Glass Universe: The Emerging Science of Wholeness*. New York: Simon & Schuster/Touchstone, 1982.

Buckley, Paul, and F. David Peat. *A Question of Physics: Ideas in Physics and the Link to Biology*. Toronto, Canada: University of Toronto Press, 1979. Later expanded into *Glimpsing Reality: A Question of Physics: Ideas in Physics and the Link to Biology.*

Cowan, Jay. *Hunter S. Thompson: An Insider's View of Deranged, Depraved, Drugged Out Brilliance*. Guilford, CONN: Globe Pequot Press/Lyons Press, 2009.

Davies, Paul. *Other Worlds: Space, Superspace and the Quantum Universe*. New York: Simon & Schuster, 1980.

Harrell, Margaret A. *Love in Transition: Voyage of Ulysses—Letters to Penelope* I. Sibiu, RO: Hermann Press, 1996.

———. *A Lecture upon the Shadow*. Partially published in *Keep THIS Quiet Too!* Sibiu, RO, & Raleigh NC: Saeculum University Press, 2012.

Henderson, Introduction. In Carl Jung, *The Earth Has a Soul: C. G. Jung on Nature, Technology, and Modern Life.*

Hillman, James. *The Soul's Code: In Search of Character and Calling*. New York: Random House, 1996.

Jung, Carl G. *Psychology and Religion*. 17th ed. New Haven: Yale University Press, 1967. Based on the 1937 Terry Lectures.

———. *Synchronicity: An Acausal Connecting Principle*. Princeton NJ: Princeton University Press, 2010. First published in 1952. Included in *The Collected Works of C. G. Jung*, vol. 8.

Works Cited

———. *Psychology and Alchemy*, 8th ed. Translated by R. F. C. Hull. Princeton, NJ: Princeton University Press (Bollingen paperback), 1980. First published in 1952. Included in *The Collected Works of C. G. Jung*, vol. 12.

———. *The Basic Writings of C. G. Jung*. Edited by Violet Staub de Laszlo. New York: Random House/Modern Library, 1959.

———. *Memories, Dreams, Reflections*. Edited by Aniela Jaffé. Translated by Richard and Clara Winston. New York: HarperCollins/Fontana Press, 1967. First published in German in 1962, English 1963.

———. *The Earth Has a Soul: C. G. Jung on Nature, Technology, and Modern Life*. Edited by Meredith Sabini. Berkeley: North Atlantic Books, 2002.

Jung, Carl G., M.-L. von Franz, et al, *Man and His Symbols*. London: Pan Books/Picador, 1978. First published in 1964.

Jung, Carl G., and Wolfgang Pauli. *The Interpretation of Nature and the Psyche*. Translated by R. F. C. Hull. New York: Ishi Press, 2012. First published in German in 1952.

Jyoti (Jeneane Prevatt). *An Angel Called My Name*. Prague, CZ: DharmaGaia Publishing, 1998.

Klonsky, Milton. "Art & Life: A Menippaen Paean to the Flea; or, Did Dostoevsky Kill Trotsky?" *American Review* #20 (April): 115–88. Published in soft cover, New York: Bantam Books, 1974.

Lanza, Robert, and Bob Berman. *Biocentrism: How Life and Consciousness Are the Keys to Understanding the True Nature of the Universe*. Dallas, TX: Ben Bella Books, 2010; I quoted from an essay that preceded the book, "A New Theory of the Universe," in *The American Scholar, Essays*, Spring 2007, http://theamericanscholar.org/a-new-theory-of-the-universe/.

Lindorff, David. *Pauli and Jung: The Meeting of Two Great Minds*. Wheaton, IL: Theosophical Publishing House, 2004.

Mensaert, Jan. *The Suicide Mozart*. Partially published in *Life, Page One*. Tienen, BE: het Toreke Museum, 2001.

Miller, Arthur I. *137: Jung, Pauli, and the Pursuit of a Scientific Obsession*. New York: Norton & Co., 2010.

Mindell, Arnold. The *Quantum Mind and Healing: How to Listen and Respond to Your Body's Symptoms*. Charlottesville, VA: Hampton Roads Publishing Co., 2004.

———. *Process Mind: A User's Guide to Connecting with the Mind of God*. Wheaton: IL: Theosophical Publishing House, 2010.

Pauli, Wolfgang, "The Influence of Archetypal Ideas on the Scientific Theories of Kepler." In Jung and Pauli, *The Interpretation of Nature and the Psyche*, 147–212.

———. *Die Alchemie als nicht geglückter Versuch eines psyco-physischen Monismus* (*Alchemy as an unsuccessful attempt of a psycho-physical monism*), Wissenschaftlicher Briefweschel met Bohr, Einstein, Heisenberg, u.a., Band 4/II: 139–43 (1953–1954). Quoted in Roth I: 88. Translated by Roth.

Pauli, Wolfgang, and Carl G. Jung. *Atom and Archetype: The Pauli/Jung Letters 1932–1958*. Edited by C. A. Meier. Translated by David Roscoe. Princeton: Princeton New Jersey Press, 2001.

Peat, F. David. *Synchronicity: The Bridge between Mind and Matter*. New York: Bantam Books, 1987.

———. *Pathways of Chance*. Pari, IT: Pari Publishing, 2005.

Roth, Remo. *Return of the World Soul I: Wolfgang Pauli, C. G. Jung and the Psychophysical Reality. The Battle of Giants*. Pari, IT: Pari Publishing, 2011.

———. *Return of the World Soul II: Wolfgang Pauli, C. G. Jung and the Psychophysical Reality. A Psychophysical Theory*. Pari, IT: Pari Publishing, 2012.

Thompson, Hunter. *Songs of the Doomed: More Notes on the Death of the American Dream Gonzo Papers* vol. 3. New York: Simon and Schuster, 1990.

———. *Kingdom of Fear: Loathsome Secrets of a Star-Crossed Child in the Final Days of the American Century*, New York: Simon & Schuster, 2003.

White, Eric Charles. *Kaironomia: On the Will-to-Invent*. Berkeley: University of California Berkeley, 1983.

White, Michael. *Isaac Newton: The Last Sorcerer*. London: Fourth Estate, 1977.

Wilber, Ken, ed. *The Holographic Paradigm and Other Paradoxes: Exploring the Leading Edge of Science*. Boulder: Shambhala, 1982.

Yogananda, Paramahansa. *Autobiography of a Yogi*. 11th ed. Los Angeles: Self-Realization Fellowship, 1947.

Articles

Weber, Renée. "The Enfolding-Unfolding Universe: A Conversation with David Bohm." In *The Holographic Paradigm*, edited by Ken Wilber, 44–104.

———. "*The Tao of Physics* Revisited: A Conversation with Fritjof Capra." In *The Holographic Paradigm*, edited by Ken Wilber, 215–48.

Wilber, Ken. "Physics, Mysticism, and the New Holographic Paradigm: A Critical Appraisal," In *The Holographic Paradigm*, edited by Wilber, 157–86.

DVDs

Quispel, Gilles. *Remembering Jung: A Conversation about C. G. Jung and His Work (with Gilles Quispel)*. Interview with Quispel by James Kirsch and Suzanne Wagner, 1977. Los Angeles: C. G. Jung Institute Los Angeles.

URLs

Beach, Chris. "Psychological Type and the Transcendent." http://www.mainejungcenter.org/index.php/programs.

Burns, Charlene. "Wolfgang Pauli, Carl Jung, and the Acausal Connecting Principle: A Case Study in Transdisciplinarity." http://www.metanexus.net/essay/wolfgang-pauli-carl-jung-and-acausal-connecting-principle-case-study-transdisciplinarity.

Chalquist, Craig. A Glossary of Jungian Terms. http://www.terrapsych.com/jungdefs.html.

Editor. "Mother of Alchemy," *JMag*. http://www.jdate.com/jmag/2011/11/mother-of-alchemy/.

Corbett, Sara. "The Holy Grail of the Unconscious," *New York Times Magazine*, September 16, 2009. Reprint. http://www.nytimes.com/2009/09/20/magazine/20jung-t.html?pagewanted=all.

Diamond, Stephen. "Redefining Reality (Part Two), Psychotherapy, Synchronicity, and the Rainmaker." http://www.psychologytoday.com/blog/evil-deeds/201001/redefining-reality-part-two-psychotherapy-synchronicity-and-the-rainmaker.

Riso, Don Richard, and Russ Hudson. "The Challenger: Enneagram Type 8." http://www.enneagraminstitute.com/typeeight.asp#.UZJYT77D9z0.

Fauvre, Katherine C., and David W. "Enneagram Type 8: Leader, Solution Master, Maverick, Protector or Intimidator." http://www.enneagram.net/type8.html.

Gillabel, Dirk. "Biography of Joska Soos." http://www.soul-guidance.com/houseofthesun/biojoska.htm.

Jung, Carl G. "Richard Wilhelm: In Memoriam," Munich 1930. http://www.jgsparks.net/guides/vF/WilhelmAddress.pdf.

———. Face to Face with Carl Jung—Part I." Video interview with Jung at eighty-four. http://www.youtube.com/watch?v=eLJsiQ4h3fY&feature=player_embedded#!

Krishnananda, Swami. Chapter 8, "Walking into the Consciousness of the Absolute." In *The Universality of Being*. Discourses given in 1996 covering the various levels of reality up to the highest state of being. http://www.swami-krishnananda.org/universality/universality_08.html.

———. Chapter 3, "Summoning Consciousness into Itself." In *The Universality of Being*. http://www.swami-krishnananda.org/universality/universality_03.html.

Lanza, Robert. "A New Theory of the Universe: Biocentrism builds on quantum physics by putting life into the equation," *The American Scholar, Essays*, spring 2007. http://theamericanscholar.org/a-new-theory-of-the-universe/.

Merry, Peter. "Sacred Space and Sacred Time beyond the Veil." http://www.petermerry.org/blog/tag/geomancy/.

Mickunas, Julian C. Lee. "Commentary on the Chidakasha Gita of Nityananda," 2011. http://yogasutras.com/Chidakasha_Gita_of_Nityananda_Julian_Lee.html.

Norton, John D. "A Peek into Einstein's Zurich Notebook." http://www.pitt.edu/~jdnorton/Goodies/Zurich_Notebook/index.html.

"Wolfgang Pauli," *Oxford Dictionary of Scientists*. Reprint. http://www.answers.com/topic/wolfgang-pauli#ixzz2JkhCEye0.

Peat, F. David. "Divine Contenders and the Symmetry of the World." http://www.fdavidpeat.com/bibliography/essays/divine.htm.

Roth, Remo. Interview with *Huffington Post*, April 24, 2012. http://www.psychovision.ch/?page_id=329.

———. "Remo F. Roth, C. G. Jung, Marie-Louise von Franz and Wolfgang Pauli," Interview with *Huffington Post*, Section III D, April 2012. https://www.facebook.com/permalink.php?story_fbid=401561173275690&id=300564096708732.

———. Post on "Psychovision: Unus Mundus" forum, June 26, 2006. http://unus-mundus.fr/viewtopic.php?t=187.

Small, Jacquelyn. "The Crisis of Initiation." http://www.eupsychia.com/myst/articles/initiation.html.

Stein, Murray. "On the Importance of Numinous Experience in the Alchemy of Individuation." http://www.murraystein.com/articles.html.

van Erkelens, Herbert. "Commentary on 'The Piano Lesson,'" *Harvest: International Journal for Jungian Studies*, vol. 48, no. 2, 2002. Reprint. http://herbert.vanerkelens.nl/2009/03/commentary-on-the-piano-lesson/.

Ven Sochu. "Turning a Tap in Adelaide, a Downpour in London." http://www.thebuddhistsociety.org/resources/previous_stories/Tap.htm.

Woodman, Marion. "Jungian Analyst Marion Woodman on her approach to therapy." http://www.youtube.com/watch?v=-q9Re6YD22M.

Yang, "Square Root of Minus One, Complex Phases and Erwin Schrödinger." In Kilmister, C. W., ed. *Schrödinger. Centenary Celebration of a Polymath*. Cambridge: Cambridge University Press, 1987. Cited in van Erkelens. http://herbert.vanerkelens.nl/2009/03/commentary-on-the-piano-lesson/.

Manuscripts

Manuscripts of Sir Isaac Newton, bought at auction by John Maynard Keynes and donated to King's College Library (KCL), Cambridge University.

Acknowledgments

I am wholeheartedly indebted to those who encouraged me through the first two memoirs. In particular, Douglas Brinkley, the Literary Executor of the Hunter S. Thompson Estate and a professor of history at Rice University, for permission to reprint materials of Hunter in the series. To fans of Hunter, my hat is off to you in appreciation of your support. For editing *Keep This Quiet!* to start the ball rolling, many thanks to Stacey Cochran. Regarding *Keep This Quiet! III—Initiations*, I thank Martin Flynn for his willingness to plunge into it in manuscript and for his stimulating response. Many thanks to Virginia Parrott Williams for her tireless developmental editing; again, she walked alongside me as I wrote, shooting pages over to her; thanks to Mary Paul Thomas for being an inspiring beta reader and errors catcher, who made this journey so much lighter. Thanks to Bernie Nelson for editing suggestions and editor Alice Osborn for her serious and sharp eye regarding final edits. Thanks to Al Miner (forty-year channel of Lama Sing) for permission to reprint extracts from his readings and for going over with me his distinctions about nuanced metaphysical definitions. Also, to Helen Titchen Beeth for reviewing her memories of the "Willy section." And Rosemary Eagles Toumey for permission to reprint a letter.

To Jyoti, thanks for being an inspiration in Rome, at the Jung Institute Zurich, and afterwards, and for reprinted paragraphs from *An Angel Called My Name*. Also undying thanks for reading the manuscript; likewise, to her husband, Russell Park, for his sensitive reading based on a long profession as a board-certified transpersonal psychologist. And to Jungian analyst, mentor to many, Puanani Harvey, who read this manuscript in retreat—bringing her years of expertise on Jung and Pauli to reassure me I was on the right track. Likewise, to Chris Van de Velde for contributing and recording some of his Inner Landscaping exercises and for being a player in the story. To my longtime friend, poet-professor-editor Frank Despriet for the deciding vote on the title and for his all-round brilliance in bringing up points. And another longtime friend, Hiltrud Wagner, for keeping me in her home during trips to Belgium.

How could I think of a *Keep This Quiet!* volume without its cover designer, Gaelyn Larrick of Waking World, who from Bali thundered to the rescue again? Also my returning interior designer, Darlene Swanson of Van-garde Imagery. And the Jung and Pauli experts and those scientists whose insights and gravitas I've been inspired by, such as physicist F. David Peat. Also Jungian author-researcher-healer Remo Roth, whom I likewise drew from, including an extract from the "Psychovision: Unus Mundus" forum. Finally, thanks to Anita Hollier, archivist at CERN in Geneva in charge of "La Salle Pauli," for generously steering me through the selection process for a Pauli photo and Julia Bidai, at the C. G. Jung Institute Zurich, for photographing the library with the permission of the Institute. And the Saeculum publisher, Didi-Ionel Cenuşer, in Romania.

Artwork Credits

The Mercurial Fountain is from *The Rosary of the Philosophers* originally published in Frankfurt in 1550

The Alembic vintage engraving is © Morphant Creation

Interior Photographs:

"C. G. Jung Institute Library": Julia Bidai

"Margaret & Chris, 2012": Hiltrud Wagner

Cover Images:

"Psychiatrist Carl Jung Reading," undated: Otto Bettmann Archives, Corbis rights management

"Wolfgang Pauli in Holland," 1949: photographer unknown, CERN collection

"Milton Klonsky, c. 1965": Robert John

"Aquarius," Zodiac signs collection: Roman Sigaev

"Zodiac signs—Aquarius" (jug): Kerstin Schoene

Index

accident: Al Miner, 10; Arnie Mindell, 24–25; Jan Mensaert, 189; Rosa Lee Harrell, 184

accident, Willy Van Luyten: 197–99, 203, 206, 222–23, 232, 234, 274; dream of car, 219, 223, 232; premonition of, 217, 222, 234

after death: dimensions, 229; dreams, 232, 273; phenomena, 239; presence, 12, 84, 90; state, 84

alchemy, 16, 58, 61, 63, 74, 94, 116, 142–44, 155, 159, 161, 165; hermetic, 66, 94, 143, 151–54, 162–65, 167; individuation and, 163; mysticism and, 158; Neoplatonic, 23, 62, 164; Newton and, 134, 141; reputation of, 143; Tao and, 164; *see also* "Prophetissa, Maria" and "*Rosarium philosophorum*"

Angel Called My Name, An, 82–83

anima, 5, 35, 52, 54, 56, 62, 66, 78, 83, 149, 151, 156, 164

anima mundi (world soul), 36, 62, 66, 150, 153, 158, 162–63

animus, 7, 35, 77–79, 81, 84, 160

archetype, (general): 7, 19, 29, 36, 38–39, 41, 45, 50, 55, 57–59, 62, 78, 84, 100, 107, 102, 112–13, 122, 124–25, 137, 140, 142–43, 148, 151, 162, 178, 221; constellated, 23, 29, 34, 45, 47, 56, 66, 58, 160, 162, 165

archetype (examples): of change, 120; of completion, 66; of the couple (*see* "Sacred Marriage"), 123; of the enemy, 78; of Home, 174; of initiation, 73; of the "mana personality," 160; of saving the Earth (*see* "archetype of Home"); of the Self, 19, 58, 165; of wholeness, 8, 136

Atom and Archetype (Pauli and Jung letters), 39, 44, 52–53, 57, 60–61, 148, 154, 159–161, 154

A.R.E., 11

Babaji, 122, 232

Baudelaire, 54-55, 116

Beeth, Helen Titchen, 216, 223, 228, 230–31

beggar, 29, 47–48, 52–55, 57–58, 61, 65–66, 116, 154–55, 156, 162, 165, 241

bell (parapsychological): Jung, 49, 142; Tienen apartment, 183, 230–33, 239–42

Bell, Mrs., 212, 230

belly, Buddha (kumbhaka), 212–13

bipod metalism, 20, 22, 24, 45, 148,

Index

157, 163, 165–66
Blankenberge, Belgium, 10, 19–20, 103, 231
Bohm, David, 30, 86, 156
boson, 31, 59, 158; Higgs, 32, 59
Breathwork, Maitri, 200, 209, 212–13, 215
Broyard, Anatole, 9–10, 79, 81, 209–11
Cayce, Edgar, 10–11, 93, 204
Charlottesville, Virginia, 3, 5–6, 8–9, 13, 105, 120, 187, 213
Christ, 15, 73, 81, 84, 90, 93–94, 99–102, 109, 111–14, 122, 127, 174–76, 227, 232; consciousness (see "Christ consciousness"); Menu (dream), 78–79
chthonic, 160, 164
collective unconscious, xx, 19, 21, 24, 48 53–54, 76, 84, 102, 152, 161, 165
complementarity, 36, 42, 58, 129, 152, 161–63, 165–66
Confrontation with the Self, 77; with the Unconscious, 77, 106, 273
coniunctio, conjunction (see "hieros gamos")
consciousness (Light), Christ, 15, 93, 122, 126; as illumination of the universal nature, 15, 132, 161, 232
cook-key, 54, 117, 155
cords, grounding, 249–51
correspondence, 49, 62, 64–65, 161, 179; meaning-, 148

"Correspondences" (Baudelaire), 55
Damascus, 88, 102, 112, 114
death, xix–xx, 4, 8–12, 14, 19-20, 35, 43, 51, 53, 73, 79–80, 82, 90, 110, 119–20, 128, 130, 133, 136, 150, 174, 184, 186–87, 199, 201, 206, 211–12, 219–22, 224–25, 227–33, 235, 237; of ego, 94–96, 122
Dhyanyogi-ji, 99, 179, 212
dome, 55, 119, 121
Dôme café, 47, 52, 54–55, 65, 116
doubling, 55, 77, 116, 120, 165, 169, 187, 195, 202, 211, 223, 225
dreams: about a car accident, 1981, 1991 (see under "accident, Willy Van Luyten"); about Jung's study, 20–22, 46, 148, 165–66; about a fountain, 73–75, 215; dreamed by Jung, 1909 (descending into the cellar), 21; dreamed by Pauli, lines under a window (see "window, Pauli"); lucid Dream of My Life, 8, 15, 138
"End Pocket, The" (Milton Klonsky), 54–55, 66, 165
energy ball, 252
Event Ball, 212, 219
Faust, 58, 142
feminine principle, 35, 46, 61, 100, 105, 114, 150, 163, 165–66
fermion, 31, 158
Fludd, Robert, 151–54, 156–57, 162–64, 166–67

fountain: mercurial (dream), 73–75, 215; Rockefeller, 4

four, fourth, 4, 8, 15-17, 19, 36, 52, 58, 60–66, 76, 84, 100, 102–103, 111-12, 128, 130, 151, 153, 155–56, 158

functions: feeling, intuition, thinking, sensation (*see* "psychological types")

gâteau, 54, 116-17, 122, 155-56

gnosis, 101

Hammadi, Nag, 101

Heisenberg, 41, 152; loan mechanism, 87

hieros gamos (coniunctio, Sacred Marriage), 58, 63, 94, 102, 123, 125, 150, 154, 163–65, 242

Hillman, James, 34-36

I Ching, xxi, 151, 166, 178

Imaginative Thinking (I. T.), 247

individuality, 76, 134, 176

individuation process, 7–8, 53, 57, 62–63, 73–74, 78–79, 84, 106, 161, 174, 273

initiation: general (Jung, Jyoti, esoteric), xix–xxi, 43, 72–73, 77, 83, 85, 102, 106; Zurich, xix–xxi, 30, 42–43, 48, 60, 71–72, 75–77, 85, 88, 92–138, 171, 174, 180, 185–88, 190–91, 194, 198, 212, 225, 232–33

Initiator, 66, 90, 92–138, 171, 173, 176, 184, 186–91, 195–97, 215, 231, 274

Inner Landscaping, 206, 208, 216–17, 228, 230–31, 247ff

internal states, violent, 49

Jung, Carl, xix, xxi, 3, 7–8, 14–25, 29, 34–35, 39, 43–46, 49–53, 55–58, 60–64, 71–85, 81, 83–85, 92, 96, 100–102, 106, 123, 142–43, 147–54; 156, 158–67, 174, 178–79, 183, 208, 218–19, 243; Institute, Küsnacht/Zurich, xix, 3, 7, 14, 16, 20, 22–23, 29, 43, 63, 77, 80, 92, 96, 98–102, 107, 148–49, 153–54, 158, 186–87, 194, 218,

Jung/Pauli letters (*see Atom and Archetype*)

Jyoti, 79, 81–85, 200, 209, 212–15, 219, 228, 237, 273

Kepler, Johannes, 62, 150-51, 153, 156-7, 163–64, 167

Kiekegaard, 98–99, 128, 226

Klonsky, Milton, xix–xx, 7–14, 19–20, 43, 54–55, 65, 72–73, 79–81, 84–85, 88, 90, 103–104, 110, 120–22, 136, 165, 175, 187, 206, 210–11, 214, 218–19, 222, 228, 231–32, 234, 273–75

kundalini, 82, 93, 99, 212, 217–18, 220–21, 232, 234, 273–74

Lauf, Detlef, 73–74, 98

Lindorff, David, 23, 45, 60–61, 65, 157

Love in Transition (Margaret A. Harrell), 47, 53, 72, 103, 107, 116, 121, 138, 154, 175, 210, 239, 241

meditation, xx, 74, 89, 94, 96, 142,

Index

151, 163, 206, 208, 217, 231
Meier, C. A., 149, 152
Mensaert, Jan, 4, 6–7, 9–10, 12, 19, 72, 80, 114, 184–87, 176, 189, 191–94, 197–200, 204–206, 214, 220, 224–28, 233
metalism, bipod (*see* "bipod metalism")
Miller, Arthur I., 16, 158
Milton Christ (*see* "Initiator")
Mindell, Arnold, 24–25, 140
Miner, Al (and Lama Sing), 10–14, 93, 126, 132, 198, 204, 231, 274
Montparnasse, Paris, 7, 48, 52, 54, 57, 116, 165
Mozart, 76, 109-10, 113–15, 175, 188–89, 192–93, 225, 227
Mysterium Coniunctionis (Carl Jung); see "hieros gamos"
Newton, 30, 42, 64, 128–31, 134, 136, 141, 150, 154, 156, 169
Nobel Prize, xix, 15, 25, 32, 61, 150, 159
Number four (*see* "four, fourth")
Number three, 15-16, 19, 53, 60–64, 84, 100, 105, 111, 153, 158
numinous, 10, 19, 15, 78–80, 103, 116, 154, 166, 178, 231, 273
Observer, 30, 32, 45, 48, 57–58, 152
Odeon café, 149, 194–95
Old Christmas (January 6), 218, 220, 232
opposites, 15-16, 18, 46, 53, 58, 61, 64, 123, 152-57, 164, 167, 172, 178, 205, 208, 241

oscillation, 51-53, 55, 156, 165
Other Worlds (Paul Davies), 86, 88, 94, 96, 100
out-of-body experiences (OBEs), 82, 190
Paracelsus, 143, 153
parade (Blankenberge/Paradeplatz), 10, 103, 231, 273
parapsychology, 12, 49; *see also* "after death," "bell, parapsychological," "Pauli effect," "psychokinesis," etc.
Paris (*see* "Montparnasse")
Park, Russell, 213, 219, 237
participatory universe, 48–49, 56, 152
Pascal, René, 176, 194–96, 201, 219, 234
Pauli effect, 54, 149, 153, 164, 166
Pauli, Wolfgang, xix, 15–16, 23–25, 34–37, 39, 43–46, 50–65, 103, 143, 147–66, 258
Peat, David, xix–xx, 32, 41, 43, 48–49, 152
personality: general, 90, 105, 109, 124, 128, 134, 175, 180, 209, 243; integration, 7, 73; levels, 92ff, 224; soul and, 35
Philosopher's Stone, 16, 63, 142
"Piano Lesson" (Wolfgang Pauli), 35–36
pilot wave (*see* "wave, pilot")
Plato, 57, 64
Princeton, 150, 159, 166
probability, 30–31, 33, 219; law of, 45
Prophetissa, Maria, 16, 19, 63–64
psychokinesis: "computer PK," 231,

233, 239; also see "Pauli effect"
psychological types, 17–19, 35, 62, 69, 78–79, 95, 114, 149, 167–68, 208
psychology-physics connection, xix, 24, 35, 39, 43, 55, 58, 148, 153–54, 158, 162–65
quantum mechanics (QM), 30–32, 36, 41, 100, 143
Quispel, Gilles, 101-102
radioactivity, 23, 64, 156, 159–62, 164–66
rainmaker, xxi–xxii
Romania, 53, 116, 165, 193
Rome, 79–85, 273
Rosarium philosophorum (The Rosary of the Philosophers), 74–75, 94
Roth, Remo, 63, 151, 158, 161–67
Sacred Marriage (*see* "hieros gamos")
sanskara, 209, 217–18, 268
Secret of the Golden Flower, The, 142, 151, 163
Self, the, 7, 19, 24, 57–58, 61, 63, 66, 73–74, 77–78, 84, 95, 101, 148, 159, 161, 165–66, 190
seventeenth century, 23–24, 62, 66, 128–29, 134, 142, 150, 154, 157, 167
shaman (*see* "Soos, Joska")
Snoep, 3, 5, 96, 172, 185–87
Soos, Joska, 269–70
soul: group, 12–15, 96, 125, 132, 175, 218, 223, 228, 231, 233; universal nature of each soul, 15, 132, 161, 232

spirit and matter, entanglement of, 123, 135
Standard Model (particle physics), 31–32
Stein, Murray, 71, 73
subpersonalities, 80, 114
Swami Krishnananda, 161, 265
symmetry, 41, 143, 152, 154, 211
synchronicity, 7, 23, 25, 41, 43–46, 48–49, 52, 54–55, 58, 64–65, 98, 101, 131, 136, 148, 157, 159–62, 165–66, 171, 178, 185–86, 201, 222, 220, 267
Tao, 53, 98–99, 142, 150–51, 163-64, 166, 178–79
Tienen, Belgium, 185–86, 191–92, 200–201, 214, 216–17, 219, 226, 241
Thompson, Hunter, 3–7, 15, 125–26, 195, 198, 209–10, 224, 232–42
transpersonality, xx, 100, 112, 122, 124, 127, 134, 189, 213, 219
triggers, 41, 116, 123, 135, 215; visual, 47, 49–50, 52, 57
unconscious, collective (*see* "collective unconscious")
unconscious, the, xix–xx, 7–9, 15–19, 21–22, 37, 39–43, 49–58, 62, 66, 74, 77, 80, 88, 90, 103, 106, 116, 118, 124, 147, 149, 153–54, 156–58, 161–62, 165–66, 171–73, 178–79, 228, 239
Valentinus, 101–102

Van de Velde, Chris, 183, 206–208, 217–18, 231, 240, 247ff
Van Luyten, Willy, 183-84, 186, 191, 196–240, 242
Von Franz, Marie-Louise, 18–19, 22, 63, 151, 158
wave function (state vector), 31; collapse (wave packet reduction), 31–32, 40, 90, 128, 239
wave, pilot (informational), 24, 57
wave symbol, 53 (*see* "oscillation")
Weber, Renée, 30, 86
Wheeler, John, 48, 89
Wilber, Ken, 30–31, 86

Wilhelm, Richard, 142, 151, 178
window: accident foreseen through, 234; beggar at, 47, 52, 54–55, 57, 61, 65, 116, 155; Leibniz and (windowless monad), 57; Odeon café and, 149; psyche and, 58; Pauli: lines under, 51–55, 60–61, 65; scarabeid beetle seen through, 160
Woodman, Marion, 16, 78, 84
World Clock (vision), 51–52, 60
yin-yang, 164, 166
Yogananda, 122, 232
yogi, 99, 102, 122, 161, 212, 264, 274

About the Author

Margaret A. Harrell was three times a fellow at MacDowell Colony for artists in New Hampshire. She has degrees from Duke University (history) and Columbia University (contemporary literature). An author of seven books in the *Love in Transition/Space Encounters* series (published in English in Romania), she moved back to the United States from Belgium in 2001. She has since published a coffeetable guidebook to the series, featuring her color cloud photography. Her memoirs followed: *Keep This Quiet! My Relationship with Hunter S. Thompson, Milton Klonsky, and Jan Mensaert* (2011) and *Keep THIS Quiet Too! More Adventures with Hunter S. Thompson, Milton Klonsky, Jan Mensaert* (2012). They feature letters Gonzo journalist Hunter S. Thompson wrote her while she was copy editing his first book, *Hell's Angels,* and after. She is also the author of *Marking Time with Faulkner* (literary criticism). She teaches advanced guided meditation centered in the "light body," in addition to being a photographer and editor. For more, visit http://www.hunterthompsonnewbook.com or http://www.lightangel.net.

www.ingramcontent.com/pod-product-compliance
Lightning Source LLC
Chambersburg PA
CBHW050621300426
44112CB00012B/1595